The French Revolution and Napoleon

The French Revolution and Napoleon

Crucible of the Modern World

**LYNN HUNT AND
JACK R. CENSER**

Bloomsbury Academic
An imprint of Bloomsbury Publishing Plc

B L O O M S B U R Y
LONDON · OXFORD · NEW YORK · NEW DELHI · SYDNEY

Bloomsbury Academic

An imprint of Bloomsbury Publishing Plc

50 Bedford Square	1385 Broadway
London	New York
WC1B 3DP	NY 10018
UK	USA

www.bloomsbury.com

BLOOMSBURY and the Diana logo are trademarks of Bloomsbury Publishing Plc

First published 2017

British Library Cataloguing-in-Publication Data

A catalogue record for this book is available from the British Library.

ISBN:	HB:	978–1–4742–1372–1
	PB:	978–1–4742–1371–4
	ePDF:	978–1–4742–1373–8
	ePub:	978–1–4742–1374–5

Library of Congress Cataloging-in-Publication Data

Names: Hunt, Lynn, 1945- author. | Censer, Jack Richard, 1946- author.
Title: The French Revolution and Napoleon : crucible of the modern world / Lynn Hunt and Jack R. Censer.
Description: London; New York, NY : Bloomsbury Academic, 2017. | Includes bibliographical references.
Identifiers: LCCN 2017010879| ISBN 9781474213721 (hb) | ISBN 9781474213714 (pb)
Subjects: LCSH: France—History—Revolution, 1789–1799. | France—History—Consulate and First Empire, 1799–1815. | Napoleon I, Emperor of the French, 1769–1821.
Classification: LCC DC148. H863 2017 | DDC 944.04—dc23 LC record available at https://lccn.loc.gov/2017010879

Cover design by Cyan Design
Cover image: Napoleon Bonaparte haranguing the army before the Battle of the Pyramids, July 21, 1798. Painting by Antoine Jean Gros, oil on canvas, 3,89 x 3,11 m. Castle Museum, Versailles, France (© Leemage/Corbis via Getty Images)

Typeset by RefineCatch Limited, Bungay, Suffolk
Printed and bound in Great Britain

To find out more about our authors and books visit www.bloomsbury.com. Here you will find extracts, author interviews, details of forthcoming events and the option to sign up for our newsletters.

Contents

List of illustrations

Tables

Figures

List of maps

Preface

The French Revolution ended two centuries ago, but its highs and lows still haunt present-day politics. The crucible of that revolution forged the modern terms and forms of political action: left and right as political designations; propaganda, terrorist, and revolution as new political terms; democratic government elected by universal manhood suffrage, the use of terror to suppress political dissent, and an authoritarian police state as new political forms. Universal human rights and democracy ran up against the constraints of national security in a seemingly perpetual war that ultimately brought one of the most extraordinary generals in all world history to power, Napoleon Bonaparte. He made himself emperor and through military conquest ruled over much of Europe. French occupation redrew boundaries and recast laws and institutions, and its effects could be felt for generations afterward.

The nearly constant combat that took place between 1792 and 1815 rewrote the rules of warfare and brought revolutionary ideas to virtually all the corners of the world. The French introduced national conscription and the inculcation of patriotism in the ranks of a citizen army, which enabled them to field mass armies fired with fervor for their nation. Nationalism took flight, and France's enemies soon learned how to turn it back against the French. Wherever the French triumphed, however temporarily, they introduced revolutionary reforms such as the abolition of serfdom and the legal institution of religious toleration. Traditional rulers took fright and eventually adapted techniques they learned from the French to shore up their own threatened authority.

The ideals of liberty and equality had a life of their own independent of military conflict, and they proved impossible to eradicate even after Napoleon had fallen from power. In the revolutionary vortex the most basic social and cultural relations came into question. Peasants challenged their noble overlords, workers demanded attention to their needs, religious minorities seized the opening for participation, women claimed a voice in political affairs, and mixed-race people and African slaves smashed the chains of their subjugation. Newspapers popped up like mushrooms after a rain; composers, novelists, and playwrights cultivated new styles; and printmakers flooded markets everywhere with revolutionary and counter-revolutionary images.

When Bonaparte came to power, he curbed participation and publication and showed how a cult of personality could buttress the power of property-owners and new political elites. The world took notice as the conflicts between revolutionary ideals, traditional regimes, and new style authoritarianism spread far and wide.

The resonance of these momentous events hardly diminished over time. The French themselves have only come to terms with their revolutionary heritage in the last decades, but more important, aspiring revolutionaries, generals of people's armies, would-be military dictators, and human rights activists around the world continue to study the models developed during the French revolutionary and Napoleonic era. When the Bolsheviks fought among themselves about the direction of the Russian Revolution in the 1920s, one of their most influential leaders, Leon Trotsky, made constant references to events during the French Revolution. He even cited specific speeches from 1794. The Universal Declaration of Human Rights adopted by the United Nations in 1948 begins with a first article that is directly drawn from the 1789 French Declaration of the Rights of Man and Citizen. The Vietnamese victor over the French army at Dien Bien Phu in 1954, General Vo Nguyen Giap, had memorized every detail of Napoleon's battles (true, he was a history teacher before the struggle for independence). Finally, to this day in the People's Republic of China, astute observers wonder aloud about whether the Chinese will ever exit from their "Thermidorian reaction" like the one that followed upon the fall of Maximilien Robespierre in 1794 (the month on the revolutionary calendar was called Thermidor). In an interview published in 2000, for instance, one Chinese intellectual concluded about the Chinese revolution, "No matter how far revolution goes, Thermidor lies in wait."[1] It is virtually impossible to think about revolution or empire without reference to the events that took place between 1789 and 1815.

Contemporaries of the events immediately grasped their epochal significance. Only a few months after the French Revolution began in July 1789, the Anglo-Irish politician Edmund Burke wrote, "It looks to me as if I were in a great crisis, not of the affairs of France alone, but of all Europe, perhaps of more than Europe. All circumstances taken together, the French Revolution is the most astonishing that has hitherto happened in the world."[2] The Revolution had just started, and the world had yet to witness the abolition of nobility, the first successful slave uprising in world history, the execution of King Louis XVI and his wife Marie-Antoinette, a campaign of de-Christianization, a vicious civil war, not to mention nearly a quarter century of fighting across the globe, and the rise, after Burke's death in 1797, of an obscure Corsican to become emperor of the French and the ruler by surrogate of much of Continental Europe. Confronted with the intensity and dizzying rapidity of these changes, contemporaries alternately rejoiced, worried, and felt horror at what was happening, but no one escaped the power of these unexpected and far-reaching events.

These world-shaping experiences generated unending controversies, not least among scholars. Every generation has its own version of the French Revolution, but three broad questions have shaped the debates of the last 225 years: Was the French Revolution good or evil? What motivated political leaders and factions in their struggle for power? Which structural conditions best explain the overall trajectory of events? Over time, interest has shifted away from the first question toward the second and especially the third one, and this book reflects that shift. Yet even the question about good or evil still lingers in writing about the French Revolution because the events raise so many enduring challenges: How much violence is justified in the pursuit of a more equal and just society? What should take priority, individual rights or national security? Does revolution inevitably create a pressure for war with internal and external enemies? Does revolution necessarily end in authoritarianism? We do not intend to give explicit answers to these questions but rather hope to provide a compelling account that will encourage readers to think about their own responses.

Two literary masterpieces of the nineteenth century give a sense of the range of possible opinions expressed about the French Revolution. The anticlerical, pro-republican Jules Michelet produced a seven-volume history of the French Revolution (1847–1853) that only covered developments from 1789 to 1794 but did so in such passionate and lyrical terms that it still bears re-reading today. For him the Revolution was fundamentally good because it was made by "the people," meaning the common people of France; peasants, artisans, and workers. This mystical, enthusiastic, laughing, determined people was his only hero; the political leaders always fell short. The fundamental principle of the Revolution, he insisted, was "the triumph of right, the resurrection of justice."[3]

At the other end of the spectrum, the cultural historian and literary critic Hippolyte Taine published four volumes on the French Revolution (1878–1890) as part of his series, *The Origins of Modern France*. His view of the fundamental evil of the Revolution can be found in his own summary of his first volume: "Popular insurrections and the laws of the Constituent Assembly [1789–1791] end in destroying all government in France." Revolution was evil because it meant anarchy, "the dictatorship of a mob."[4] The revolutionary leaders were too incompetent to surmount the violence and devastation. When it came to Napoleon Bonaparte, Taine granted that he ended the revolution and brought the mob to heel, but he remained a "military adventurer" who cared "only for his own advancement."[5]

The structural conditions shaping the French Revolution obsessed two great nineteenth-century pioneers of sociology, Alexis de Tocqueville and Karl

Marx. A contemporary of Michelet, Tocqueville showed little interest in the question of good or evil or revolutionary leaders. His overriding concern was to explain how a revolution made in the name of liberty and equality could produce terror and Napoleonic despotism. In his classic *The Old Regime and the Revolution* (1856), he sought the answers in the structure of the monarchical regime itself, which had steadily eroded aristocratic participation and local liberties and centralized power in the hands of the king. France had already learned to be servile, and Bonaparte simply used the promise of equality to eliminate political liberty. The French Revolution thus inaugurated, in Tocqueville's view, the unending modern struggle between his version of true political liberty and the dangerous promises of equality.

Karl Marx (1818–1883) believed, in contrast, that equality had to trump the chimerical promises of political liberty, which only served to maintain the privileges of the ruling classes. For him the struggle was not between liberty and equality but between the ruling and oppressed classes. In his view, the French Revolution took the essential first step toward an eventual communist revolution; it was a "bourgeois" revolution that overthrew aristocratic feudalism and ushered in the modern state required by capitalism. Capitalism in its turn would be overthrown by a proletarian revolution that would bring about communism, that is, the abolition of private property. Class struggle drove both revolutionary processes. Although Marx never got around to writing his projected history of the French Revolution, it came up again and again in his work, especially as he traced the unraveling of its legacy in the revolutions of 1848 and the Paris Commune of 1871. He said little about Napoleon but clearly considered him a sign of the failure of the republican experiment; for him Napoleon represented the interests of the leading bourgeois and also the conservative peasants.

Debates about the role of specific political leaders and factions dominated the writings of the two great early twentieth-century historians of the French Revolution, Alphonse Aulard (1849–1928) and Albert Mathiez (1874–1932). Although they both embraced the republican ideal, Aulard preferred those leaders who sought to moderate the use of terror while Mathiez, Aulard's student, vigorously defended Robespierre and his allies who had used terror to save the republic. Unlike Mathiez, Aulard chose to consider Napoleon at some length in his general history of the French Revolution. In Aulard's view, Napoleon was a despot who undid all the political liberties of the republic while maintaining the gains in social equality.

Mathiez was the first of several generations of historians of the French Revolution in France who identified themselves as Marxists and in some cases, members of the communist party. Mathiez led the way in writing about the social dimension of the Revolution, especially the difficulties created by food shortages for the working classes in Paris. Robespierre pursued his draconian policies, Mathiez insisted, because they benefited the lower classes and because the Parisian lower classes demanded them. Enthusiasm for social histories of the working classes grew in response to the influence of Marxism and Mathiez's own example. His successor in the Chair of the History of the French Revolution at the University of Paris (Sorbonne), Georges Lefebvre (1874–1959), shifted attention to the peasants, who, he argued, had good economic reasons to join in the Revolution, from which they benefited. Like Aulard, Lefebvre maintained a balanced view in his biography of Napoleon; the emperor was an enlightened despot who rejected democracy but also hated religious intolerance, legal inequality, and feudalism.

Since the next two holders of the Sorbonne Chair, Albert Soboul (1914–1982) and Michel Vovelle (1933–), were both Marxists and members of the communist party, it might have seemed that the Marxist interpretation of the French Revolution would carry all before it. But as communist regimes began to unravel in the 1980s, the Marxist hold on the history of the French Revolution came under intense fire. Using the evidence and criticisms first offered by Anglo-American critics of the Marxist view, a former communist turned anti-communist, François Furet (1927–1997), leveled a barrage against the Marxist "vulgate." He maintained that neither the outbreak nor the major conflicts of the Revolution could be explained by class struggles. The Revolution had a dynamic all its own that was shaped first and foremost by the language and ideology of politics; picking up where Tocqueville left off, he argued that the democratic language of the power of "the people" created an opening for proto-totalitarian politics in which Robespierre, derided by Furet as a mediocrity, or Napoleon, lauded as a genius, could claim to speak for the people and justify the stifling of dissent.

Furet's revival of interest in politics, and especially the language of politics, reflected broader trends that developed in the study of history in the last half of the twentieth century. An emphasis on social factors and groups, often inspired by Marxism, had grown to prominence among historians in the 1950s, 1960s, and 1970s. Cultural history, which includes the study of political rhetoric and culture, attracted increasing attention in the 1980s, 1990s, and early 2000s. As the debate about Marxism died down, women's and gender history and the history of the revolution in the colonies gained traction. Studies of women's participation (and exclusion) and of slave movements against the plantation regime in the Caribbean have taken the history of the French Revolution in exciting new directions. The two authors of this book have taken part in these developments. Jack Censer has analyzed the role of the press in the Old Regime and the French Revolution, and Lynn Hunt has written about political culture, gender relations, and human rights, including the rights of mixed-race and slave peoples. Such studies are crucial for understanding this pivotal period, for politics is about more than lawmaking or institution building;

it depends on public opinion, and therefore the press, and in this time of upheaval, the role of women, the status of the family, and race relations all became subjects of intensive controversy.

The recent attention to the history of slavery and the colonies is part of a wider shift in historical studies toward interest in globalization and global history. This book aims to put social, cultural, and global concerns together in an attempt to understand how the French Revolution shaped the modern world. The global perspective offers a significant new dimension. First, the Revolution had such wide resonance because it grew out of a global competition for colonial resources. When France allied with the British North American colonies against Great Britain, it jump-started an Atlantic-wide circulation of ideas of rights, representation, and republicanism. The outbreak of revolution in France gave new shape and currency to those ideas which then traveled to much of the world. Wars between the revolutionaries and the monarchs who opposed them changed boundaries and regimes in Europe and opened the way to the spread of notions of liberty, equality, and national independence across Europe and into South America and parts of Africa and Asia. Moreover, once the French Revolution had ended, discussion of its meaning had only begun. The traditional order could no longer go unexplained; the ideologies of conservatism and liberalism grew up in direct response to the impact of the French Revolution. A global approach makes sense of the exceptional resonance of the ideas, movements, and political forms that emerged from the crucible of the French Revolution.

1

1789: A world overturned

Great revolutions often begin when a small spark sets off a mighty blaze. On July 12, 1789 Parisians heard the rumor that the king's minister of finances, Jacques Necker, had been fired. A rich banker from Geneva, Necker had been brought in to prevent an impending bankruptcy, and he supported growing public demands for fiscal accountability. Leading aristocrats at King Louis XVI's court vehemently opposed him; Necker was not French, noble, or Catholic. While Necker slipped away under orders to keep silent, hostile crowds gathered in the streets. Emotions ran especially high in the Palais-Royal, a complex of theaters, restaurants, cafés, bookshops, and gambling dens built onto the grounds and gardens owned by the Duke of Orleans, the king's fabulously rich cousin and ardent supporter of reform. Seizing the occasion was a 29-year-old lawyer from northern France named Camille Desmoulins. He jumped on to one of the café tables, waved a pistol, and urged those gathered around him to take up arms and put green ribbons on their hats because green, he said, was "the color of hope." It was also the Duke's color.

After a mad scramble for green ribbons, people paraded busts of Necker and the Duke and insisted that all the theaters close their doors. When news came of some soldiers attacking demonstrators, the crowd began to pillage gun shops. Early the next morning church bells rang to signal alarm. Men and women spilled into the streets, demanding arms wherever they could be found. Reports flew of troops marching toward the city. At city hall an emergency committee set up a citizen's militia to keep order, as the thousands of soldiers sent to Paris by the king withdrew to temporary encampments outside the city. Regiments of French Guards now threatened to take the side of their fellow citizens against the many foreign troops deployed by the king. On July 14, Desmoulins found himself in a crowd of 7–8,000 people that demanded rifles at the Invalides hospital for veterans. They got the rifles but needed powder and cartridges. Many then set off for the Bastille prison on the east side of the city. The late medieval fortress with walls 78-feet high and 10-feet thick loomed over some of the poorest neighborhoods of the city.

Long feared as the secret prison for the crown's critics and guarded by Swiss soldiers who had no intention of giving up their stores of ammunition, the Bastille had come to embody despotism itself. Thousands of people armed with knives, axes, swords, pikes, and a few old muskets laid siege to the building. After scores had fallen victim to the Swiss firing from above, French Guards appeared with five cannon and opened a breach in the walls (Figure 1.1).

The aristocratic head of the prison, Marquis de Launay, considered detonating explosives stowed in the fortress that could have caused much death and destruction, but was convinced to surrender, only to be dragged to city hall where he was beaten and stabbed to death. His head was cut off and paraded on a pike for all to see. Several Swiss soldiers met similar fates, as did a leading city official accused of conspiring with de Launay. Desmoulins

FIGURE 1.1 *The Taking of the Bastille*
The artist, Jean-François Janinet, shows the moment when the French Guards and armed civilians have broken into the inner courtyard of the prison. The Swiss Guards are firing on them from above. Etching and aquatint, Paris, 1789.

arrived too late to see the taking of the Bastille, but he spent the night with others patrolling the streets of Paris in case the king's army should decide to take action. "I was certain," he wrote to his father breathlessly, that "the incredible taking of the Bastille in a fifteen minute assault had caused consternation at the chateau of Versailles [the king's residence] and the camp [the army encampment]." As would soon become clear, the fall of the Bastille prison started a revolution that would ultimately change the destiny of Europe and much of the world.[1]

Similar uprisings rocked towns and cities across the country, showing that the king could not fire a popular minister and crush political opposition without provoking resistance. Young activists like Desmoulins were prepared to risk their lives by speaking publicly for immediate reform. Hundreds of thousands of ordinary people were ready to act, sometimes with violence and a frightening sense of retribution. Why had they joined the movement for change? What had brought them into the streets? The army had proved to be unreliable, and some aristocrats, such as the king's own cousin, had joined the opposition. How had Europe's richest and most populous nation, ruled from time out of mind by kings and aristocrats, come to this tipping point?

An empire in trouble

Global competition is the simplest answer to those questions. The huge deficits incurred in competing with Britain opened the way to constitutional change in France and eventually to social and cultural revolution. Although the French kings tried to reform their finances and administration over the course of the 1700s, they could not surmount the challenges posed by competing for global resources, which required ships, sailors, merchants, administrators, money, and when necessary, as was often the case, soldiers to fight and yet more money to pay them. The cost of defending a far-flung empire pushed the French king to the edge of bankruptcy, and to avoid it he convoked an Estates-General, a body of delegates that had not met for 175 years. From the moment of its first meeting in May 1789 the king began to lose control of the situation. Steady growth in the population and increasing government commitments to providing welfare and ensuring social order added to the shortage of funds that was the immediate cause of the upheaval of 1789.

If the French kings had been content to stay home and fight the usual land wars against their longtime enemies the Austrian Habsburgs, there likely would have been no revolution in 1789. But France needed overseas outposts, oceanic trading connections, and colonies in order to keep up with their maritime rivals (see Map 1.1). Spain and Portugal had already conquered the New World territories rich in gold and silver by the mid-sixteenth century, so France, Britain, and the Dutch Republic had to settle for the leftovers: North America, the Caribbean islands, India, and Indonesia. The leftovers turned out to have unexpected potential, in large part because of the dramatic expansion of the violent enslavement of Africans and their bondage on plantations growing sugar, cotton, and coffee for a rapidly growing consumer market. As the slave trade and commerce with Asian countries expanded, the relative balance of imperial power shifted dramatically in favor of the northern Atlantic countries. Portugal and Spain dominated the slave trade until 1650 but by 1675, the Dutch had taken over, carrying more than half of the slaves transported from Africa to the New World in their ships. Dutch dominance faded quickly, however; by 1700 the British had surpassed the Dutch and everyone else. The French desperately tried to catch up.

Competition between the British and French proved especially intense because they both aspired to dominate commerce in the Caribbean and India. With the forced labor of African slaves, more than a million of whom were transported to the Caribbean islands just between 1750 and 1775, French and British owners developed a plantation system to produce sugar, coffee, and cotton, goods that could not be produced in Europe but were in increasing demand. The southern British North American colonies and the Caribbean islands imported slaves as fast as they could be shipped and churned out unimaginable wealth alongside the wreckage of black African lives. One French colony, Saint-Domingue (now Haïti), stood out both for its unparalleled production of wealth and its extreme numerical imbalance between whites and black slaves. In 1789 Saint-Domingue supplied half the world's exports of coffee and sugar; it accounted for two-thirds of the goods imported to Europe from all the French colonies, including those in Africa and around the Indian Ocean. Saint-Domingue alone generated twice as much revenue as Spain's richest colony, Mexico. With 500,000 African slaves, 30–40,000 whites, and 32,000 free people of color, it also had the largest percentage of slaves. With half as many people, the principal British Caribbean colony Jamaica produced only a third of the goods of French Saint-Domingue.

The slave trade depended on a wider global commerce. British and French traders bought slaves with textiles purchased in India and cowries (shells) from the Maldive Islands off the Indian coast; cowries made up one-third to one-half of the purchase price of slaves in Africa in the 1700s because Africans preferred these particular shells to gold or silver. Commercial rivalries thus necessarily extended across the globe. According to the French government's own secret estimates, in 1788 France dominated trade in the Caribbean, Spain enjoyed the lion's share with South America, Britain had a slight edge in

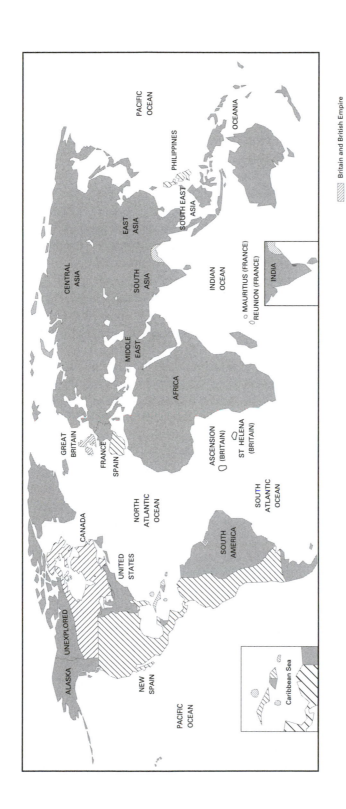

MAP 1.1 *British and French Imperial Competition*

trade with the newly independent United States, and the British and Dutch far outstripped the French in trade with China and India, the latter being the source of textiles and cowries for the slave trade.[2]

Since commercial rivalries were increasingly global, it is not surprising that European wars became more global, too. Skirmishes in the Seven Years' War, 1756–1763 (known in the US as the French and Indian War) actually began in 1754 when the British sent a colonial militia to stop the French from building forts in the Ohio River Valley (now Pennsylvania). To protect its interests on the European continent, Britain allied with Prussia in 1756, and in response, France signed a mutual defense treaty with its longest-standing enemy, the Austrian Habsburgs. War soon raged worldwide with battles in Europe, India, North America, South America, and Africa; the fighting involved, at one time or another, all the major European powers. While the land war in Europe ended in stalemate, the British drove the French out of their major settlements in Canada, India, and sub-Saharan Africa (Senegal). By the terms of the peace agreement, France was forced to give up all its military bases in India and almost all of its colonies in Canada in addition to ceding Louisiana to Spain.

The French alliance with Austria did not end with the peace; in 1770, the heir to the French throne, the eventual Louis XVI (r. 1774–1792), married one of the daughters of Maria Theresa, the Austrian ruler. Marie-Antoinette was not yet fifteen years old and joined a court where many still despised the Austrians and feared her influence. Eight years went by before she gave birth to a daughter and three more before she produced a male heir to the throne, but by then she had a less than enviable reputation for extravagance. The paternity of her children, the costs of her wardrobe, the names of her reputed lovers, and her Austrian connections provided endless grist for the rumor mills. By contrast to his all too vivacious wife, Louis seemed timid, taciturn, and more interested in books and tinkering than the theater or court gatherings. He was only a year older than his wife, and for reasons that still animate debate today, he could not consummate the marriage for seven years.

As king after 1774 Louis had trouble making up his mind, a trait that would prove fatal later on. He dithered about joining the North American colonists in their struggle for independence from Great Britain, but by 1778, the opportunity to avenge the losses in the Seven Years' War proved too enticing, and France concluded a military alliance with the Americans. Spain allied with France, and Britain declared war on the Dutch in reaction to their supplying arms to the North American rebels. Fighting took place in North and South America, the Caribbean, and India. This time the French came out on the winning side but the decision to support the rebels had two momentous consequences; it vastly increased the crown's debt, and it jump-started an Atlantic circulation of republican and democratic ideals that would before long undermine the French monarchy and monarchical and aristocratic systems all over Europe.

As finance minister during the American war, Necker had raised the necessary funds for France's participation by borrowing rather than increasing taxes. Borrowing in itself was not the problem, for the British had borrowed too. Per capita taxation, the ratio of debt to GNP, and the ratio of taxes to GNP were all lower in France than in Britain, but the proportion of debt service to tax revenues was higher. The French government paid a higher rate of interest (about 6 percent) to borrow than the British (about 3 percent) because the French had no national bank to organize government loans and the French king did not submit his accounts to any public body for approval, rendering default more likely. The French crown kept borrowing in a vain effort to make ends meet. As a result, the interest on the debt consumed ever-larger portions of the budget. By 1789, interest payments ate up nearly half of the year's incoming revenue.

France's success in the American war nonetheless had promised a reversal of fortunes. In the peace settlement of 1783 France got back some territory in India and Senegal and stood poised to extend its international commerce. In 1785 the French government re-established the French East India Company, and in the late 1780s, the French sent off more vessels than ever before to the Indian Ocean, surpassing the British and Dutch in this regard, though not in revenues gained. So confident were the French that the government signed a free trade treaty with Great Britain in September 1786, suddenly opening French markets to cheap British textiles. The French even overtook the British in slave trading. Between 1787 and 1791 the French shipped 40 percent of the slaves taken from Africa, the British only 23 percent, a dramatic turnaround (except for those enslaved) from the late 1770s.

Maintaining an empire, even in peacetime, required great expense; in 1788, the war department, which included the army and cavalry, was the single biggest French budget item after interest on the debt, and next in line was the department of the navy and colonies. French officials kept close tabs on all their competitors, large and small (see Table 1.1). While they must have prided themselves on spending more per capita on the French people than most powers and less proportionately on their military, by the French government's account the French and British spent more on their militaries than any of the other European powers, including the Ottoman Empire.

Although French wealth increased dramatically after 1783, the king found himself chronically short of funds. Ironically, the migration of foreign bankers to Paris after political upheavals in Geneva, the Dutch Republic, and Belgium only worsened the situation because with more money available and more bankers willing to arrange loans, the ministers just kept borrowing. The higher rate of interest paid by the French made government bonds more attractive,

TABLE 1.1 France and its competitors, 1789

European governments kept close tabs on each other and often sent agents (spies) to gather information about their competitors and even their allies. Most governments provided little public information about their finances. The information given below was most likely gathered by Necker and his subordinates for presentation to the Estates-General in 1789. The French government was running a serious deficit but so too, it claimed, was Great Britain. The French clearly considered the Ottoman Turks part of their world but not did gather information on powers further away such as China.

Country	Territory[a]	Population	Population Density	Revenue	Military cost	General Expenses	Military as % of General Expense
France	27,490	24,800,000	902	486,000,000	155,300,000	614,000,000	25
Great Britain	16,667	10,800,000	648	312,000,000	90,000,000	408,000,000	22
Ottoman Empire	130,000	50,000,000	385	250,000,000	60,000,000	200,000,000	30
Austrian Empire	34,820	19,500,000	560	215,000,000	79,000,000	208,000,000	38
Russia	160,000	23,800,000	148	160,000,000	86,000,000	130,000,000	66
Spain	12,920	8,400,000	650	140,000,000	50,000,000	180,000,000	28
Prussia	30,358	6,200,000	204	96,000,000	55,000,000	88,000,000	63
Portugal	5,028	2,500,000	497	72,000,000	20,000,000	58,000,000	34
Dutch Republic	1,736	2,400,000	1,382	68,000,000	42,000,000	87,000,000	48

[a] The territory is given in square leagues of 2,000 *toises*. A league was equivalent to about 4 km.

Source: British Library, Additional MSS 74100, *Aperçu de la Balance du Commerce de la France Année – 1789, Ensemble le Relevé de la Population des Finances et Forces Militaires des Principales Puissances de l'Europe*. It is unclear how this collection of handwritten tables came into the hands of the British government. The French compiled information about 14 other countries as well but they have been excluded as they were not the main competitors. We have calculated population density from the figures given for territory and population as well as the ratio of military to general expenses.

Questions on Table 1.1

1. What advantages did France enjoy over Great Britain and the Austrian Empire?
2. Which countries had the biggest deficits (gaps between revenues and expenses)?

as long as the crown was able to pay the interest. After a speculative boom, fueled in part by foreign investments, ran its course between 1785 and 1787, the ensuing bust undermined confidence in government securities. Although the French had signed a formal alliance with the Dutch Republic in 1785, their precarious financial situation kept them on the sidelines when Prussia invaded with British collaboration in September 1787 to quash a revolt against the Dutch stadholder. Greater humiliation followed; in August 1788, France partially suspended its payments, a move tantamount to bankruptcy. Necker was called back to the position he had held between 1776 and 1781; he returned a hero, but he faced a political maelstrom that even he could not surmount.

The global circulation of subversive ideas

In the past, the deficit would not have produced a major political crisis. Louis XIV arrested his biggest lender in 1661, kept him in prison, and confiscated his holdings. French kings exercised wide-ranging authority, and during the eighteenth century, the crown continued to use various expedients such as manipulating the currency, raising new taxes, putting surtaxes on old ones, demanding loans from various corporate bodies, and firing finance ministers whenever a change of policy was required. By 1788, however, the government's creditors, which included many foreign investors, enjoyed the protection of an amorphous yet nonetheless newly powerful public opinion. This more assertive public was French but also European, Atlantic, and even global. It grew out of new social spaces and international networks that spread ideas and habits that challenged the status quo.

Over the course of the 1700s, alongside the building of public theaters and the organization of the first art exhibitions and music concerts open to the public, provincial academies were established in most big towns and cities in France; in them local notables discussed scientific discoveries and the country's social problems but stayed away from political disputes. More threatening to the old ways were the masonic lodges that appeared in France and Italy for the first time in the 1720s and spread rapidly to central and eastern Europe despite condemnation by the Pope; the "freemasons" got their name from stonemason guilds in Scotland in the 1600s and in the early 1700s, which had been turned into a new kind of social gathering for the middle and upper class in England. From there masonry was exported to the continent and to the North American and Caribbean colonies. By 1789 even Saint-Domingue had 20 masonic lodges. Masons looked for their "brothers" when they traveled, thereby putting together an international network receptive to new ideas. Since masons wrote "constitutions" for their lodges, it is perhaps not surprising that many of the prominent leaders of the French Revolution belonged to masonic lodges, but so too did many aristocrats who eventually opposed revolution. Because the lodges met in secret, their role in fostering revolutionary ideas remains controversial to this day.

New products and new social customs contributed to the growth of the public. Although the very first French cafés dated back to the late 1600s, coffee drinking soared in France after planters turned to coffee-growing in the Caribbean colony of Martinique in the 1720s. By 1789 the French colonies produced two-thirds of the world's coffee and had even supplanted Yemen as the chief supplier to the Ottoman empire; many considered it a "French" drink. Paris had 1,600 cafés by 1789, and where there were cafés, there were most often also newspapers. France only got its first daily newspaper in 1777, but newspaper readership increased greatly during the American war. Although the French government censored domestic publications, many educated French people read political news in French-language papers published in the Austrian Netherlands or the Dutch Republic and distributed widely in France.

The new public proved receptive to the ideas of the intellectual movement known as the Enlightenment. Ranging from Philadelphia and Cap Français (Saint-Domingue) to Moscow and bringing Italian jurists, French social critics, Scottish moral philosophers, German playwrights, and North American reformers into conversation with each other, the Enlightenment was not an organized party but rather a set of overlapping intellectual and social circles. Its adherents championed legal equality, religious toleration, an end to judicial torture and cruel punishments, and a measure of greater political participation. Enlightenment writers such as Montesquieu, Voltaire, and Rousseau challenged the Christian view that Adam and Eve's fall in the Garden of Eden had made evil an integral part of human nature. Instead the *philosophes* (French for philosophers) argued that a creator God had endowed humans with the skills and abilities to comprehend and reshape their world through exploring nature and discovering its laws. Moreover, this benevolent God gave humans the facility to align themselves with natural morality that could then inform government.

Out of the Enlightenment came an emphasis on universally valid "natural rights" or "rights of man," the eighteenth-century predecessor to human rights. *Rights of man* gained currency as a term in French in the 1760s as the *philosophes* sought a new and more politically powerful way of expressing the view, previously associated with natural law or natural rights (the terms are the same in French, *droit(s) naturel(s)*), that a universal philosophical principle could guarantee equal respect and individual freedom for all people. In a society where privileges had been distributed according to status, region, religion, and gender and were justified by church teachings and long-standing monarchical and aristocratic traditions, universal human rights offered a radically different vision.

Given the potentially subversive nature of Enlightenment ideas, it is not surprising that the king's ministers and the Catholic Church initially tried to block them; in fact, the government censored all domestically published work right up to 1789. But condemnation and police seizure of banned Enlightenment writings in the 1740s and 1750s gave way in the 1760s and 1770s to greater laxity, in part because even Louis XV and Louis XVI and some high-ranking nobles and many clergy came to believe that reforms were needed. Books published could now be tacitly rather than officially permitted, a status that did not provide the equivalent of a copyright, so these works might be pirated or prosecuted. Although Enlightenment publications often criticized the Catholic Church, many Catholic clergymen took up ideas of reform and even contributed to them. They read Enlightenment writers, corresponded with them, wrote for Enlightenment publications, and joined masonic lodges.

Explicitly forbidden books were published in countries along France's eastern and northern borders and then smuggled into France and sold under the counter in bookstores. Rather than try to stem the tide, in the 1780s the government focused on stopping the most outrageous attacks on Queen Marie-Antoinette and other courtiers. The government even paid spies to find and buy out entire press runs. Despite these efforts, inflammatory and sometimes frankly pornographic books and pamphlets continued to reach readers and fed into a growing underground stream of disdain for a supposedly degenerate upper aristocracy.[3]

Political rights were not the only subjects of growing controversy. Economic and geopolitical competition with Great Britain fueled a great burst of French debate about the economy, which had influence far beyond France's borders. Breaking with traditional writers who questioned the virtue of emphasizing wealth, the "economists" or "Physiocrats" sought to liberate productive forces and increase wealth through scientific study of what would come to be called after them "economics." Blazing the trail was François Quesnay, a physician at Louis XV's court who turned to writing treatises about the need for free trade in grain and investment in agriculture. In 1763 the king's government declared freedom of trade in grain only to retreat under pressure of rising prices and growing disorder in 1770. In 1774, when a disciple of the Physiocrats, Jacques Turgot, became chief finance minister of the new king Louis XVI, he restored free trade in grain and then went even further and abolished the guilds, whose rules in the name of imposing standards of quality strangled competition in the labor market. Turgot's reforms, too, had to be withdrawn after widespread unrest, but the lasting influence of these conflicts can be seen in the determination of the 1789 leaders to replace restrictions on the economy with a faith in free trade.

The general ideas of the Enlightenment and of rights took on much more urgency when the American independence movement began putting them into practice. Thomas Jefferson's words in the Declaration of Independence of July 1776 showed that independence meant more than simple separation from Great Britain; it signified a revolution in the name of equality.

> We hold these truths to be self-evident, that all men are created equal, that they are endowed by their Creator with certain unalienable Rights, that among these are Life, Liberty and the pursuit of Happiness—That to secure these rights, Governments are instituted among Men, deriving their just powers from the consent of the governed.

By this account, governments derived their legitimacy from the defense of rights, not from dynastic inheritance or historical traditions (though the document also cited King George III's attacks on the colonists' historic rights). When the American colonists followed this bold commitment with new state and federal constitutions, their example galvanized many in the world. In Russia, for example, Alexander Radishchev wrote an "Ode to Liberty" to the Americans, saying "What you have, indeed, is what we thirst for." As soon as it appeared, Tsarina Catherine the Great banned it and exiled the author. Radicals in Britain, the Dutch Republic, and many Italian states similarly took heart from the American experiments. But nowhere was the fallout more consequential than in France.

The French public's interest in American developments intensified when Benjamin Franklin arrived in Paris in December 1776. Wearing an American fur hat over his own gray hair rather than a powdered wig, the 70-year-old envoy was the most famous American in the world thanks to his scientific experiments with electricity and his long career as a printer, publisher, and writer. A freemason for more than 40 years, he was promptly elected a member of the new Paris Lodge of the Nine Sisters, which soon included among its members Voltaire, many other illustrious figures of the French Enlightenment, and some 40 foreign members. Franklin came to enlist French support for American independence, and even before he gained it, he had helped inspire young men such as the 19-year-old Marquis de Lafayette to disregard official orders and sail as a volunteer to the colonies. Lafayette served on the staff of his fellow freemason George Washington. When France officially joined the war effort, thousands of soldiers and sailors came over and many went home, like Lafayette, enthusiastic about the new republic and what it augured for the world. As another young aristocratic officer recounted, "it naturally turned out that though we were originally animated to declare ourselves the partisans and champions of liberty by a purely warlike impulse, we ended up by being filled with enthusiasm for it in all good faith."

A traditional social structure under pressure

In one or another way, international trade, Enlightenment writings, and excitement about the American experiment created new fissures in French society. Some nobles invested in trade, went to America, participated in the Enlightenment, and joined masonic lodges, while others resisted any hint of change in their status. International trade made some middle-class families very rich, and new ideas and organizations such as the masonic lodges stoked their demands for change. Since a million jobs in mainland France depended on colonial investments and internal commerce also boomed, all but the most remote rural people gained access to new products and new opportunities. The king and his ministers embraced Enlightenment-inspired projects for reform of taxation, the judiciary, and the economy only to have to withdraw them when faced with withering opposition from social groups with different ideas, in some cases from nobles who wanted to protect their privileges, but in others from the urban lower classes who resented the higher prices that resulted from the freeing of the grain trade. The traditional social structure was coming undone but it still had deep pockets of resistance to change.

Of the 28 million inhabitants in France in 1789, only 170,000 were clergy and 140,000 were nobles, in other words, just over 1 percent of the population. That 1 percent controlled nearly half the land and claimed almost all the official leadership positions in French society and politics (Figure 1.2). Nevertheless, the rapidly growing involvement of France in overseas and colonial commerce was changing not only the consumer habits of the French population at home but also the attitudes of French people toward their traditional elites. International trade quadrupled over the course of the eighteenth century and colonial commerce rocketed to ten times higher than it had been in 1700. Traditional elites participated in these changes to some extent, but status increasingly depended on wealth.

Even as cracks widened in French society and Enlightenment writers criticized Catholic authorities for their intolerance and bigotry, the Catholic Church continued to enjoy great influence. Ordinary people appreciated the efforts of their local priests who usually lived very modest lives. The church had social as well as moral authority: births, marriages, and deaths had to be registered by the local parish; and the church supervised primary education and all 348 secondary schools (open only to boys). Because the practice of Calvinism had been outlawed in 1685 and remained so until 1787, Protestants had to send their children to private boarding schools or to Calvinist Geneva. By law, Calvinists could not own land in the colonies. The Catholic Church owned 10 percent of French land and collected an annual tithe of about 10 percent, often directly from the peasants' harvest. The tithe, a tax and not a voluntary offering, contributed two-thirds of the church's revenues which in

À faut espérer q'eu jeu la finira ben tôt.

Un Paisant portant un Prélat, et un Noble.

Allusion aux empots dont le poids retombait en entier sur le peuple. MM. les Eclesiastiques et les Nobles non seulement ne payoient rien, mais encore obtenoient des graces, des pensions qui épuisoient l'Etat, et le Malheureux cultivateur pouvoit a peine fournir à sa subsistance.

FIGURE 1.2 *The Game Must End Soon*
This satirical print shows a peasant carrying a clergyman and a noble. The text below explains that the image refers to the unequal burdens of taxation; the clergy and nobles are exempt from most taxes so the peasants have to shoulder the greatest burden. Traditional social relations are coming into question. Anonymous hand-colored etching, 1789.

total amounted to about 150–180,000,000 *livres* (hereafter abbreviated as l.) a year, a sum equal to the crown's receipts in 1788 from direct taxes (levied directly on individuals as opposed to taxes on goods for sale). Protestants made up only 2–3 percent of the population, Jews even less, but Protestants played a disproportionate role in overseas commerce in cities such as Bordeaux and Marseille, where they benefited from international connections with other Protestant merchants and bankers. In 1789 revolutionary legislators would begin a long and often violent process of dismantling the prerogatives of the Catholic Church, bringing it more closely under the control of the state.

Although commercial wealth was increasing, nobles, especially the richest and those with the oldest pedigree, remained on top.[4] Whether rich or poor, and noble title did not guarantee lasting wealth, nobles claimed exemption from the principal land tax (the *taille*), and, more important still, noble families dominated the high ranks of the church, the judiciary, and the armed forces. One-third of the land in France belonged to nobles. The Duke of Orleans himself owned 5 percent of the land in France, and with an income of 7.5 million l. a year, he was second in wealth only to the king. (An average urban worker made 200–300 l. a year, one-tenth as much as a provincial lawyer.) Although noble status had traditionally been considered incompatible with participation in commerce, in fact many nobles invested in overseas commerce, including the slave trade, and some of the greatest noble families held land in Saint-Domingue and other colonies. Moreover, men who made great wealth through commercial investments could buy noble status for their families either directly from the king or by buying judicial or administrative offices that conferred nobility after a certain passage of time. "Sword nobles," who held positions as military officers, insisted on their distinction from "robe nobles," so-called after the robes worn by judges, because robe nobles came from non-noble or more recently ennobled families. In 1781 a royal order required every noble requesting appointment as a military officer to show that his family had held noble title for at least four generations, thus shutting out the sons of recent robe nobles.

At the bottom of the social structure were those in farming. Four out of five French people lived in the countryside and of these 80 percent tilled the land. Yet this mass was far from immobile or unaffected by France's increasing overseas entanglement. The term "peasant" covers a wide range of circumstances from the desperate 10 percent at the very bottom who lived off aid provided by others to the 5–10 percent at the top who farmed large tracts of land and enjoyed considerable prosperity. Half the peasants had no land or just a tiny allotment and worked for others. This impoverished group was extremely vulnerable economically. Many left their home villages in search of work elsewhere, and sometimes they left for places far away, joining the army, moving across the border or even making their way to the colonies. Those who had land often worked it under sharecropping or tenant-farming arrangements, though the upper crust of the peasants might own substantial land or combine some personal property with other lands they rented or sharecropped.

Most peasants paid a variety of seigneurial dues to "lords" who could be nobles, clergy, or rich commoners who had bought seigneurial rights along with the property. Between one-quarter and one-half of peasant income went to the combination of seigneurial rights, the church's tithe, and state taxes, with the latter taking the largest chunk. The precariousness of existence for many made smuggling salt or tobacco extremely attractive; in the case of tobacco, a colonial product, peasants could earn three or four month's worth of income in just one run. The government claimed a monopoly on both, salt being an essential preservative, and enforced it through a system of private tax-farming corporations that demanded the death penalty for smuggling in some cases. The crackdowns added to the pervasive hatred of the tax farmers and the growing criticism of the royal government.

While peasants with little or no land faced hardship whenever grain harvests fell short, their fate did not compare to that of the textile workers in many big towns and cities who confronted desperate conditions in the spring of 1789. In the northeastern town of Troyes, for instance, two-thirds of the 28,000 inhabitants worked in the cotton industry, and because of overproduction and competition from the more mechanized English manufacturers that followed the signing of the free trade treaty in 1786, at least 10,000 textile workers were unemployed by the end of 1788. Meanwhile, the price of bread, the main staple of the poor, was rising rapidly due to a bad harvest in 1787 and bad weather in the summer and winter of 1788. In Troyes, the price of raw wheat rose 230 percent between June 1788 and July 1789; the price of bread rose more than 40 percent. Rioting over the price of food became increasingly common in many towns.

Largely immune to these short-term fluctuations were the middle classes or "bourgeois" (so-called because most lived in *bourgs*, that is, large villages or towns): lawyers, non-noble officials, doctors, *rentiers* (living off their investments or *rentes*), merchants, and manufacturers. They constituted about 10 percent of the French population and owned about 15 percent of the land. They made up the bulk of the new public because they were literate and educated; provincial academies, masonic lodges, art exhibitions, and public concerts were all located in towns and cities, not to mention major domestic markets and international ports. Virtually all of the middle classes had extensive exposure to the global economy, either directly as investors or traders, or indirectly as consumers of global products such as sugar, coffee, and Chinese or imitation porcelain.

In a country where noble status could be purchased by great wealth, the top ranks of the "bourgeoisie" or middle classes often emulated the ways of the nobility, but since the chances of moving up were limited in practice to the ultra-rich, they also had reason to feel resentful, especially since the middle classes were the fastest growing segment in French society, tripling in number over the course of the eighteenth century. Events in 1788 and 1789 would bring these resentments to the boiling point.

In between the middle classes and poor workers of the towns stood the artisans and shopkeepers, who sometimes owned a shop but could also be individual women who sold coffee or *crêpes* in the street. In Paris by the time of the Revolution 40 percent of households had a coffee pot, and artisans and shopkeepers sometimes had snuffboxes, too. Workers used clay or ceramic pipes. For both workers and artisans coffee and sugar had become staples of life, not just luxuries. Artisans and shopkeepers—and their wives—were much more likely to be literate than unskilled workers. They often had a servant, their own furniture and linens, and a greater variety of clothing than unskilled workers. But the less well-off among them remained susceptible to the food shortages of 1788–1789, and they would form the backbone of crowds demanding government intervention.

The constitutional crisis of 1789

The debt crunch in France opened the door to a constitutional crisis that proved revolutionary because of the influence of new ideas, an expanded public, and the sufferings caused by unexpected food shortages. Recognizing the need for tax reform to make more palatable the increases that were necessary to pay down the debt, Louis XVI convened a special assembly of notables in February 1787. It had last been summoned in 1626. Of its 144 members, at most five were non-nobles. The king hoped that they would enable him to bypass the Parlement of Paris that was responsible for registering crown decrees. The notables refused to ratify the reforms, however, and the king then had to turn to the Parlement of Paris. It too refused and demanded that the king call an Estates-General, with representatives from the clergy (First Estate), nobility (Second Estate), and Third Estate (everyone else). An Estates-General had last met in 1614. Other rifts followed. Among his many powers, the king could order the Parlement to register its approval of new loans. When Louis XVI did so in November 1787, the Duke of Orleans and various magistrates protested. The king used *lettres de cachet* (secret letters that circumvented legal channels) to order the Duke exiled to his country estate in northern France and to imprison two judges.[5]

In response, the Duke and the judges portrayed themselves as defenders of liberty. The judges had long represented themselves as necessary barriers to royal overreach, a kind of constitutional guarantee against despotism. They defended the historic rights of the parlements that through the centuries made up an unwritten but nonetheless influential "constitution." The king's supposedly absolute powers had always been limited by the expectation that he would consult his ministers, the courts, leading nobles, and provincial Estates in the regions that had them by custom. When the Paris Parlement denounced the use of *lettres de cachet* in 1787 as "injurious to reason" and "obviously repugnant to human nature," they were echoing Enlightenment views that had made their way into the public domain. Five years before, a French nobleman, Honoré Gabriel Riquetti, Count of Mirabeau, had anonymously published an influential exposé of *lettres de cachet* and of the prisons to which victims were sent. He had first-hand experience, having been consigned to prison by *lettre de cachet* by his father, a leading Physiocrat, first for overspending and then for having run away with a married woman (he was married himself). Mirabeau soon became a celebrity writer. In his 1782 book he repeatedly referred to the *lettres de cachet* as contrary to "natural rights" and the "rights of man," phrases now increasingly in fashion.

As the tide of criticism continued to swell, the king's government decided in May 1788 to create new courts to challenge the authority of the Paris Parlement and the 12 other provincial parlements. Louis XV had tried something similar between 1770 and 1774 but those reforms had been withdrawn when he died and his grandson Louis XVI succeeded him. Now the angry judges demanded the immediate convocation of the Estates-General and heatedly denounced the despotism of the king's ministers. As nobles and clergy rallied to the side of the parlements (most of whose judges were nobles), riots broke out in towns with parlements. In August, the king retreated and agreed to give up the plan for new courts, move up the date of the Estates-General to May 1, 1789, and recall Necker. In Paris people celebrated in the streets and burned in effigy Necker's predecessor. The United States ambassador to France, Thomas Jefferson, reported that when the police tried to stop the Parisians, they attacked several guard posts and fought pitched battles in which some protestors died. The king's authority was crumbling.

Up to this moment, the nobles had been the champions of resistance to despotism. All this changed in the blink of an eye when the recalled Parlement of Paris decreed in September 1788 that the Estates-General should meet following the rules established in 1614 that gave one vote to each of three estates (clergy, nobility, and commoners). These rules seemed to give the nobles veto power over the proceedings, since most expected the clergy, led by noble archbishops and bishops, to vote in lockstep with the Second Estate. A flood of angry pamphlets demanded twice as many deputies for the Third and voting by individual head, which would mean that a few defections by nobles or clergymen would give the Third Estate the upper hand. The Parlement of Paris relented in December and supported the doubling of the Third's number of deputies, and the king agreed to it in late December 1788 but left unresolved the issue of voting by head. The political damage to the Parlement's reputation could not be undone.

In *What is the Third Estate?*, a fiery manifesto published in January 1789, a non-noble clergyman, Emmanuel Sieyès, lambasted the nobility: for him, the nobles were simply a "burden for the Nation," not a part of it. "If we remove the privileged order, the Nation will not be something less but something more." According to Sieyès, the Third Estate did all the useful work in society and yet they were told: "Whatever your services, whatever your talents, you will only go so far; you will go no further. It would not do for you to be honored." "Careers open to talents" (rather than birth) would become one of the most powerful slogans of 1789. Most French people nonetheless still fervently hoped for national unity around reform, and even Sieyès stopped short of directly demanding the removal of the nobility.

Like many of the American revolutionaries such as Jefferson and Alexander Hamilton, Sieyès had been influenced by the Scottish Enlightenment philosopher Adam Smith's book *Wealth of Nations* (1776). Taking up the Physiocratic ideal of *laissez-faire* (literally "let alone," meaning get rid of excessive governmental regulation of the economy), Smith nonetheless went beyond them in important respects: he did not consider agriculture to be the only pillar of the economy, and he drew attention to the productivity that could be gained in manufacturing by the division of labor. Sieyès's critique of the nobility drew on this emphasis on productivity; in Sieyès's view, the nobles contributed nothing useful to the nation. In pamphlets like Sieyès's, seemingly abstract Enlightenment ideas about the economy, social relations, and constitutions made their way into the very specific political debates of the time.

The elections to the Estates-General

Even as the pamphlet war over the composition of the Estates-General heated up the political atmosphere, the process of electing deputies drew everyone's attention. Although the colonies were explicitly excluded, the king asked every village and town in mainland France to draw up a list of grievances to forward on with those elected as their delegates to the regional meetings; altogether some 40,000 lists were drafted, creating in the process of discussion and voting an unprecedented level of political mobilization. A cacophony of voices could be heard, yet it did not drown out the clear expression of deep political and social differences that now divided the nation.

Although 24 Protestants were elected among the 663 deputies to the Third Estate, only Catholic clergy could be elected to the First Estate's deputation.

The rules for elections of the clergy, set out by the government, gave each of the 60,000 ordinary parish priests the right to participate in person in the regional meetings of the clergy, while the 26,000 monks, 55,000 nuns, and 29,000 Cathedral staff, chaplains, or administrators had to choose representatives, one per monastery or nunnery (nuns had to choose male proxies) and one for every 10 clergy attached to Cathedrals. As a consequence, the widely shared expectation that noble bishops and archbishops would run the show was confounded: three-fourths of the 330 deputies elected for the First Estate were parish priests, hardly any were monks, and the noble hierarchy, though represented, was dramatically outnumbered. Would the parish priests take the side of the Third Estate?

The 171 grievance lists drawn up by the regional meetings of the clergy offered no clear response to that question. They supported such constitutional reforms as periodic meetings of the Estates-General and the suppression of *lettres de cachet* and offered to give up the clergy's tax exemptions; the church paid only a voluntary contribution to the state, usually about 3 percent of the church's income. But most meetings of the clergy avoided taking a stand on voting by order or by head, an ambiguity that would have momentous consequences a few months later. Only a third of the clergy's grievance lists mentioned Protestants; those that did opposed any further extension of rights to them.

All nobles had the right to participate in the meetings of the nobility, the Second Estate, and those who owned lands to which seigneurial rights were attached could send proxies to all of the regions in which they held such lands. Female fiefholders, mainly widows, (a fief was land to which seigneurial rights were attached) could choose proxies, too. Since the Duke of Orleans had fiefholdings in 29 different regions, he not only sent surrogates but also circulated pamphlets with model grievance lists, one of which was written by Sieyès. The distribution of 100,000 such pamphlets later gave rise to conspiracy theories, among them about the hidden hand of freemasonry. The Duke was the Grand Master of all the French freemasons, and Sieyès belonged to the Nine Sisters lodge.

The Duke was not the only reform-minded aristocrat. When agitation began in the fall of 1788 on the question of voting by head or order, a group of high-ranking nobles started meeting in Paris in what came to be called the Society or Committee of Thirty (though it actually had about 50 members). Some were judges in the Parlement of Paris, but half were from ancient military families. Among the latter were the hero of the American War of Independence, Marquis de Lafayette; the early abolitionist and famous mathematician, Marquis de Condorcet; and Mirabeau.

Joining this illustrious group were two clerics: Sieyès and the aristocrat Charles Maurice de Talleyrand-Perigord, who had become a clergyman because with a limp he could not aspire to military command. Talleyrand represented a type that could only flourish in the conditions of the late eighteenth century; he had no personal interest in becoming a clergyman but was forced to do so by his parents who considered him unsuitable for heading a major aristocratic family. He pursued his clerical career with worldly ambition and never hesitated to seduce women or gamble or read forbidden authors. Sieyès came from a much more modest background; he was the fifth of seven children of a minor tax collector in southern France who had sent his son to become a cleric as a route to social advancement. Recently appointed Bishop of Autun, Talleyrand was elected to the Estates-General as a deputy for the clergy. Sieyès failed in his attempt to be elected a deputy for the First Estate, but was chosen at the last minute to represent the Third Estate of Paris.

Reform-minded nobles ran into a wall of resistance from their conservative counterparts in the provinces. The Duke of Orleans sailed through as a deputy, but Lafayette only got a spot when he agreed to a traditionalist list of grievances drawn up by nobles in his home region. Condorcet failed to be elected in either his provincial seat or Paris, even though he had already made a name for himself as a writer on constitutional and electoral questions. Mirabeau's conservative younger brother was elected for the nobility of a region in central France, but Mirabeau himself had to settle for election as a deputy of the Third Estate from Provence, in southern France.

The liberal nobles, who wanted to make common cause with the Third Estate, gained little traction against the conservatives who drafted grievance lists that stubbornly defended honorific distinctions such as the exclusive right to bear arms, walk first in any public procession, and adorn their castles and coaches with coats of arms. Three-quarters of the 322 nobles elected as deputies to the Estates-General were titled (prince, duke, marquis, count, etc.) as opposed to only one in twenty who held titles among all the nobles in the kingdom. The nobles did support constitutional reform; they advocated regular meetings of the Estates-General, but with voting by order. They also argued for the abolition of *lettres de cachet* and new measures to confront the crown's debts; in short, they wanted a greater say in the nation's affairs and saw the crown as the major impediment. Even though the nobles agreed to give up some of their fiscal privileges, they had nonetheless opened the road to bitter conflicts over their status, especially once it became known that the crown spent almost as much on pensions and payments to courtiers, including the king's brothers, as it did on the navy and all the colonies combined.

When peasants made their voices heard in the grievance lists drawn up at the village level (see Document 1.1, at the end of the chapter), they complained bitterly about their burdens. They demanded a decrease in or outright elimination of consumption taxes on salt and alcoholic beverages; moderation of the main land tax (*taille*); the suppression of a host of noble privileges, such as exclusive rights to hunting and raising pigeons; and the abolition of seigneurial dues, such as payments to the lord on the sale of one's property or to use the winepress or oven—monopolies of the lord. Peasants sent these demands along with many peasant delegates to the 200 regional meetings of the Third Estate, but only one peasant was ultimately elected as deputy to the Estates-General. A filtering process took place as voting moved from the local parishes to the regional assemblies of the Third Estate. This did not mean that peasants had given up making their voices heard; in just a few months they would do so in resounding fashion.

In the 290 biggest towns and cities in France, occupational and professional groups first met separately to choose delegates to the town meetings and often to write their own lists of grievances. Like the peasants, urban artisans and small shopkeepers wanted a lessening of their tax burdens, especially the taxes on consumption, and a fairer overall tax system that eliminated noble privileges. Women were excluded from these meetings; domestic servants, who made up as much as 10 percent of the population of cities, were unrepresented because they did not belong to guilds; and textile workers were underrepresented because textile production was no longer controlled by the guild system.

Yet even the most ordinary men demonstrated great interest in the pressing constitutional issues of the day. When 39 master shoemakers of Angoulême, a small town (population 11,000) in southwestern France, met in February to choose a delegate to the town meeting, they drew up a grievance list that began by demanding meetings of the Estates-General every five years and went on to ask that all French people, whatever their estate, pay taxes proportionate to their incomes.[6] Their own specific complaints did not prevent them from seeing the broader issues. As the grievance lists and delegates made their way first up to the town assemblies and then to the regional meetings of the Third Estate, ordinary men like the shoemakers still had a voice but a fainter and fainter one.

Lawyers, officials, and big property-owners dominated the regional elections for the Third Estate. Two-thirds of those elected as deputies to the Estates-General had had some training in the law, whether as mid-level judges, lawyers, or notaries. They were elected in far greater numbers than the richest members of the middle classes: bankers, manufacturers, and merchants of the slave port cities such as Nantes and La Rochelle. Merchants had been well-represented at the town level; in Troyes, for example, though only 13 percent of the delegates to the town meeting were merchants or clothiers, a third of those sent to the regional meeting fell in that category. But less than 10 percent of the Third Estate deputies as a whole came from the commercial classes, and none of them were artisans or shopkeepers.

The grievance lists drawn up by the regional meetings of the Third Estate carried forward many of the demands of the peasants and urban workers but prioritized them differently: the top four subjects on the peasants' lists were taxation in general, the salt tax, the tax on alcoholic beverages, and the state's salt monopoly while the top four subjects on the regional grievance lists were taxation, the powers of provincial Estates, regular meetings of the Estates-General, and voting by head in the Estates-General. The lower-level assemblies had focused on basic economic issues, but at the regional meetings the involvement of the educated middle classes led to increased emphasis on more abstract political matters. Moreover, many of those attending regional meetings had seen sample *cahiers* that emphasized constitutional issues, such as voting by head.

By the middle of April 1789 most of the elections had taken place, except for Paris. Regulations for elections in Paris were not published until April 13 and to the shock of many they called for meetings by district rather than occupational group. The 60 Paris districts were supposed to meet on April 21 and immediately select delegates to a city-wide assembly that would then choose 20 deputies for the Third Estate (the nobles and clergy met separately to pick their deputies). Rather than simply convene and select delegates, however, many of the sixty local assemblies insisted on organizing themselves; they threw out the presidents named by the king and elected new ones and drew up grievance lists, even though they had not been asked to do so.

In this way, a new shadow government of Paris took shape, especially as some district assemblies continued to meet. The scene of the action then shifted to the general assembly, which only finished electing deputies on May 23, more than two weeks after the Estates-General opened. Although officially disbanded, the Paris electoral assembly reconvened at the end of June and promptly began operating as a parallel city government. Its president as of early July was Médéric Moreau de Saint Méry, a 39-year-old lawyer born in Martinique. An expert on Saint-Domingue and a freemason, Moreau saw no contradiction between his enthusiasm for revolutionary politics and his impassioned defenses of slavery.

But others did. The question of slavery gained new urgency after Jacques Brissot organized an abolitionist club, The Society of the Friends of Blacks, in February 1788. The 35-year-old lawyer and member of the Nine Sisters masonic lodge was known for his treatises on legal reform, his knowledge of the new United States, and his unsavory past as a pornographic pamphleteer. The club, an affiliate of the English and American abolitionist societies, promptly attracted many of the liberal nobles of the Society of Thirty, including Lafayette, Condorcet, and Mirabeau. In response, the planters began to mobilize. In September 1788 delegates from the planters of Saint-Domingue brought a petition to the king requesting representation in the Estates-General.

After being refused, secret assemblies began meeting back on the island to elect deputies. Brissot took the lead in insisting on exclusion of any such deputies from the Estates-General. When the Estates began meeting in early May, the question of colonial representation was still unresolved. But then so were many other burning issues.

The Estates-General meets

As the deputies spilled into Versailles for the opening procession of May 4, 1789, they brought soaring hopes for reform but also deep worries. The electoral process had raised the political temperature to a fever pitch, and at the same time the country faced a dangerous food emergency. A severe drought in the spring of 1788 had damaged crops resulting in two-thirds the normal grain production and an even more catastrophic wine harvest. Then the winter of 1788–1789 turned into one of the coldest ever recorded. Outside work stopped, wine froze and burst the barrels, iced-over rivers made it impossible to grind or transport grain, and everywhere poor people scrounged for firewood just to stay alive.

The prices of grain and therefore bread rose continuously through 1788 and into 1789; by April 1789 they were 75 percent higher than in 1787 with the next harvest still months away. Since bread and flour made up as much as 95 percent of the diet of the poor and average workers spent about half their earnings on them even in good times, the price increase could only be disastrous for poor peasants and workers. Riots over the cost of bread began in August 1788 and continued into 1789. Just days before the opening of the Estates-General, workers at a wallpaper factory in eastern Paris heard rumors that their wages would be reduced, and in a fury, sacked the house of Jean-Baptiste Réveillon, the factory owner and one of the delegates to the Paris electoral assembly. Troops fired on the crowd, killing more than 200 according to the British ambassador. Two rioters were executed the next day. To say tempers were on edge hardly begins to capture the anxiety of the moment.[7]

The deputies could afford to eat, and in fact their arrival jump-started the development of the restaurant as a place to dine (*restaurant* comes from the French word for "restoring"), but they had to keep the food shortage in mind even while preparing for the Estates-General. Many felt apprehensive. Adrien Duquesnoy, a 30-year-old lawyer and Third Estate deputy from eastern France, wrote on May 3 that he and many others believed "the government wants to wear us down with famine and fatigue." In this scenario, the deputies would talk and talk, accomplish little, and eventually give up and go home. Duquesnoy recounted the remarks supposedly made by one of the titled noble deputies about his Third Estate counterparts: "Let us go see how they look, these beasts that are going to overrun us."

The majestic opening procession of May 4 did nothing to calm fears. The deputies were told to assemble at 7 a.m. but the king did not arrive until three hours later. "An individual does not make a nation wait for three hours," complained Duquesnoy. The Duke of Orleans was cheered, the kings' brothers heard only silence, and the queen, despite a few feeble murmurs of "Vive la Reine!," was greeted with loud insults. The deputies of the Third Estate insisted on marching together rather than by region, and when the parade many hours later finally reached the church where mass was to be celebrated, the master of ceremonies demanded that the Third Estate deputies who had taken seats in the front move to the back behind the clergy and nobles. Compromise was not in the air.

OPENING OF THE ESTATES-GENERAL (Short phrases in bold face and capital letters refer to the timeline of important events given at the end of each chapter)   On May 5 Louis XVI opened the meeting in Versailles, and Necker gave such an endless speech on the state of the finances that a clerk had to read it when he lost his voice (Figure 1.3). The king said nothing on the question of voting by order or by head, and the next day the deputies of the Third Estate found themselves in a separate room from the other two estates. They had received no instructions on how to proceed, and other than Mirabeau hardly any of the deputies had a national reputation. Given his checkered past as a writer of pornography and political pamphlets for financiers, Mirabeau did not enjoy universal esteem. Duquesnoy described him on May 7 as "a ferocious, rabid beast; he has the look of a tiger. He only speaks in convulsions; his face tenses up, and he whistles with rage." Nothing, however, was going to stop Mirabeau either inside or outside the meetings; he and Brissot both immediately began publishing newspapers to influence opinion. Desmoulins had rushed to Paris and on May 5 he told his father that he had written to Mirabeau asking to become a collaborator on the "much discussed gazette." The government promptly banned both papers but Mirabeau just changed the name of his from *Journal des États Généraux* to *Lettres du Comte de Mirabeau à ses Commettants* (Constituents) and claimed that he was simply reporting back home.

Even as the deputies of the Third argued about what to do first, two momentous developments were unfolding: the emergence of a political press and political caucusing. The success of Mirabeau's maneuver made continuing restriction of the press impossible to sustain. Within a year, 90 periodicals would appear including some dozen dailies; a year later the total rose to over 120. Political journalists like Desmoulins became celebrities; Desmoulins himself earned as much as 10,000 l. a year, more than many Old Regime officials and five times as much as a provincial lawyer.[8]

FIGURE 1.3 *The Opening of the Estates-General, May 5, 1789*
This print is part of the many subscription series that were launched in 1789 and afterward to try to capture the unfolding history of events. Because it was part of a series, we know the names of the designer, Charles Monnet, the engraver, Isidor Stanislas Helman, and even the publisher, Nicolas Ponce. Etching and engraving, 1790.

Although most deputies hoped to sway opinion through their oratory in the hall, some began meeting over dinner to plan strategy, in particular, deputies from Brittany known as "the Breton Club." In the run-up to elections in Brittany a group of young lawyers had become increasingly radicalized by the opposition of Breton nobles to any suggestion of reform. Once the meetings opened in Versailles, the Bretons welcomed others of like mind including Desmoulins, Mirabeau, Sieyès, and a 31-year-old lawyer from northern France, Maximilien Robespierre, a close friend of Desmoulins from school days. Mirabeau sarcastically said of the socially awkward Robespierre, "this man will go far: he believes everything he says." Robespierre was destined to become the single most controversial figure of the French Revolution but at this moment he was simply one of many trying to shape the country's future with no clear blueprint at hand.

THE NATIONAL ASSEMBLY Most of the Third Estate deputies hoped for compromise with the other two estates but the Breton Club members determined to hold out for vote by head. After many efforts at conciliation failed, the deputies of the Third Estate decided to act unilaterally. On June 8, Sieyès, just elected from Paris, read a motion at the Breton Club calling on the other two estates to meet with the Third for a joint verification of credentials; the Third Estate deputies voted nearly unanimously for it on June 10. On June 12 three parish priests joined the Third, and another 19 followed soon after. On June 17, in front of a gallery packed with 4,000 spectators, the deputies voted to adopt the name National Assembly, a term Sieyès had not used in his motion on June 8 but now endorsed. The first decree passed by the Assembly took control over taxation and promised to work with the king to fix the principles of "national regeneration."[9]

TENNIS COURT OATH With the stroke of a pen, a constitutional revolution had been set in motion. But would it hold? Was Louis XVI willing to become a constitutional monarch sharing power with an elected assembly? Were the nobles and clergy ready for the obliteration of estates in favor of an assembly in which the Third Estate delegates enjoyed a clear majority? Half of the clergy's deputies decided to join the National Assembly, but the Duke of Orleans got only 89 votes for his motion to the nobles to do the same. High-ranking nobles furiously lobbied the king for intervention. On June 20 the deputies found themselves locked out of their hall on the grounds that it had to be refurbished for a royal session in which the king would reveal his decision. The deputies ended up nearby in an unused indoor tennis court of the palace where they swore an oath, called thereafter the Tennis Court Oath, not to separate until they drafted a workable constitution. On June 23, Louis XVI announced his decision in person to the deputies; he summarily rejected the National Assembly and ordered each estate to meet separately and vote on almost all matters by order. When commanded to disperse, the deputies refused, and Mirabeau shouted, "We will not leave our seats except by the force of bayonets." Louis backed down. Or was he simply playing for time while loyal soldiers moved into Paris and Versailles?

In an ominous sign, armed soldiers now guarded the hall, but 47 liberal nobles nevertheless decided to join the National Assembly. The mere mention that Necker was going to resign brought a huge crowd to his house begging him to stay; when he said he would, people celebrated by racing through the streets torches in hand and crying "Long Live the National Assembly," "Long Live Necker." The carriages of conservative nobles and clergy were hooted or even stoned. On June 27, fearing a popular uprising or mutiny of the French Guards, the king ordered all the clergy and nobles to sit in the new assembly. The king's indecisiveness was fast becoming a decisive factor.

The deputies, the people, and social revolution

Soldiers, many of them Swiss or German mercenaries, kept streaming toward Paris and Versailles, only eleven miles apart from each other. Desmoulins claimed 30,000 soldiers were surrounding Paris; some deputies spoke of 50,000. No one knew for certain. Given the growing tendency of the French Guards to sympathize with the public, the government seemed determined to rely on its foreign contingents. On July 8 Mirabeau warned of the consequences of the deployment of foreign troops; "Do those who advised these measures foresee the consequences that they will entail for the security itself of the throne? Have they studied the history of all peoples and seen how revolutions start?"

FALL OF THE BASTILLE   Louis now gave in to pressure from those pushing him to act; he would fire Necker and replace all the major heads of departments. On July 5 he ordered reinforcement of the garrison of the Bastille with Swiss soldiers and on July 11, the day he sacked Necker, he wrote to the Paris commander, "if there is a general insurrection we cannot defend the whole of Paris and you must confine yourself to the plan for the defense of the Bourse [stock exchange], the Royal Treasury, the Bastille and the Invalides." Faced with crowds arming themselves in Paris, the commander instead ordered the soldiers back to their camps and fled the scene. Only the Bastille garrison held out, until it fell on July 14 (see Map 1.2).

As events unfolded in Paris, the deputies in Versailles met in twelve-hour shifts and slept armed with pistols and swords. When the smoke cleared in Paris on July 15, the king had to yield. He vowed to work with the National Assembly, whose existence he now recognized. On July 16 he recalled Necker, and the next day he went to Paris, escorted by the deputies. The citizens' militia known as the National Guard assured security; it had been set up by the Paris electors and was commanded by Lafayette. Filled with middle-class men, the National Guard allayed fears about the intervention of the army and the potential violence of the working classes. Passing by 200,000 armed citizens, the king arrived at city hall where the new mayor handed him a tricolor cockade, a rosette of red, white, and blue ribbons, to put on his hat. It signaled adherence to the new order. The tricolor had replaced the green of the Duke of Orleans; red and blue were the colors of Paris, white the color of the monarchy.

The British ambassador astutely remarked that Louis XVI was "more a captive than a king, being led along like a tamed bear." The ordinary people of Paris had flexed their muscle; they had armed themselves, attacked the most imposing symbol of royal power at the Bastille prison, and demonstrated a terrifying passion for retribution against those seen as traitors to the people's will. They had no doubt been alarmed by the continuing rise in the price of

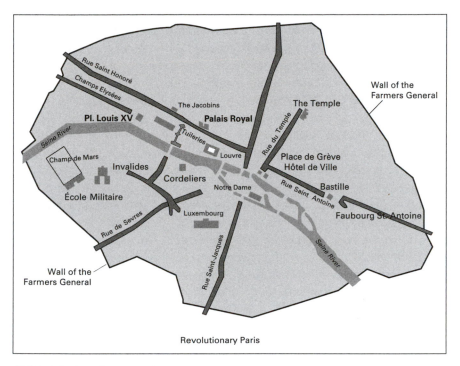

MAP 1.2 *Revolutionary Paris*

bread, which reached its apex for the year precisely on July 14, but they had been motivated even more by their desire to defend the new political order.

The people in arms had saved the deputies, but popular fears of conspiracy and reactions of vengefulness would prove hard to contain. On July 22, a royal official suspected of plotting to hoard grain was dragged out of city hall, hanged from a lamppost, and mutilated. The crowd later presented his severed head to his son-in-law who was similarly murdered and dismembered. Lafayette and other city leaders had tried vainly to ensure the safety of the captives but failed. Denouncing these "bloody and illegal executions," Lafayette tendered his resignation but under pressure agreed to stay on.

Paris was far from alone in experiencing paroxysms of violence. Food riots rocked many towns and cities from July 12 onward, and when news filtered out of Necker's dismissal local revolts threatened to topple municipal administrations. In Rouen, Nantes, Lille, Strasbourg, Grenoble, and many other cities, huge crowds demanded action on grain prices and arms. Popular pressure forced city councils to set up emergency committees to organize militia units (soon called the National Guard on the model of Paris) and to distribute grain. Over the summer the emergency committees, which often included numerous artisans and shopkeepers, took on increasing responsibility and sometimes displaced the councils altogether. Scores of local revolutions thus reinforced the changes in Paris and Versailles.

RIOTS IN THE COUNTRYSIDE The rapidly unfolding events aroused not only enthusiasm but also deep anxieties. Did anyone imagine that the defenders of the Old Regime would just sit back and let events take their course? In late July and early August, when the harvest had yet to come in, the new National Guard units confronted a mounting rural panic that historians have labeled the Great Fear. Rumors of secret plots to starve the people moved in chain reaction across much of the country. Unnamed aristocrats were supposedly hiring brigands to burn the crops in the fields. If an unknown man, or worse yet a gang of beggars appeared, villagers would spread the word and gather together with pitchforks and scythes to defend themselves. As warnings escalated from village to village, hundreds and even thousands of people would flee to nearby towns or cities, demanding that National Guard units protect them.[10]

In many places, but especially in southeastern and south central France, peasant self-defense turned into attacks on the seigneurial or "feudal" regime. In 1788 poor peasants had rioted against rising grain prices. Writing down their grievances in the spring of 1789 had shifted peasant attention to *féodalité* or the feudal system according to which noble lords could still claim all kinds of seigneurial dues from their peasant tenants. After arming themselves against brigands in July, peasants quickly turned against the signs of seigneurial or feudal privilege: they attacked chateaux, burned the lord's records of their dues, ripped out the lord's private pews in the parish church, and even tore down weathervanes and coats of arms. In a final symbolic gesture, they sometimes planted a liberty tree or maypole in front of the lord's manor, a practice then picked up in Paris and other big cities.

END OF "FEUDALISM" While some noble deputies back in Versailles feared the worst for their properties, all the deputies fretted about the course of events. Was not the spread of rural panic and rebellion itself a sign of conspiracy to wreck the credit of the new assembly? Was British money behind the nearly simultaneous cries of alarm in the countryside? As violence swirled, many officials of the monarchy abandoned their posts and even went into hiding. Nothing had been decided about a new government but the old one was melting away. Something had to be done, and so the Breton Club planned a spectacular intervention; the Duke of Aiguillon, one of the richest men in France, would step to the podium in a night session on August 4 and propose a phased-out indemnification of seigneurial dues. Hearing of the plans, another noble deputy jumped ahead of him and put forward something much more radical, abolition of seigneurial dues without compensation.

Before long, a kind of spell took hold as clergy, nobles, and commoners outdid each other in volunteering to give up privileges, not only the suppression of the remnants of feudalism but the end as well to the buying and selling of offices, the clergy's fees and the tithe, and all exemptions from taxes. "Posterity will never believe," wrote one deputy, "what the National Assembly did in the space of five hours."

It remained to be seen, however, just what form these various proposals would take. After a week's discussion, on August 11 the Assembly announced that it "entirely destroys the feudal regime," but while eliminating noble privileges such as dovecotes and the exclusive right to hunting, the deputies distinguished between feudal rights derived from serfdom, which were abolished without compensation, and those covered by written contracts, which had to be indemnified. At the same time, the Assembly abolished venality of office and all tax exemptions, whether for nobles, clergy, towns, or regions; opened all official positions to merit alone; and promised to eliminate the tithe once other means of supporting the Catholic Church could be established. The decree announced the arrival of a new regime of equality under the law, but still left most peasants dissatisfied. Violence in the countryside subsided but did not disappear.[11]

Many hoped to present the principles animating the new regime in a declaration of rights that would serve as a preamble to France's first written constitution. The American Declaration of Independence in 1776 had spoken of the "self-evident" truth that all men were endowed with "certain unalienable rights," but it had not defined those rights beyond promising life, liberty, and the pursuit of happiness. The new United States Constitution ratified in 1788 did not include a bill of rights until 1791, when the first ten amendments were approved. In fact, the United States Constitution made hardly any mention of rights, and the rights articulated in the first ten amendments only prevented the new government from being overly intrusive. On July 11 Lafayette presented to the National Assembly his draft of a declaration; he had developed it in conversation with the US ambassador, Jefferson, who also rather high-handedly offered a draft of his own. Sieyès and Mirabeau proposed their own versions, but on August 26, after great debate about whether such a "metaphysical" statement was even necessary, the deputies finally approved 17 articles sent forward by a largely anonymous committee (see Document 1.2, at the end of the chapter).

DECLARATION OF THE RIGHTS OF MAN AND CITIZEN Despite its origins in a cat's cradle of parliamentary trade-offs, the Declaration of the Rights of Man and Citizen set out a powerful, universal vision of the foundation of all government on the recognition of rights. It said nothing of the king, the Catholic Church, or the nobility, or for that matter, of Protestants, women, or slaves. It insisted, as the American Declaration of Independence had, on the equality of rights of all men but left open the definition of the French citizen. As Sieyès had articulated in his January defense of the Third Estate, "common utility" was to be the only standard for social distinctions, not birth into a privileged order. The declaration also proclaimed freedom of expression and freedom of religion as long as they did not undermine public order; conservatives hoped that this wording would allow government monitoring of the press and prevent the extension of political rights to Protestants. The bold promise of a right of insurrection was balanced by an equally strong article that demanded obedience to the law.

The deputies had chosen an abstract language in part in order to paper over deep differences of opinion. That abstraction and the universal reach of the claims would have both an energizing and a less attractive aggrandizing effect. The abstraction—"men," "every man," "every citizen," "the nation"—opened the door to Protestants, Jews, men without property, free blacks, women, and slaves to demand equal rights, which they did over the following months and years. At the same time, the universalism of the claims eventually cleared a path to French intervention in the affairs of other, supposedly less free countries. As the 32-year-old veteran of the American war, Duke Mathieu de Montmorency, proclaimed during the debates, the United States "set a great example in the new hemisphere; let us give one to the universe." It would not be long before such sentiments would justify occupation and even annexation of foreign territories.

The great debate on the declaration of rights had shown conservatives the importance of mobilizing to counter the influence of men such as Mirabeau and Sieyès. As the Breton Club and its allies began to sit together in the assembly hall on the presiding member's left side, those who opposed radical measures began to sit together on the right, giving rise to the modern notion of political "left" and "right." The deputies on the right also began to meet together to plan strategy. At their center was Jean-Joseph Mounier, a talented legal scholar and judge from Grenoble who favored a constitutional monarchy on the English model, in which the king shared power with a legislature made up of an elected lower house and an upper house with lifetime members like the House of Lords in the English Parliament. Although he failed to get the assembly to agree to a two-house legislature or an absolute veto for the king, Mounier did achieve the substantial victory of a "suspensive" veto in which a veto would hold unless three successive legislatures voted to overturn it.

As with the consideration of the declaration of rights, the debate about the veto demonstrated the influence of Enlightenment writings about freedom, constitutions, and rights. At the same time it also revealed the depth of divisions about the conclusions that should be drawn from those writings. Hardly anyone imagined that France could become a republic, since most believed that republics would only survive in small states like Geneva, Venice, or the Dutch Republic. England seemed a more likely model than the new United States because like France England had been governed by a monarch for centuries. Although the experience of the United States showed that constitutions could be fashioned on new principles, in most respects the United States was simply too different to serve as an exemplar; it only had 4 million inhabitants, of whom 700,000 were slaves and 150,000 were Native Americans. The biggest city, Philadelphia, had 40,000 people whereas Paris housed 16 times that number.

MARCH ON VERSAILLES   Even though the deputies on the political right protected the king's authority to a great extent, they could neither force the king to cooperate nor keep the lid on mounting discontent in Paris. Louis XVI kept putting off the official proclamation of the Declaration of the Rights of Man and the first constitutional decrees. After stabilizing for a while, the price of bread rose ominously again. On October 4 the king gave voice to his reservations about the declaration of rights. By then rumors of an incident in Versailles had stirred up the Parisian populace; the king's bodyguards had given a banquet on October 1 for a newly arrived regiment that included many foreigners and during the celebration, at which the king and queen were present, the soldiers trampled the tricolor cockade and ostentatiously paraded black ones, the color of Marie-Antoinette. Once again the Paris crowd swung into action, but this time, unlike July 14, women took the lead. Working women had been standing in the long lines for bread and worrying about how to make ends meet for their families, but they also followed the political affairs of the moment, in this case with rising anger. They intended to make their voices heard.

On October 5, groups of market women gathered at the Paris city hall where they demanded to know why officials had accomplished so little. Determined to press their case with the deputies in Versailles, they set off in a steady rain, brandishing broomsticks, pitchforks, and swords (Figure 1.4). When they arrived, 7,000 strong, a deputation allowed into the meeting room called for punishment of the bodyguards, withdrawal of the recently arrived regiment, and action on bread prices. Mounier, as president of the assembly, then led the women through the mud to the royal palace where twelve of them went in to speak to the king. Louis XVI agreed to rush grain supplies to Paris. Mounier returned to find other wet and disheveled women now occupying seats in the assembly, including his own. Meanwhile Lafayette had arrived with 20,000 National Guards to ensure order. That night a group of men went to Mounier's house and threatened to cut off his head; he withdrew from the assembly soon after.

Early the next morning, a small group of protestors broke through the palace doors, killed two bodyguards, and raced toward the queen's private quarters where they had every intention of killing her. She barely escaped through a secret door as the intruders stabbed and shredded her bed.

À Versailles À Versailles du 5 Octobre 1789

FIGURE 1.4 *Women's March to Versailles, October 5, 1789*
Working women drag a cannon and brandish pikes and bayonets on their way to
Versailles to meet the king and the deputies. Note the middle-class woman on the
far left whose participation seems less than voluntary. Anonymous, hand-colored
etching, 1789.

Lafayette brought the king out on a balcony to calm the crowd but they
insisted on seeing the queen too. The king had to agree to bring his whole
family immediately back to Paris. An astonishing nine-hour procession of
60,000 people made its way to Paris accompanied by the heads of the two
guards on pikes. The deputies of the National Assembly moved their meetings
to Paris a few days later.

No one was entirely certain why events had taken the course they had.
Many blamed the Duke of Orleans and Mirabeau, and in fact a judicial inquiry
set up a few weeks later targeted their suspected role in trying to discredit the
king in order to make way for Orleans as regent or king. Now that newspapers
were no longer censored, many spread the idea of hidden conspiracies. In his
newspaper *Le Patriote français*, Brissot claimed that there was no food
shortage, just a manipulation of prices to upset ordinary people. While
denouncing "the rash and illegal executions" and insisting the "riot" had been
set in motion by "enemies of the public good," he concluded that the plotting
actually had the opposite effect because it brought the king and the assembly
to Paris where they could be watched by the people.

A fundamental dynamic had been set in motion that would drive the
revolution forward for the next five years. While the deputies fought over the

shape of the future government of the nation, lower-class people on occasion intervened, first to protect the revolution from hostile forces, then to push their representatives to act more quickly and more decisively. Collective violence, whether in the form of demonstrations, riots, price-fixing, or retribution against perceived enemies of the nation, lurked beneath the surface of the waves of legislative debate. Violence could be mobilized by political factions once it erupted, but it could not be fully controlled. Successive leaders discovered this truth the hard way, usually as they were falling from power.

Documents

DOCUMENT 1.1

Complaints, grievances, and protests of the parish of Saint-Beury in Burgundy

In the spring of 1789, peasants, all over France, when requested by the King to give their concerns, answered. Some wrote a few paragraphs, others pages of complaints. Although this grievance list from the French heartland did not focus on taxes as many others did, it provides profound insights into the rural mentality. Here the peasants clearly express an ideal: they owed loyalty to the seigneurs who consequently should protect them. But the unworthy lords exacted unfair payments, controlled too much of the land, and enjoyed privileges denied to their "vassals." By referring so explicitly to the "leftovers" from "the tyranny of feudal times," the peasants appeared to dismiss the entire seigneurial regime, which they equated with feudalism. In addition, the grievance lists expressed resentment, however obliquely, toward the royal government, which required them to work on the roads, creating terrible hardships. Here again they used the term "tyranny," a political reference that, though common enough among the educated, is surprising here. Framing all these complaints were core beliefs: the hard-working peasants faced poverty and multiple injustices, which could only be galling in a society of "free men."

The parish of Saint-Beury includes four hamlets: Beurizot, L'Hé, Lignière, and Verchisy. Situated at the head of the valley of Saint-Thibault, its soil is difficult to cultivate; it produces wheat and a little mixed wheat and rye; there are several small vineyards. Much of the terrain is mountainous and scarcely arable. The meadows are abundant; the woods, reserved to the seigneur, exist in sufficient amount, but are so overused that they do not suffice for heating, still less for general use, even for use in ploughs. The inhabitants work hard but are reduced to the greatest misery. The parish includes 94 households.

. . . . . .

In 1788, a big road opened that cut through the parish.

. . . . . .

May one complain here of the tyranny exercised by this route during the recent construction? Squads of armed constables forced unfortunate people to work and tore them away from the necessary and pressing work of the countryside. Men, women, and livestock, all were assigned to this job. One wagon of stones, found a half-league [1. 5 miles] from the road cost 10 sols [approximately ½ *livre*].

. . . . . .

The vassals owe homage and submission to their seigneur and the seigneur owes justice to his vassals where they live. To go four leagues to find one's judge is necessarily an issue because of the expense for the vassal. A woman whose husband dies leaving her with four, six, ten children, cannot without considerable expense take three or four people to a judge so far away to be approved as guardian.

. . . . . .

Seigneurial rights never expire; the rights of individuals end after 30 years. Why this difference in a society of free men?

. . . . . .

An individual, when inheriting property and having it recorded, has to pay the seigneur for rights and bills 29 years in arrears at a value of 100 *livres* against an inheritance often not worth over 50. He cannot simply give up the property as payment; he has to pay, even when he has bought back the right, if he has lost the title [verifying the redemption]. What injustice!

. . . . . .

Salt is an almost indispensable necessity; it costs 14 sols [a pound] in Burgundy. The expense of this commodity means that the majority of the most impoverished cannot use salt because if they do, they cannot buy bread – which is more necessary still. Oh, how painful is their life!

. . . . . .

This parish wishes that each be judged by his peers and demands the entire abolition of *mainmorte* [the seigneurial right to a portion of the deceased peasant's estate], a leftover from the tyranny of feudal times.

Source: Victor Flour de Saint-Genis, ed., *Cahier de doléances du Tiers-état de la paroisse de Saint-Beury en Auxois* (Paris: Imprimerie nationale, 1901), available at http://gallica.bnf.fr/ark:/12148/bpt6k42415d/f7.image. r=feodalite%20.langEN (consulted April 24, 2015).

Questions on the grievance list

1 List as many reasons as you can for the grievances of the peasants.

2 Why did many wealthy people and nobles fear these demands?

3 How were problems addressed by the August 4 decrees?

DOCUMENT 1.2

Declaration of the Rights of Man and Citizen, 1789

The drafting of the declaration left almost everyone unsatisfied, but after six days of impassioned debate, the deputies needed to move on to other tasks. On August 26, 1789 they therefore voted to postpone further discussion until they had completed writing a new constitution. They never returned to the subject. Some had wanted a declaration of duties alongside that of rights; some wanted much longer explanations of the articles; others considered the very idea of a declaration an unnecessary distraction from the need to create new administrative, fiscal, and electoral rules. The declaration focused on abstract and general principles, and in so doing, opened the door to a series of unanticipated discussions about rights, including the rights of religious minorities, men without property, free blacks, slaves, and women.

The representatives of the French people, constituted as a National Assembly, and considering that ignorance, neglect or contempt of the rights of man are the sole causes of public misfortunes and governmental corruption, have resolved to set forth in a solemn declaration the natural, inalienable and sacred rights of man: so that by being constantly present to all the members of the social body this declaration may always remind them of their rights and duties; so that by being liable at every moment to comparison with the aim of any and all political institutions the acts of the legislative and executive powers may be the more fully respected; and so that by being founded henceforward on simple and incontestable principles the demands of the citizens may always tend toward maintaining the constitution and the general welfare.

In consequence, the National Assembly recognizes and declares, in the presence and under the auspices of the Supreme Being, the following rights of man and the citizen:

1 Men are born and remain free and equal in rights. Social distinctions may be based only on common utility.

2 The purpose of all political association is the preservation of the natural and imprescriptible rights of man. These rights are liberty, property, security and resistance to oppression.

3 The principle of all sovereignty rests essentially in the nation. No body and no individual may exercise authority which does not emanate expressly from the nation.

4 Liberty consists in the ability to do whatever does not harm another; hence the exercise of the natural rights of each man has no other limits than those which assure to other members of society the enjoyment of the same rights. These limits can only be determined by the law.

5 The law only has the right to prohibit those actions which are injurious to society. No hindrance should be put in the way of anything not prohibited by the law, nor may any one be forced to do what the law does not require.

6 The law is the expression of the general will. All citizens have the right to take part, in person or by their representatives, in its formation. It must be the same for everyone whether it protects or penalizes. All citizens being equal in its eyes are equally admissible to all public dignities, offices and employments, according to their ability, and with no other distinction than that of their virtues and talents.

7 No man may be indicted, arrested or detained except in cases determined by the law and according to the forms which it has prescribed. Those who seek, expedite, execute or cause to be executed arbitrary orders should be punished; but citizens summoned or seized by virtue of the law should obey instantly, and render themselves guilty by resistance.

8 Only strictly and obviously necessary punishments may be established by the law, and no one may be punished except by virtue of a law established and promulgated before the time of the offense, and legally applied.

9 Every man being presumed innocent until judged guilty, if it is deemed indispensable to arrest him, all rigor unnecessary to securing his person should be severely repressed by the law.

10 No one should be disturbed for his opinions, even in religion, provided that their manifestation does not trouble public order as established by law.

11 The free communication of thoughts and opinions is one of the most precious of the rights of man. Every citizen may therefore speak, write and print freely, if he accepts his own responsibility for any abuse of this liberty in the cases set by the law.

12 The safeguard of the rights of man and the citizen requires public powers. These powers are therefore instituted for the advantage of all, and not for the private benefit of those to whom they are entrusted.

13 For maintenance of public authority and for expenses of administration, common taxation is indispensable. It should be apportioned equally among all the citizens according to their capacity to pay.

14 All citizens have the right, by themselves or through their representatives, to have demonstrated to them the necessity of public taxes, to consent to them freely, to follow the use made of the proceeds, and to determine the means of apportionment, assessment, and collection, and the duration of them.

15 Society has the right to hold accountable every public agent of the administration.

16 Any society in which the guarantee of rights is not assured or the separation of powers not settled has no constitution.

17 Property being an inviolable and sacred right, no one may be deprived of it except when public necessity, certified by law, obviously requires it, and on the condition of a just compensation in advance.

Source: La Constitution française, Présentée au Roi par l'Assemblée Nationale, le 3 septembre 1791 (Paris, 1791).

Questions on the Declaration of Rights of Man and Citizen

1 Since the Declaration emerged as a compromise between conservatives and the more liberally minded deputies, find articles that contain both points of view.

2 Even before the Revolution, the French believed that institutions like the *parlement* had the right to limit royal actions. How did this claim evolve in the Declaration of Rights?

TIMELINE TO CHAPTER 1

May 5	Opening of the Estates-General.
June 17	Third Estate calls itself the National Assembly.
June 20	Tennis Court Oath defies royal authority.
July 14	Fall of the Bastille.
July 14–Aug. 4	Riots in the countryside.
August 4	Deputies vow to end "feudalism".
August 26	Declaration of the Rights of Man and Citizen approved.
October 5–6	March on Versailles by the Parisian populace ends with the royal family brought to Paris.

QUESTIONS ABOUT CHAPTER 1

1 What were the most important global trends that led to the French Revolution? Be sure to consider changes in commercial and financial patterns.

2 Examine the seizure of the Bastille. Consider the role of ideas, social and economic problems, and other general matters. Which do you think mattered most: these general considerations or the specific acts of individuals?

3 Why did some wealthy people and nobles join the movement to change the French form of government in 1789?

4 Compare the actions of the king leading up to the seizure of the Bastille with his efforts in subsequent months up to early October. Can you draw conclusions about his motives?

5 Although the king and assembly played central roles in the Revolution, the working classes in Paris as well as in the countryside erupted. Compare the goals of the two groups and the effects of their actions.

2

The power of the people, 1789–1792

A new chapter opened in October 1789 when a popular demonstration forced the king and the National Assembly to move to the capital city. Camille Desmoulins wrote irreverently to his father on October 8, "*Consummatum est*" [It is finished—Jesus's last words on the cross], and then recounted how the queen had been forced to invite market women to dine with her in Paris. He begged his father for money so that he could install himself properly in Paris and gain a position as commander of the National Guard or as an official with the Paris government. His pamphlets had gained him notoriety, but he craved for more direct political influence so he set up a newspaper of his own the next month.

The October days of 1789 had revealed the power of the people; as Desmoulins wrote in one of his pamphlets, "When the people do not get justice, they get it for themselves." But just what were the powers of the people and how should they be exercised? Even Desmoulins worried about the effects of popular violence. The deputies had declared that sovereignty rested in the nation, not the king, but what form would sovereignty take? In a series of startling developments over the next three years, the sovereign nation first became a constitutional monarchy and then turned into a republic with the first nationwide institution of nearly universal male suffrage ever seen in the world. Noble status was abolished, the properties of the Catholic Church were confiscated, and equality under the law was given explicit expression in new law codes and entirely new administrative and tax systems. Bishops were elected by the citizenry, as were, for a time, even army officers. In short, the revolution first tore up and then rewrote the political agenda for Europe and eventually much of the rest of the world. Between 1789 and 1792, previously unimagined forms of political organization, political participation, and political ideology emerged. The power of the people permeated every realm of life in France and soon promised to revolutionize much of the Western world.

Trans-Atlantic and trans-European radicalism

The French were not alone in pursuing democratic aspirations. They were tapping into a sense of destiny shared by many across the Atlantic world. In the 1770s, 1780s, and 1790s supporters of fundamental change called themselves "patriots." Benjamin Franklin revitalized the term when in a letter of July 1773 he saluted the "many Thousand true Patriots [that] New England contains."[1] The term then began to circulate around the Atlantic to signify resistance to oppressors and demands for popular sovereignty. For the British North American colonists like Franklin, it stood for those who wanted independence as a nation in order to guarantee their rights. The Dutch "patriots" were those who wanted to take power away from the stadholder and his favorites and put it in the hands of the people. One of the early Dutch supporters of the American cause, Joan Derk, Baron van der Capellen tot den Pol, published an anonymous pamphlet in 1781 titled "To the People of the Netherlands." In it he made arguments clearly derived from the American example: "You [the people] are the members, the owners, and masters of the national society which bears the title of the *United Netherlands*. The great ones, on the contrary, are but directors and treasurers of this society." The true patriot, he insisted, was willing to stand up for his rights.

Van der Capellen belonged to a growing trans-Atlantic circle of supporters of revolution. He had previously translated into Dutch the pamphlets that the Welsh Unitarian minister Richard Price wrote in favor of the American rebels. Price's 1776 pamphlet *Observations on the Nature of Civil Liberty* sold 60,000 copies in a few days; Franklin, Jefferson, and John Adams were among those who made it a point to visit him in London, so grateful were they for his support. In May 1779 Price wrote to his Dutch translator, "How grievous is it to think that the body of mankind should in almost all countries be so dreadfully debased by oppression and slavery? But you stand forth their protector and friend." When his own pamphlet was banned, Van der Capellen managed nonetheless to get it translated into English, French, and German. He befriended Adams when the American envoy came to the Dutch Republic in 1781 seeking support for the colonists. The upper-class Dutchman helped raise money and even loaned some of his own fortune.[2]

While Dutch agitation grew, the people of Geneva attempted their own revolution. In April 1782 armed lower-class residents occupied city hall after an elite council had refused to extend citizenship to watchmakers and new immigrants to the city. The French, still occupied with fighting the British in the Caribbean, the Mediterranean, and India, refused to countenance any change so near their border; a joint French-Swiss-Savoyard army restored the traditional magistrates, forcing leaders of the revolt to flee. Brissot had rushed to Geneva to witness events and afterward wrote a pamphlet extolling the revolution. He had been prompted to intervene by his new patron and friend, Etienne Clavière, a 47-year-old banker and one of the leaders of the revolt. They met each other in Neufchâtel, the Swiss center for publishing works forbidden in France; there they also met Mirabeau who had come looking for a publisher for his book on *lettres de cachet*. A close collaboration soon ensued in which Clavière provided money, ideas, and even prose, eventually helping to write Mirabeau's speeches and journal articles in 1789. All three ended up in London at the same time in 1784, joining circles of Genevan refugees, French writers, North Americans, and British sympathizers such as Price.

The Geneva revolutionaries did not call themselves "patriots" but their Dutch counterparts did when they raised the flag of revolt. Van der Capellen's effort had unleashed a pamphlet war, and slowly but surely the patriots organized militias, held demonstrations, and took control of city governments. The stadholder had his supporters, too, and the two sides began fighting each other in what approached an armed civil war. When the stadholder's wife was arrested by a patriot militia in June 1787, her brother, the king of Prussia, sent in 26,000 troops to restore the stadholder's full authority. The British government had supported the stadholder all along and when the French proved incapable of intervening to stop the Prussians, the British signed alliances with the Dutch and the Prussians. In 1788 Abigail, the wife of John Adams, wrote from London to a friend, lamenting "poor Holland, like a sheep has it been deliverd (sic) to slaughter, panic struck she has submitted, discouraged and disheartened, unassisted by France her ally, who could not, or would not interfere."[3] Thousands of Dutch patriots fled to France.

Many more fled just south of the border into the Austrian Netherlands (now Belgium and Luxembourg), where they would witness yet another revolution, this one in defense of local liberties. Joseph II, older brother of Marie-Antoinette, emperor of the Holy Roman Empire and ruler of the Austrian Netherlands, tried to enforce the same Enlightenment-inspired reforms he had instituted elsewhere in his lands including abolishing torture, affording greater toleration to Protestants and Jews, eliminating monasteries he considered superfluous, modernizing the university curriculum, and reducing the independence of town governments and regional estates. The Belgians resisted these changes, claiming they violated the fundamental laws in place for centuries. After riots were suppressed in 1787, the Belgians began secretly organizing, and in October 1789 a makeshift army defeated Austrian forces. These events were closely followed in France; in November 1789 Desmoulins began publishing a weekly called *Révolutions de France et de Brabant* (Brabant was the most significant province of the Austrian Netherlands and the primary site of conflict between the Belgians and the Austrians) in which he reported on the Belgian revolution as it unfolded.

UNITED BELGIAN STATES Despite moral support from France and inspiration from the example of the United States of America, the new United Belgian States, proclaimed in January 1790, crumbled under the weight of internal divisions and external pressures. Unlike their French counterparts, those who had set up the new government wanted to maintain the powers of the nobility and the Catholic Church. Their opponents, who called themselves "democrats," wanted a measure of popular participation, not just independence from Austria. Rather than organizing for defense against the Austrians, the new leaders drummed up violent pro-Catholic mobs to force many democrats to flee for their lives. Lafayette tried to intervene with personal negotiations to bring the two sides together, but in November 1790 Leopold II succeeded his brother Joseph and reoccupied Belgium with the consent of the Prussians, Dutch, and British. Lafayette had by then given up in disgust, convinced that the Belgian government was a "monstrosity of privilege, a conspiracy of nobles and clergy against the rights and liberties of all Belgians."

The Belgian revolution showed how fast radical ideas had traveled and how eager most European powers were to stifle any attempt to follow the French path. The unfolding of events in France alarmed virtually every European sovereign and prompted defenders of traditional rule to make explicit the virtues of "conservatism." As one English aristocrat wrote to another in January 1790, "if they [the French] had been content with a liberal translation of our system; if they had respected the prerogatives of the Crown, and the privileges of the nobles, they might have raised a solid fabric on the only true foundation—the national aristocracy of a great country."[4] In this way, French events gave birth to ideology, that is, the articulation of systematic political positions on the desirability and speed of change. Conservatives took the stage first because they saw the need to defend the "old regime" against those who favored revolution.[5]

The most prominent of the conservatives was Edmund Burke, an Anglo-Irish politician who had supported the American rebels but now feared the subversive influence of the French Revolution on his British compatriots. In November 1790 he published his *Reflections on the Revolution in France*, which he had begun as a rebuke of Richard Price for supporting the French revolutionaries. Burke had been particularly outraged by women's role in the October Days when "the royal captives" were led in procession "amidst the horrid yells, and shrilling screams, and frantic dances, . . . and all the unutterable abominations of the furies of hell, in the abused shape of the vilest of women." He rejected the "paltry, blurred shreds of papers about the rights of man" and argued that reason was an insufficient guide in government; history, tradition, aristocracy, and religion had to be revered. If the British were to follow the French example, all learning would be "trodden down under the hoofs of a swinish multitude."

PAINE, *RIGHTS OF MAN* The offhanded reference to "a swinish multitude" set off a firestorm of controversy. Even John Adams, the second president of the United States, who shared some of Burke's reservations about the French Revolution, called the remark "impolitic, inhuman and insolent." Burke's broadside let loose an avalanche of responses across the Atlantic world. Just three months after Burke's publication, Thomas Paine rushed into print the first part of his *Rights of Man*, subtitled *Being an Answer to Mr. Burke's Attack on the French Revolution*. Paine's 46-page pamphlet *Common Sense*, published in 1776, had been widely credited with pushing the Americans to demand independence from Britain, and Paine, the first international revolutionary, had become friends with Jefferson, Lafayette, and even Burke himself, who supported the Americans.

Now back in England, the self-educated and increasingly radical Paine lambasted Burke and all he defended: rather than mindlessly support tradition, Paine insisted, "Every age and generation must be as free to act for itself, *in all cases*, as the ages and generations which preceded it." Writing in a deliberately folksy style, Paine laid out the arguments that would guide British radicals for generations; armed with reason, the people had the right to demand a government that represented their interests, not those of the church, the aristocracy, or the monarch. So vociferous were Paine's criticisms of monarchy that he had to flee to France to escape prosecution for seditious libel when he published the second part of his book in 1792. In 1793 a court in Edinburgh convicted another radical of sedition just for encouraging his hairdresser to buy and read a copy of the book. Though always short of funds Paine gladly waived royalties so that cheap editions could be printed anywhere a willing printer could be found; 50,000 copies sold in just the first three months of publication, quickly outpacing Burke.

WOLLSTONECRAFT, *RIGHTS OF WOMAN* The English writer Mary Wollstonecraft published *A Vindication of the Rights of Men* even before Paine entered the fray, but it did not have the impact of her subsequent tract of 1792, *A Vindication of the Rights of Woman*, now considered the founding text of the women's rights movement. In the earlier work, Wollstonecraft had objected to Burke's "mortal antipathy to reason," and in the *Rights of Woman*, she repeatedly called on reason to argue that the rights of women must be subjected to the same test as the rights of men. Because women could be educated to use their full powers of reason, only prejudice could explain their exclusion from "the natural rights of mankind."

Wollstonecraft is one of the most extraordinary figures of the entire era. Encouraged by Richard Price who also inspired Paine, Wollstonecraft aimed to make a living from her writing, an aspiration that was nearly impossible for men, much less women, who were barred from universities and all professions. Derided by her critics as a "hyena in petticoats," her influence nonetheless spread far and wide. A 1799 magazine article in the United States concluded that her work "quickly became a staple commodity at the circulating libraries." No wonder the rulers of Europe feared the power of the French example; it seemed that everything could now be questioned including the role of women.

Starting over from zero

Even as the contesting of tradition in the name of reason, the rights of man, and the power of the people spread across Europe, the French faced an unprecedented set of challenges at home. On August 4, they had effectively decreed the end of the old regime, but now they had to build a new one, which included: drafting France's first written constitution; setting up new electoral, administrative, financial, and judicial structures; and, most urgently, dealing with the deficit and the growing debt. On August 7, Necker informed the deputies that the treasury was running out of money. They agreed to guarantee a new loan for 30,000,000 l. at only 4.5 percent interest but when that failed to find subscribers they offered 5 percent for 80,000,000 l. Only about half was subscribed. They also decreed the continuation of the old tax system until the new one could be put in place. In early October they instituted a one-time "patriotic contribution," but it raised only about 32 million l. when the government needed 80 million l. just to make ends meet for 1790.

NATIONALIZATION OF CHURCH PROPERTY   Necker hoped to convince the deputies to turn the *Caisse d'Escompte* (Discount Bank) into a national bank to stabilize finances. The *Caisse d'Escompte* had been set up in Paris in 1776 with private funding under state supervision to facilitate the transfers of bills of exchange and keep funds flowing at relatively low rates of interest. It loaned money to the state, and its paper circulated within Paris like money. Mirabeau and Brissot, with Clavière's help (he had moved to Paris in 1784 and become a major speculator on *Caisse d'Escompte* shares), led the charge against Necker's plan. In November the deputies moved toward a different and fateful solution; acting on the suggestion of Talleyrand, himself a bishop, and with strong support from Mirabeau, the deputies voted to nationalize all the property of the church, valued at between 2 and 3 billion l., and use it as a guarantee for the issue of paper called *assignats* scheduled to earn 5 percent interest (reduced a few months later to 3 percent). The treasury would release 400,000,000 l. of *assignats* in 1000 l. units to its creditors (including officials who had bought their offices and would now be reimbursed) and in theory the paper would be used to buy church lands or be redeemed with gold and silver gained from direct sales of land; the *assignats* would then be retired from circulation and in this way liquidate the government's debt.

Circumstances dictated otherwise. As taxpayers refused to pay until a new tax system was installed, the treasury ran dry. It took six months for the deputies to put in place a system for selling church properties by auction, and even longer to take possession of the properties and collect the sale proceeds. In September 1790, therefore, Mirabeau convinced the deputies to issue 1.2 billion l. of *assignats* (including the 400 million previously authorized) in values down to 50 l.; these bore no interest and circulated as money (Figure 2.1). Mirabeau made it a matter of patriotism and cited the example of the Americans who faced a similar crisis. "I can hear Americans saying to the French: 'During our Revolution we created an unsound paper currency, yet that paper saved us. . . . And you who have also a revolution to carry through; . . . You who have commenced your career like men will not finish it like children!'" In June 1791 another 600 million had to be authorized, and depreciation set in as the amount of paper in circulation increased. By the end of 1791 the *assignats* had lost 14 percent of their face value, and the slide showed no signs of stopping.

Sale of church lands—and later those of the king's personal domain as well as property of those who emigrated to oppose the Revolution—profoundly altered the property structure in France. The Catholic Church lost its land, and clergy became salaried functionaries of the state. The nobility lost much land,

FIGURE 2.1 Assignat *of 200 Livres*
The first *assignats* featured pictures of the king in profile. Paper, 1789–1790.

even though some was reclaimed after 1815. From the bits and pieces of evidence that have been collected, it appears that both peasants and middle-class town people gained land, creating a society in which land became especially desirable as an investment. Two important long-term consequences followed: France became a country of small-property-owners, and investment that might have gone to trade and industry funneled instead into land. As a consequence, France industrialized more slowly than Britain or even Belgium.

CIVIL CONSTITUTION OF THE CLERGY While the sale of nationalized lands democratized landholding to some extent (the share owned by the middle classes increased even more than that of the peasants), the wholesale reorganization of the Catholic Church ended up destroying any possible consensus around the new order. The deputies thought they were following the wishes of their fellow citizens for reform of clerical abuses; they abolished monastic vows, suppressed all religious orders that did not contribute to charity work or teaching, and drew up a Civil Constitution of the Clergy in July 1790 that specified the number of bishops, reduced the number of parishes, set the salaries of all clerics, and provided for their election by citizens. The king grudgingly accepted the new clerical organization, but the Pope remained ominously silent. Thirty bishops who had been deputies and voted against the Civil Constitution published a manifesto against it. Opinions on both sides hardened, and in reaction, in November 1790 the deputies required all clerics to swear an oath to the new Civil Constitution; those who refused would be fired.

The oath ripped apart the church and divided the population. A papal brief of March 1791 condemned both the Declaration of the Rights of Man and Citizen and the Civil Constitution of the Clergy and another in April declared as schismatic all those clerics who did swear the oath. Only a handful of bishops took it and just over half the parish clergy. Supporters of the revolution considered the "refractories" (those who refused) counter-revolutionary, and over time increasingly harsh measures would be enforced against them. While the "constitutional" church got considerable backing in the Paris region and the southeast, it was largely rejected in Alsace and Lorraine and in western France, where only about a quarter of the clerics took the oath. The ground was sown for future resistance to revolutionary authority. Given the Pope's hostility, the deputies now felt free to annex the small papal territories of Avignon and Comtat Venaissin in the south, citing the vote of the people of Avignon for incorporation. An ominous dynamic took shape; as resistance to the revolution grew, those who supported it began to urge sterner measures against opponents alongside more aggressive moves to expand French territory.[6]

Even while the fiscal and ecclesiastical crises were unfolding in tandem, the deputies somehow found the time to restructure the government from top to bottom. The lasting success of many of these measures is all the more surprising given the chaotic conditions in which the deputies labored. When they moved to Paris in October 1789, they had no place to meet. After considering fifteen different sites, they settled on a riding school just west of the residence of the king in the Tuileries palace; the hall was much deeper than it was wide which made communication of any sort difficult. The sessions proved difficult to control: the presidency rotated every two weeks, as many as 1,000 deputies (fewer over time as nobles and clergy abandoned their seats) jostled for attention, and a thousand or more citizens watched the proceedings in anything but respectful silence. "They discuss nothing in the Assembly," complained Gouverneur Morris in a letter to George Washington in January 1790. "Those who intend to speak write their names on a tablet and are heard in the order that their names are written down, if the others will hear them, which they often refuse to do, keeping up a continual uproar till the orator leaves the pulpit."

Yet by working in committees and caucuses outside the assembly hall, the deputies managed to pass legislation that rationalized every aspect of French civic life. In December 1789 they set up electoral and administrative systems based on the principle that every part of France be subject to the exact same rules. "Active citizens" (men who paid a tax bill equivalent to at least three days' wages) voted for electors (men who paid a tax bill equivalent to at least ten days' wages) who then chose the council and mayor of their municipality and, with electors from surrounding areas, councils for the district and regional department. For the first time since 1685, when Calvinism was outlawed, Protestant men gained the right to vote and hold office. In February 1790 the deputies agreed to redraw the map of France, replacing the traditional provinces, which often had their own Estates and tax and legal codes, with 83 departments of more or less equal territory (see Map 2.1). The departments were named after local rivers and mountains, thereby erasing references to the past and establishing instead a nation literally grounded in the laws of nature. Towns competed with each other to be named capital of the department because the new judicial and administrative structures would be centered there. The departments have continued to function as the basis of French government right up to the present.[7]

In November 1789 all the parlements were suspended, and in August, September, and October 1790 a new judicial structure took shape, achieving what the ministers of Louis XV and Louis XVI had tried but failed to accomplish: elimination of the buying and selling of offices, suppression of the parlements and other Old Regime courts, and the establishment of uniform, elected judicial offices throughout the country. The establishment of new criminal court procedures took longer to put in place, but certain principles went into operation almost immediately: judicial torture was eliminated as were such corporal punishments as mutilations, branding with hot irons, and whipping; the *lettres de cachet* were abolished; and families were no longer punished by confiscation of their property for crimes committed by one of their members.

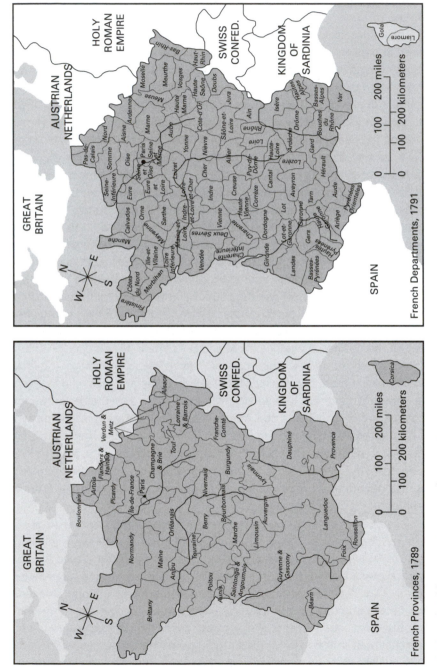

MAP 2.1 *Old Regime Provinces become Departments*

After re-establishing freedom of trade in grain and abolishing all internal tolls, the deputies had to rebuild the tax system. They tried to collect the various consumption and property taxes of the Old Regime in 1790, but ended up with less than a third of what they anticipated, in part because they abolished the system of tax farming by which the state contracted the collection of consumption taxes to private individuals who paid the state a set amount and then harvested the taxes through their own personnel. The new tax system that went into operation in January 1791 relied heavily on a land tax (75 percent of direct taxes) but included as well a personal property tax (20 percent of direct taxes) and a tax on trade and commerce. Ironically, because the new taxes removed all the local exemptions and variations that had characterized the Old Regime's hodgepodge of levies, many found themselves scheduled to pay more taxes to the state than before, on paper sometimes as much as 50–60 percent more. Moreover, the new administrators did not have the time or resources to conduct thorough property evaluations, so they ended up using the Old Regime tax rolls as their basis for assessment. In western France, the increase in taxes may have contributed to growing ferment against the revolution, and almost everywhere peasants expressed disappointment that their burdens did not diminish. On the other hand, the transfer of control of public funds to salaried officials and to a treasury department using modern accounting enabled France to mobilize the immense resources necessary to fight the wars against much of Europe that would start in 1792.

In April 1791, the sudden death of Mirabeau stunned the nation. Thunderously eloquent, ugly yet charismatic, a libertine known for his scandalous affairs, Mirabeau always seemed larger than life (Figure 2.2). To assure the public that the cause was natural, an autopsy was conducted in front of no less than 56 witnesses, 26 of them physicians. Faced with popular pressure for an imposing commemoration, the deputies turned a newly built church into a secular Pantheon of revolutionary heroes and voted to bury Mirabeau there. A 6-hour-long funeral procession that included all the deputies of the National Assembly drew at least 300,000 spectators. Across the country demonstrations and memorial services celebrated "the modern Demosthenes who has been taken from Europe." At Troyes, for instance, a 20-foot high funeral stand held an urn inscribed, "At the voice of Mirabeau Aristocracy falls and Liberty rises."

A new kind of civic religion was taking shape that included insignia such as the tricolor cockade and public festivals. In the first of such organized public gatherings, villages and towns all over France celebrated the anniversary of the fall of the Bastille on July 14, 1790 with a Festival of Federation. In Paris, Lafayette led a mass rally at the Champ de Mars, a military training ground on which the Eiffel Tower now stands. On a triumphal arch constructed for the

FIGURE 2.2 *Satirical Print about Mirabeau*

Satirical prints helped mobilize opinion against every political faction and leader, Mirabeau included. If the viewer had any doubts about the artist's meaning, the text below makes it clear: "M-r-b-u in his study, inspired by his private adviser [the devil]. Bad son, bad husband. The Catiline of France." Cataline was a Roman Senator known for conspiring against the republic and for being charged with adultery. As with many such prints, this etching from 1790 was produced anonymously.

occasion one inscription read, "The rights of man were unknown for centuries; they have been re-established for all of humanity." Soldiers, national guardsmen, and officials swore their fidelity at the "altar of the fatherland" in front of a huge crowd of spectators wearing tricolor cockades. The king, without his crown or scepter, then promised to uphold the constitution and the laws. The English writer Helen Maria Williams had just arrived in Paris. For her, despite a pelting rain, the festival was "the most sublime spectacle which, perhaps, was ever represented on the theatre of this earth."[8]

The constitution that was finally completed in the summer of 1791 made the king a salaried chief executive but one with considerable independence; he chose his ministers, ambassadors, and military commanders and could veto legislation. He now had to work through a one-house legislature elected by male property-owners; two-thirds of adult men met the criteria for "active citizens," that is, for voting. Among them were Jews who gained equal civil and political rights in September 1791; the Sephardic Jews of the southwest of France had already been accorded such rights in January 1790. In exchange Jewish communities had to give up their autonomous status and separate laws governing marriage and inheritance. No other state had granted equal political rights to its Jewish population (some states in the new United States did, but not all), but the emancipation also began a debate that continues up to the present about the compatibility of particular community interests and customs with a more general notion of French citizenship. Women did not get the right to vote, though two prominent writers argued they should. In July 1790 Condorcet published an article on the rights of women in which he insisted, "Since women have the same qualities [as men], they necessarily have equal rights." The playwright Olympe de Gouges deliberately twisted the wording of the Declaration of the Rights of Man and Citizen in her pamphlet of September 1791 called *The Rights of Woman*; echoing article 1, she wrote, "Woman is born free and remains equal to man in rights." (see Document 2.1, at the end of the chapter). Many questions about rights remained on the table for discussion.

The king's flight

A shocking event cast a shadow on the new constitution even before it went into effect: the king tried to flee Paris and join troops loyal to him near the eastern border. Louis believed that once he was safely out of Paris the rest of France would eagerly return his full powers.

FLIGHT TO VARENNES   Late in the night of June 20–21, 1791, the king and his immediate family slipped out of Paris dressed as ordinary middle-class citizens but with coaches and an entourage that inevitably attracted attention.

Louis left behind a letter insisting that he had only agreed to the new laws under duress. The carriages lumbered along slowly, however, and forty miles from the border of the Austrian Netherlands, ruled by Marie-Antoinette's brother Leopold II, a postmaster recognized the king. Local units of the National Guard halted the travelers in Varennes, and the royal family had to return to Paris under heavy guard. They were greeted this time with hostile silence. Brissot, Condorcet, and others began to speak openly of establishing a republic, but the majority in the Assembly were still committed to constitutional monarchy and adopted the view, in some cases cynically but in others sincerely, that the king had been misled by his advisors (Figure 2.3).[9]

News of the failed escape traveled far and wide thanks to the explosive growth of the press after May 1789. More than 500 newspapers appeared in Paris between May 1789 and October 1791, with another 150 or so being published in provincial cities and towns. These remarkable numbers completely dwarf the 252 newspapers that appeared in the entire country in the four decades of gradual press expansion between 1751 and 1788. Many newspapers disappeared quickly; half of those published in Paris lasted a month or less, but others proved more durable. Desmoulins' *Révolutions de France et de Brabant* continued for nearly two years, and he went on to edit another newspaper in 1793.

Some publications aimed to provide neutral reporting, but most took sides. The range was astounding, from the *Actes des Apôtres* [Acts of the apostles], a satirical aristocratic journal that specialized in scurrilous attacks on its opponents, to the bloodcurdling prose of Jean Paul Marat's *L'Ami du people* [Friend of the people]. In his issue of June 22, 1791, published before the royal family's humiliating return to Paris, Marat called the king a "perjurer," "unworthy of a throne," and so consumed with a desire for absolute power that he would soon turn into a "ferocious murderer." He went on to argue for the establishment of a "supreme dictator" who would weed out the counter-revolutionaries. Marat had not previously been among those most critical of the king; for him as for many others, the flight was the last straw.

When the news flew through Paris on June 21, 1791 that the king had disappeared (no one yet knew where he had gone), 800 men met at the Jacobin Club to discuss their options. Fearing the worst—an attempt to take Paris and the deputies by military force—Robespierre rose to speak and declared himself happy to give his life for the freedom of the fatherland. In response, Desmoulins shouted, "we will all die before you," and all those present rose as one to swear that they would defend Robespierre to the death. The melodramatic scene reflected the synergy between Jacobin Club meetings, unfolding political events, and newspapers. Newspapers reported on sessions of the club, many clubs subscribed to newspapers, and

FIGURE 2.3 *Maligning the King and Queen*
The royal family's failed attempt to flee France provoked an explosion of writing and prints critical of the king and queen. This hand-colored etching from 1791 shows the king and queen as monstrous animals. The title reads, "the two make only one," meaning that they are the two halves of one monstrosity.

news of club meetings helped shape interpretations of events as they unfolded.

Although true political parties with national organizations and slates of candidates did not emerge until relatively late in the 1800s, "patriots" and their opponents had quickly discovered the potential of political clubs in 1789. In February 1789, even before the meeting of the Estates-General, Sieyès, prompted by the Duke of Orleans, organized the Valois Club, which brought together leading nobles and political figures such as Lafayette, Talleyrand, Condorcet, and Mirabeau. Clubs drew on a long tradition of voluntary associations that included religious confraternities, guilds, and in the 1700s, masonic lodges and scientific and literary societies. None of these had been explicitly political, however. Another of the earliest political clubs was the Society of Colonists or Massiac Club; "Massiac," like most club names, came from the residence where it met. White planters from the Caribbean islands set up the club in August 1789 to defend the slave regime. The Jacobin Club, of much greater and lasting influence, emerged from the Breton Club of deputies in Versailles when the deputies moved to Paris in October 1789.

Officially its name was Society of the Friends of the Constitution but everyone called it the Jacobin Club after its meeting place. It met in a former Dominican monastery in the rue Saint-Honoré near the National Assembly; the Dominicans were nicknamed Jacobins after their original address in Paris (rue Saint-Jacques, Jacques being *Jacobus* in Latin, hence Jacobins) (see Map 1.2 for location and Box 2.1 for genealogy).

Originally a place for deputies to talk politics outside the cumbersome assembly hall, the Jacobin Club in Paris soon had corresponding and then collaborating affiliates across the country. The number of clubs rose from 19 at the end of 1789 to 312 a year later. When some anti-revolutionary municipalities tried to prevent the formation of such clubs, the deputies voted in November 1790 to affirm the freedom to "assemble peaceably and to form free societies." By July 1791 there were 921 Jacobin clubs across France. In many places, the example of the Jacobins encouraged the

BOX 2.1 GENEALOGY OF THE JACOBIN CLUBS (1789–1792)

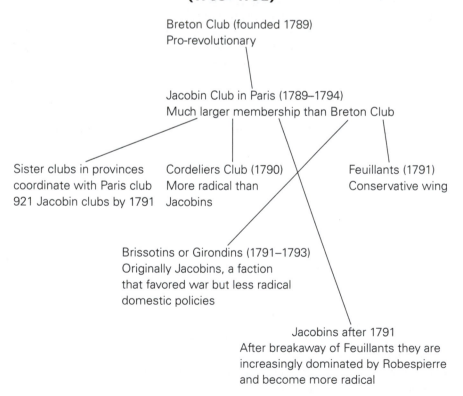

Breton Club (founded 1789)
Pro-revolutionary

Jacobin Club in Paris (1789–1794)
Much larger membership than Breton Club

Sister clubs in provinces
coordinate with Paris club
921 Jacobin clubs by 1791

Cordeliers Club (1790)
More radical than
Jacobins

Feuillants (1791)
Conservative wing

Brissotins or Girondins (1791–1793)
Originally Jacobins, a faction
that favored war but less radical
domestic policies

Jacobins after 1791
After breakaway of Feuillants they are
increasingly dominated by Robespierre
and become more radical

formation of other clubs, whether clubs of women, of soldiers, or specific neighborhoods. In April 1790, the Cordeliers Club (its official title was Society of the Friends of the Rights of Man and Citizen) appeared in the district of that name in Paris, not only to provide a forum for non-voting men and women but also to push toward a more rapid realization of revolutionary ideals. Desmoulins belonged to the Cordeliers Club, which included many others like him willing to advocate a republican form of government after the failed escape of the king.

The Cordeliers organized protest marches in the days after the royal family's return to Paris, and with various other popular clubs in Paris they urged their fellow citizens to come to the Champ de Mars on July 17, 1791 to sign a gigantic petition asking the National Assembly to reconsider its reinstatement of the king. Most deputies considered this an attack on their authority and they prevailed upon the mayor of Paris to declare martial law. Sent to break up the meeting, the National Guard fired on the crowd; 50 people lost their lives on the same field used for the Festival of Federation the previous year. Anyone trying to mount a demonstration faced immediate arrest, and a number of journalists, including Desmoulins and Marat, were forced into hiding until a general amnesty was declared in September.

The talk of a republic and violent denunciations of the king prompted most of the deputies who belonged to the Jacobin Club to leave it and form a rival club across the street, called the Feuillants after the building in which they met. They considered the Jacobins responsible for the agitation; the Jacobins originally supported the idea of a popular petition, but they withdrew from the campaign once the Assembly voted to reaffirm the inviolability of the king. One of the leaders of the Feuillants, Antoine Barnave, a 29-year-old Protestant lawyer from Grenoble, had spoken vociferously in the Assembly on July 15, 1791 in defense of inviolability. The king had neither forfeited nor abdicated the throne, he insisted, and his inviolability was crucial to the stability of the nation. Only Robespierre, Grégoire, and a few other deputies remained in the original club. At the urging of sister clubs in the provinces, about sixty deputies eventually returned to the original club, but for the moment the Jacobins found themselves on the defensive.[10]

A new set of deputies

On the suggestion of Robespierre, the deputies of the National Assembly had disqualified themselves from election to the Legislative Assembly that took over in October 1791. The 742 deputies seated in the Legislative were therefore all new, even though many had made reputations in local politics or as journalists; they were younger on average (forty-one as opposed to forty-seven years old) and only 10 percent were priests or nobles now that voting no longer took place by order. Although the Feuillants had dominated the final months of the previous assembly and leaders such as Barnave stayed in Paris to try to shape policies, Feuillant dominance was far from assured. At least 200 deputies were Jacobin members or sympathizers and they had a charismatic spokesman in the new assembly in the person of Brissot, elected along with Condorcet from Paris.

These two men made an odd couple of leaders of the radical left. The perennially indebted firebrand Brissot took up any cause that promised radical rupture with the past; he led the abolitionists, had been a secret republican for years, and was among the first to adopt the Quaker custom of wearing unpowdered hair. Condorcet was a noble, a brilliant mathematician, and the esteemed friend of a long list of Enlightenment luminaries that included Voltaire and the minister Turgot. Jefferson and Paine regularly frequented his wife Sophie's glittering salon in Paris. Although Condorcet, too, embraced abolitionism and republicanism, he appeared timid in public and preferred to mold opinion by writing, and even his writing tended toward the abstract and academic. But now he was ready to throw off his inhibitions and join in the battle, writing acerbic newspaper articles and speaking in the assembly when the occasion demanded.

The new assembly faced a set of festering problems, including violence in the colonies, continuing peasant dissatisfaction with the required compensation for seigneurial rights, the refractory clergy, the departure of nobles hoping to organize a counter-revolution, and inevitably, the role of the king. New expectations and uncertainties had prompted fermentation and then upheaval in the Caribbean. The white planters of Saint-Domingue had sent delegates to Versailles in 1789 to demand representation in the Estates-General and to lobby for freedom of trade in the colonies (the government restricted trade in the colonies to French shipping) and greater local autonomy. They wanted to prevent any challenge to the lucrative slave trade or slavery, which required countering the influence of the abolitionist Society of the Friends of Blacks among whose members were Lafayette, Mirabeau, Brissot, and Condorcet.

After initially refusing representation to the colonies, the National Assembly admitted six deputies from Saint-Domingue in July 1789. Guadeloupe's two deputies were admitted in September, and in October two deputies from Martinique joined them, one of whom was Moreau de Saint-Méry, who had led the Paris electors in revolt. Now he devoted himself to preventing any interference with the slave regime. The news from the Caribbean was alarming; free people of color demanded full political rights, slaves began to hold secret meetings, while some white planters contemplated moves toward independence. Fearing the loss of colonial commerce and the prospect of the British moving into the French sphere, the deputies had voted in March 1790 to exempt the colonies from the constitution. Barnave, as spokesman for the Colonial Committee, insisted that the deputies reassure the colonies "against those who, with criminal plots, would seek to bring trouble there, to excite uprisings there." Frustrated with the deputies' inaction on the rights of free people of color, a wealthy mixed-race slave-owner named Vincent Ogé returned from Paris, where he had met with the leading abolitionists, and led an uprising in Saint-Domingue against the white planters in October 1790. He was defeated and executed by the old methods, being broken on the wheel as an example to the thousands of free people of color in the colony.

The deputies in France did not intend to let the colonists go their own way, however. As agitation spread among the slaves in spring 1791, the National Assembly voted on May 15, over the objections of the colonial deputies, to grant political rights to free men of color in the colonies who met certain conditions. Grégoire, a member of the Friends of Blacks, published an open letter to the free people of color of Saint-Domingue celebrating their "reintegration" into the "fullness of their rights," which had not been given to them as a gift but rather recognized as a debt that needed repaying; "to have failed to do so would have been a crime on our part and a stain on the constitution," Grégoire insisted. Even though the number who benefited from the decree was quite small, probably only a few hundred, the white planters reacted in fury, organizing themselves to resist both the government in France and the increasingly restive slaves of their plantations.

SLAVE REVOLT   In August 1791, after months of secret planning, a slave insurrection erupted in Saint-Domingue. Bands of slaves burned down sugar plantations and killed whites. Within two weeks, they swelled to a force of some 15,000 and attacked the major town of Le Cap (or Cap français). Located on the northern coast, Le Cap was the colony's major port. It had a population of about 16,000 (just a bit smaller than Boston at the time) of whom at least 10,000 were slaves. The 3,500 white residents looked to the garrison of 1,000 soldiers for help, but though they were able to hold the town, within days all the plantations within 50 miles had been ruined. In one of its final acts, the National Assembly revoked the May 15 decree giving some free blacks rights, on the grounds that it was encouraging fermentation among the slaves. The deputies had not yet received word of the spreading slave revolt; in fact, the rebel slaves set fire to Le Cap just as the National Assembly was concluding its business. Their fight had only begun.

Toward the end of October 1791, the Legislative Assembly began to receive alarming reports about the unfolding slave revolt. Despite the efforts of Brissot to keep alive the cause of free people of color, the confusion of events in Saint-Domingue and the slowness in getting news left the deputies unable to decide on a course of action. Brissot himself believed that the white planters had deliberately failed to suppress the slave revolt because they thought it would help them justify their push for independence from France; in other words, even the leading abolitionists saw the revolt as part of a conspiracy to separate Saint-Domingue from France.

Moreover, events closer to home now demanded the deputies' immediate attention, in particular the refractory clergy and the increasing number of nobles who were emigrating, many of them with the intention of raising the flag of counter-revolution. Peasants in western France had already taken up arms in defense of their oath-refusing clergy. In the Breton town of Vannes in February 1791, four peasants were killed when they tried to defend the bishop who refused the oath. In April, in the Machecoul region, south of Nantes, peasants battled National Guardsmen sent to install a constitutional priest. In July, administrators at Saint-Brieuc had to declare martial law when nightly protest processions drew 200 armed men in nearby villages. Brittany was not alone. In Alsace in eastern France, the few constitutional priests had to be protected by armed guardsmen while they swore the oath. Local newspapers reported that some people yelled, "Long Live Emperor Leopold!" Leopold was the Austrian emperor.

ABOLITION OF NOBILITY   Nobles began emigrating right after the fall of the Bastille; the king's youngest brother, the Count of Artois, fled on July 17, 1789, and within two weeks many of the leading court nobles had followed his example. The march to Versailles in October 1789 prompted more departures. In June 1790 the National Assembly abolished the status, titles, and insignia of nobility. Two-thirds of the officers in the French army were nobles, and they began to desert their posts. The abortive flight of the king made an already parlous situation even more disastrous for the French army; more than 2,000 officers emigrated just between mid-September and the end of November 1791. By the end of 1791, over 6,000 officers had decamped; with half of its officer corps gone, the French army fell into a state of demoralization and confusion.

An armed counter-revolution took shape, and by late 1791 more than half of the nobles who had sat in the National Assembly had joined the emigration. Artois installed himself in Turin, the capital of the kingdom of his father-in-law, Victor-Amadeus III, King of Piedmont and Sardinia. From there, he tried to orchestrate uprisings in southern France, but his local agents succeeded only in sparking deadly street fights between Catholics and Protestants in towns with sizeable Protestant minorities. At Nîmes, a city of some 45,000 people, Protestant National Guards suppressed rioting Catholics in June 1790 and ended up killing 200–300 of them, fanning Catholic resentments against Protestants across the region. Catholic guardsmen began to meet periodically fifty miles to the north in a camp at Jalès, but the conspirators in Turin did not have the means to direct them to any precise targets.

Artois expected the rulers of Europe to support a counter-revolutionary army, but until the failed attempt at escape of Louis XVI, no one listened to him. His father-in-law even asked him to leave Turin in the spring of 1791. The Austrians worried more about the Turks, and the Russians were preoccupied with both the Turks and the Poles. The Poles had grown restive under Russian control and on May 3, 1791, with the approval of King Stanislas, Polish patriots in the *Seym* (Estates) passed a constitution, making the king a chief executive whose powers were checked by a two-house legislature. The constitution eliminated the "free veto" by which any aristocrat in the *Seym* could nullify legislation and gave middle-class townspeople political rights. While papers in London and Philadelphia congratulated the Poles on what President George Washington called their "large and unexpected strides toward liberty," Catherine the Great of Russia planned her riposte, which would come with the invasion of 98,000 troops a year later, after she made peace with the Turks.

When Louis XVI and his family returned to Paris under guard in June 1791, the attitude of Europe's rulers began to harden. In the summer of 1791, the Austrian diplomatic agent Johannes Thugut warned, "If the democratic regime there [France] ever acquires any consistency and starts to spread the misfortune with which Europe is threatened, I would not hesitate to give all my support to the most vigorous means to pull this evil up by the roots." Catherine the Great wasted no time in expressing her loathing; the former friend of Voltaire and Diderot described the revolutionaries in her letters as "brigands" and France as "the gulf of hell." "If I were M. d'Artois or M. de Condé [a leading aristocrat]," she wrote, "I would utilize these 300,000 French knights: they would save the country or I would die." In July 1791 Austrian Emperor Leopold II sent a letter to his fellow monarchs urging collective action, and the next month he and Frederick William II of Prussia issued the Declaration of Pillnitz threatening to intervene to restore Louis XVI to his full powers. In fact, however, they made no specific plans to do so. Marie-Antoinette, who spent hours every day sending detailed dispatches to her friends and agents, urged her brother to hold back for fear of making the royal family's position even more difficult. On September 12, 1791, she wrote to her longtime confidant, the Austrian ambassador Florimund Mercy Count of Argenteau, "My God! Is it possible that . . . I am destined to spend my days in such a century and with such men!"

Although some nobles had gone as far as Vienna or London, thousands clustered in places near one or another French border such as Brussels, Turin, or Koblenz. On the very day that Louis XVI tried to flee, the older of his two brothers, the Count of Provence, escaped to Brussels disguised as an Englishman. There he met his brother Artois and the two of them went on to

Koblenz, whose ruler, the Elector of Trèves, was their uncle. By November 1791, deputies in the Legislative Assembly were railing against an army they overestimated as 20,000 men strong led by 5,000 officers, with arms, horses, and supplies bought with "foreign gold." In early November, they voted measures to sequester the properties of *émigré* nobles and condemn them to death if caught. Later the same month, in response to reports of the growing religious unrest in western France, they took away the pensions of refractory clergy, ordered their surveillance, and under certain conditions provided for house arrest or even imprisonment. The king vetoed both laws.

War and radicalization

Faced with a recalcitrant king and nobles openly preparing to fight back, the deputies began to listen to calls for a pre-emptive war. War would soon change everything, including the nature of government, yet hardly anyone could see in advance how fateful and perhaps fatal it would turn out to be for the revolution. The flight of the king and his family had already excited talk of war, but at issue then was the threat of invasion. In its issue of June 25–July 2, 1791, the pro-Jacobin newspaper *Révolutions de Paris* had pointed across the border that the king had tried to reach: "why are legions of slaves on a war footing in all the neighboring states?" By late November 1791, the deputies closest to Brissot and Condorcet had started to call for a war of liberation. One of the "Brissotins" (followers of Brissot) called for a popular uprising across Europe: "If the cabinets of the foreign courts try to provoke a war of the kings against France, we will set off a war of the peoples against the kings." In the Jacobin Club on December 16, Brissot argued in messianic terms for an attack on the German princes who were sheltering the *émigrés*; "war alone can equalize and regenerate souls." (see Document 2.2).

Given the desertion of so many officers, however, could the army even make war? The army was undergoing an internal transformation: having been a force dominated by the aristocracy and filled out with regiments of hired foreigners, it was turning into a citizen army dependent on promotion from within the ranks. The tension between old and new had showed itself in a series of disturbances at garrisons in 1790 that culminated in a major mutiny of three regiments in Nancy in August 1790. The soldiers locked up their officers and demanded back pay, insisting on their rights. The National Assembly agreed to harsh repression by General Bouillé; one soldier was broken on the wheel, 22 were hanged, and 41 were condemned to 30 years in the galleys. Attitudes changed dramatically after the king's attempt to flee. Bouillé, a high-ranking aristocrat, helped plan Louis XVI's escape in June 1791; he was the commander whose protection Louis was seeking. When the plan failed Bouillé joined the counter-revolutionaries across the border. On June 15, 1792, in a sign of the changing times, a festival organized in Paris celebrated the release of the soldiers who had been sent to the galleys, now returning as heroes of aristocratic persecution.

As noble officers deserted, they were replaced by non-noble officers, often new men whose names had been put forward by deputies or local administrators. In the new volunteer battalions drawn from the National Guard that were recruited after the flight to Varennes, the rank and file elected their officers. It would take time to integrate the volunteers and solidify the command structure, but the war lobby was growing steadily in influence. Brissot knew that republicans were still a small minority in the Legislative Assembly. He hoped that war would force the king to reveal himself as a traitor and turn opinion against the monarchy.[11]

A group of Jacobin deputies from the Bordeaux region joined forces with Brissot and Condorcet. Because the department there was named Gironde after a local river, the group also came to be known as Girondins. Brissot moved toward them because the most prominent member in his old circle of friends, Robespierre, argued vehemently against war. In the spring and summer of 1791, Brissot, Clavière, and Robespierre met regularly at the home of Jean-Marie and Marie-Jeanne Roland; he was a leading economic expert, a disciple of Turgot, and husband and wife regularly attended the Jacobin Club once they moved to Paris in early 1791. Marie-Jeanne, or Manon for short, showed, if anything, even more interest in revolutionary politics than her husband. Now the question of war threatened to fracture these friendships as heated debates divided the Jacobins. On one side was the war lobby, which adroitly used emotional rhetoric to win over the big crowds of ordinary people attending the Jacobin club meetings, but on the other side, Robespierre got support from Desmoulins and from a rising star in Paris politics, Georges Danton, a 32-year-old lawyer from northeastern France with strong ties to the Cordeliers. Robespierre insisted that an offensive war was too risky because the army was unprepared and internal problems should be addressed first. He would be proved right, but he could not stem the rising tide.[12]

While Condorcet insisted that the French would respect the rights of man even when they were forced to make war, many in the war party explicitly linked war to the idea of a universal revolutionary movement. Foreign exiles in France had fostered this vision. The Prussian nobleman Anacharsis Cloots had begged for a place for foreigners in the Festival of Federation of July 14, 1790. They were men, he said, "whose countries would be free one day thanks to the influence of your unwavering courage and your philosophical laws." In December 1791 Cloots proposed at the Jacobin Club that war be declared the next month: "it remains only for the oppressed and ignorant peoples to suddenly shake the yoke in order to assure themselves a durable happiness under the direction of the French legislators." Cloots' vision was frankly imperialistic: "Twelve new squares will be added to the eighty-three squares [the departments of France] of the French checkerboard, whose edges will be the Rhine and the summit of the Alps, unless the interest of a free Europe requires a checkerboard that is even more extensive." Liberated peoples would greet the French with open arms, he predicted. Robespierre retorted, "no one likes armed missionaries." Even before war began the fundamental tension was already in place: the French would attract some support with their promise of liberation and rights but prolonged occupation would turn local opinion against them. Condorcet's dream of making war on states and not on peoples would prove impossible.

FRANCE DECLARES WAR   The war party got its way, in part because the king came to see the possible advantages for his own position. Although his brothers, his wife, and his ministers never agreed on a single course of action, all of them wanted war, either because the defeat of France would enable the victors to restore Louis to his full powers or if somehow victorious, the French armies could then turn around, shut down the Jacobin clubs, and install a regime that was more friendly to the monarchy. On March 1, 1792 Austrian Emperor Leopold II died and was succeeded by his son Francis II, who was much more willing to go to war; he rejected various French ultimatums. In order to push closer to war, or perhaps to shift the blame if defeat resulted, the king then agreed to name Girondins to key ministries, including Roland as minister of the interior, Clavière as finance minister, and General Charles Dumouriez as minister of foreign affairs (deputies could not serve as ministers). Finally, on April 20, 1792, the king went to the Legislative Assembly and declared war on Francis II. Only seven deputies opposed the declaration.[13]

Not surprisingly, given the reluctance of Lafayette and other commanders to send their disorganized troops into battle, attempts to take the offensive and invade the Austrian Netherlands failed. The motives of the king and even his commanders soon seemed more than suspect; one of the generals in the northern campaign was killed by his own troops because they believed he had led them into an ambush. On June 13 Louis summarily fired most of the Girondin ministers, and then on June 19 he vetoed a measure to deport refractory priests and another to set up a camp near Paris of 20,000 provincial National Guards. The Jacobins hesitated, but on June 20 a crowd invaded the Tuileries, the king's residence in Paris, and demanded that he withdraw his vetoes. Face to face with enraged demonstrators and jostled by them, Louis had to put on a red cap of liberty—one of the new symbols of revolutionary adherence favored by Brissot and worn by the Jacobins—and drink to the health of the nation, but he did not back down on the vetoes.

A contest of wills ensued. Petitions flooded into the Legislative Assembly demanding that the deputies punish the demonstrators, and on June 28

Lafayette left his army command on the northern border to come to Paris and urge the Legislative Assembly to shut down the "sect" of Jacobins and restore the king's authority. Speakers at the Jacobin Club openly called Lafayette a criminal. Fears of conspiracy ballooned on every side, as the Feuillants opposed the Jacobins and the Jacobins themselves divided. Moreover, the fears were not unfounded. Barnave had been in secret correspondence with Marie-Antoinette ever since he had personally accompanied the royal family back to Paris after the flight to Varennes. Marie-Antoinette was revealing everything she discovered about French war plans to the Austrians. Lafayette was starting secret negotiations with the Austrians for an armistice. The king corresponded regularly with his brothers plotting counter-revolution. Some Jacobins pointedly asked why the Girondins had agreed to become ministers to the king.

The Second Revolution: August 10, 1792

In this unstable situation, two elements tipped the balance and brought down the monarchy: the invasion of the Austrians and Prussians from the east and the mobilization of the common people in Paris. The Prussians joined the war in July; they might have acted sooner, since they had a mutual defense pact with the Austrians, but they had been preoccupied with Catherine the Great's invasion of Poland in May 1792. After crushing Polish autonomy, she would agree with the Prussians to a second partition of Poland in 1793 (the first had occurred in 1772). In late July the Duke of Brunswick, commander of the allied armies, issued a manifesto warning the French: "if the least violence be offered to their Majesties the king, queen, and royal family, and if their safety and their liberty be not immediately assured, they [the allies] will inflict an ever memorable vengeance by delivering over the city of Paris to military execution and complete destruction." The threat backfired; it set in motion the forces that would bring down the French monarchy and endanger monarchs everywhere else.

The Legislative Assembly had already declared "the fatherland in danger" on July 11 prompting thousands of young men to volunteer for the army in an outpouring of nationalist fervor. The king now accepted the deputies' request for provincial National Guards to come to Paris, in theory for the July 14 celebration. By the end of July, 5,000 had already arrived, including a large contingent of workers and artisans from Marseille who came singing a recently composed "War Song for the Army of the Rhine." Forever after known as "La Marseillaise" in honor of those who made it famous, it urged the French to "march on" and fight the "horde of slaves, traitors, and conspiratorial kings." (It is now the French national anthem.) Instead of moving to a military camp outside of Paris, most of the provincial volunteers stayed in Paris where their representatives met with leaders of the Jacobins, Cordeliers, and other popular clubs to develop a common plan of action.

The prospect of invasion galvanized the local neighborhoods of Paris. The city had been divided into 48 sections in 1790, each with its own electoral assembly that was supposed to disband after voting. In late July the deputies allowed the Paris sections to meet as often as needed (*en permanence*) as a war surveillance measure. Without authorization the sections followed the example of Danton's section, called *Théâtre-Français*, and abolished the distinction between active and passive citizens, inviting everyone to participate. The Cordeliers Club met in this neighborhood, and Paris had at least 20 other political clubs that at times drew hundreds of participants, including women. Some clubs aimed to include workers and artisans; these men were called *sans-culottes* because they wore trousers rather than the knee breeches— *culottes*—of prosperous men. Even in such clubs, however, educated professionals, merchants, or major employers usually took the leadership positions, as they did in the sections. When the sections set up a central committee to coordinate their responses in late July, political pressure on the Assembly and the king soon reached a bursting point.[14]

On August 3, the mayor of Paris presented a petition to the Assembly on behalf of 40 of the sections of Paris that demanded the immediate removal of Louis XVI, "the first link in the counter-revolutionary chain," and the convocation of a National Convention to determine the future of the nation. Militants hoped that the deputies would finally agree to act, but the Tuileries palace was being fortified by as many as 4,000 police, volunteer nobles, National Guards from the more conservative sections, and Swiss Guards. As the deputies stalled, the insurgent sections decided to take action alongside the provincial volunteers. On the evening of August 9 church bells sounded the general alarm across the city and National Guard units mobilized in many sections. In the morning, militants seized arms where they could find them, and the delegates of the sections, meeting at city hall, declared themselves the "insurrectional Commune [municipality]," shunting aside the Feuillant city council. Danton played a leading role; previously elected as chief prosecutor of the city, he advised the Commune, which ordered the arrest of the royalist commander of the Paris National Guard because he had organized the reinforcement of the Tuileries. The commander was shot and killed by an unknown assailant on the steps of city hall.

At the same time, thousands of provincial volunteers and armed men from the sections converged on the Tuileries palace dragging several cannon. They may have hoped that a final show of force would resolve the situation peacefully. In fact, National Guards and police defending the courtyard began to abandon their positions and even some of the Swiss Guards followed them.

Journée du 10 Aout 1792.

FIGURE 2.4 *The Revolution of August 10, 1792*
Another subscription print by Monnet and Helman, published by Ponce (see Figure 1.3), shows the crowd attacking the Tuileries palace. The clouds and smoke take up so much space because they provide the engraver Helman ways of showcasing his talents, even when capturing a bloody, chaotic event. Etching and engraving, Paris, 1793.

The king and queen were persuaded to seek refuge in the nearby Legislative Assembly. After the royal family left, the Swiss Guards and volunteer nobles inside the palace opened fire, killing dozens and capturing many of the cannon (Figure 2.4).

Reinforcements from the sections raced to the Tuileries and outflanked the Swiss, pushing them back into the palace and overwhelming them in chaotic hand-to-hand combat. The remaining Swiss tried to flee but their bright red uniforms made them easy targets for an enraged population; 60 were summarily executed right outside city hall after giving themselves up. Over 1,000 people died: 600 Swiss Guards, 100 noble volunteers, and 400 insurgents. The palace was sacked and set on fire.

ARREST OF LOUIS XVI A second revolution had brought down the monarchy on August 10. Once again ordinary people intervened to transform the course of events. With the king and queen cowering nearby, the galleries in upheaval, and delegations from the sections demanding action, the deputies yielded to the Girondins. They agreed that the king be suspended (not yet removed altogether) from his functions and his future decided by a National Convention that was to be elected, following the lead of the Paris sections, by nearly universal male suffrage; only servants were excluded. The king and his family were escorted to the Temple fortress in northern Paris and put under house arrest. Within days, crowds had torn down statues of kings in the major public squares of Paris.

As more than half of the deputies ceased attending after August 10, Brissot and the Girondins could call the shots in the Assembly. They removed the king's appointed ministers and installed an executive council of ministers to run the country; Roland was reinstalled as minister of the interior and Clavière as finance minister, and in a concession to Paris activists, Danton was named minister of justice. When Danton made Desmoulins his chief of staff, the journalist wrote to his father, "Despite all your prophecies that I would never amount to anything, I have now been elevated to the highest grade in our legal profession." With the effective end of the veto, the Assembly passed legislation to deport priests who refused the oath and introduced a divorce law, unprecedented for its time, which allowed divorce on the grounds of abuse, abandonment, or even mutually agreed incompatibility.

The divorce law underlined the state's new control of family matters and the deputies' belief in the supremacy of legal contracts between individuals. The state would regulate marriage and divorce, not the churches, and because marriage was seen to be a contract, like all legal contracts it could be broken under certain circumstances. The deputies likewise believed in free trade in goods and labor; in March 1791 they abolished the guild system of masters and apprenticeships that had organized labor under the Old Regime, and in June they forbade any union of workers or employers. Strikes were outlawed at the same time. Such laws did not prevent workers from joining political clubs, however, and over the next two years they would continue to make their voices heard. Although women did not get the right to vote or hold office, they did have equal rights to divorce and began to get equal rights to inheritance. The National Assembly had already abolished primogeniture, by which the eldest son inherited the bulk of the property, and the Legislative Assembly decreed equal inheritance for girls in all intestate successions. That rule would be extended to all inheritance in 1793.

The Girondins only controlled the Assembly and the provisional executive branch; the Commune still ran Paris and within days after August 10, Robespierre had joined it. The Commune and the 48 sections had their own surveillance committees and continued to meet night and day, contesting the authority of the deputies and demanding retribution against the traitors of August 10. They arrested Feuillants and "anti-civic" authors and printers and demanded that every property-owner take down all busts, statues and decorations associated with monarchy or nobility such as the fleur-de-lys or coats of arms.

The desertion of Lafayette (he then spent five years in Austrian and Prussian prisons for having supported the revolution in the first place) and his staff surprised no one, but now the allied armies began to advance, taking the eastern frontier town of Longwy on August 23 and then the heavily fortified town of Verdun on September 2. The road to Paris opened, and panic set in even before news had arrived of the fall of Verdun. At this moment, Danton gave his single most famous speech to the deputies, insisting that "we need audacity, more audacity, and yet more audacity to save France." Tragically, audacity was about to take a very different form. Because surviving Swiss Guards, nobles, and refractory priests had been locked up in Paris prisons, rumors flew that a prison breakout would be timed to coincide with the arrival of the invading armies.

SEPTEMBER MASSACRES On September 2, the Commune and the sections went into emergency meetings. Later that day, as church bells rang and cannon fired to sound the alarm, a mob killed a group of prisoners being transferred from one prison to another. Crowds then broke into the prisons either executing everyone in sight or, under the influence of delegates from the Commune, holding impromptu "tribunals of sans-culottes" as the newspaper *Révolutions de Paris* described them, to weed out supposed counter-revolutionaries from common criminals. Over five days, eager volunteers using swords, axes, pikes, or clubs slaughtered more than 1,100 people, including the queen's favorite Princess of Lamballe, whose mutilated remains were paraded under Marie-Antoinette's Temple window. "Nothing more natural or reasonable," responded *Révolutions de Paris*. Finally on September 6, the Commune went as a body to stop the killing.

Hardly anyone objected at the time, though soon the September Massacres would become a bitter source of conflict among revolutionaries. The editor of *Révolutions de Paris*, Louis Prudhomme, published a multi-volume work in 1796 decrying the crimes of the revolution and blaming Danton, Robespierre, and the Commune for the massacres; "we cannot decide which is the more heinous crime, massacring one's fellows or praising the massacres." Yet his own newspaper had joined the general refrain of praise at the time. Brissot and Roland were convinced that Robespierre had plotted to have them killed during the massacres, which certainly contributed to the rift to come, but they did nothing to stop the killing. Condorcet, the great defender of rights, was silent, too. The massacres had seemed inevitable and smaller versions took place outside of Paris. Yet violence then subsided, never to be repeated in the same, virtually anarchic, fashion. Attention turned to mobilizing for war and to the meeting of the constitutional convention—elections were already taking place—that would soon push France into new territories, both on the ground and in the imagination.

The power of the people had made itself felt but with mixed results and emotions for everyone concerned. The French had moved a long distance toward democracy by instituting nearly universal male suffrage and offering rights to religious minorities, a model that most countries would not follow until late in the next century, if then. Women remained excluded from voting and officeholding, as they were everywhere else, and the question of the rights of free people of color and slaves was far from resolved. Popular intervention had proved to be critical in the process of democratization but it also could turn mercilessly violent. Violence in the streets would become an issue again in the next phase of the revolution, but over the long run it would be overshadowed by the brutality of nearly constant warfare which would shake all of Europe and much of the world beyond for the next generation.

Documents

DOCUMENT 2.1

Olympe de Gouges, *The Rights of Woman* (1791)

As the National Assembly went about the business of creating institutions and practices commensurate with liberty and equality, the playwright and political activist Olympe de Gouges (1748–1793) raised questions about the place of women's rights in the new revolutionary organization of France. While the Declaration of Rights of Man and Citizen promised great individual liberties, it made no mention of women's rights. Gouges sought to right this wrong through her Declaration of the Rights of Woman, which paralleled the earlier Declaration but with reference to women. Gouges went beyond the Declaration to include specific remedies to the particular problems faced by women.

Preamble

Mothers, daughters, sisters, female representatives of the nation ask to be constituted as a national assembly. Considering that ignorance, neglect, or contempt for the rights of woman are the sole causes of public misfortunes and governmental corruption, they have resolved to set forth in a solemn declaration the natural, inalienable, and sacred rights of woman: so that by being constantly present to all the members of the social body this declaration may always remind them of their rights and duties; so that by being liable at every moment to comparison with the aim of any and all political institutions the acts of women's and men's powers may be the more fully respected; and so that by being founded henceforward on simple and incontestable principles the demands of the citizenesses may always tend toward maintaining the constitution, good morals, and the general welfare.

In consequence, the sex that is superior in beauty as in courage, needed in maternal sufferings, recognizes and declares, in the presence and under the auspices of the Supreme Being, the following rights of woman and the citizeness.

[Gouges then follows the order of articles in the Declaration; for reasons of space, most of them are eliminated here.]

4   Liberty and justice consist in restoring all that belongs to another; hence the exercise of the natural rights of woman has no other limits than those that the perpetual tyranny of man opposes to them; these limits must be reformed according to the laws of nature and reason.

     . . .

11 The free communication of thoughts and opinions is one of the most precious of the rights of woman, since this liberty assures the recognition of children by their fathers. Every citizeness may therefore say freely, I am the mother of your child; a barbarous prejudice [against unmarried women having children] should not force her to hide the truth, so long as responsibility is accepted for any abuse of this liberty in cases determined by the law [women are not allowed to lie about the paternity of their children].

     . . .

13 For maintenance of public authority and for expenses of administration, taxation of women and men is equal; she takes part in all forced labor service, in all painful tasks; she must therefore have the same proportion in the distribution of places, employments, offices, dignities, and in industry.

     . . .

Postscript

Women, wake up; the tocsin of reason sounds throughout the universe; recognize your rights. The powerful empire of nature is no longer surrounded by prejudice, fanaticism, superstition, and lies. The torch of truth has dispersed all the clouds of folly and usurpation. Enslaved man has multiplied his force and needs yours to break his chains. Having become free, he has become unjust toward his companion. Oh women! Women, when will you cease to be blind? What advantages have you gathered in the Revolution? A scorn more marked, a disdain more conspicuous. During the centuries of corruption you only reigned over the weakness of men. Your empire is destroyed; what is left to you then? Firm belief in the injustices of men. The reclaiming of your patrimony founded on the wise decrees of nature; why should you fear such a beautiful enterprise? . . . Whatever the barriers set up against you, it is in your power to overcome them; you only have to want it. Let us pass now to the appalling account of what you have been in society; and since national education is an issue at this moment, let us see if our wise legislators will think sanely about the education of women.

Women have done more harm than good. Constraint and dissimulation have been their lot. What force has taken from them, ruse returned to them; they have had recourse to all the resources of their charms, and the most irreproachable man has not resisted them. . . .

Under the former regime, everyone was vicious, everyone guilty. . . . A woman only had to be beautiful and amiable; when she possessed these two advantages, she saw a hundred fortunes at her feet. . . . The most indecent woman could make herself respectable with gold; the commerce in women [prostitution] was a kind of industry amongst the highest classes, which henceforth will enjoy no more credit. . . .

Other examples even more touching can be provided to reason. A young woman without experience, seduced by the man she loves, abandons her parents to follow him; the ingrate leaves her after a few years and the older she will have grown with him, the more his inconstancy will be inhuman. If she has children, he will still abandon her. If he is rich, he will believe himself excused from sharing his fortune with his noble victims. If some engagement ties him to his duties, he will violate it while counting on support from the law. If he is married, every other obligation loses its force. What laws then remain to be passed that would eradicate vice down to its roots? That of equally dividing [family] fortunes between men and women and of public administration of their goods. It is easy to imagine that a woman born of a rich family would gain much from the equal division of property [between children]. But what about the woman born in a poor family with merit and virtues; what is her lot? Poverty and opprobrium. If she does not excel in music or painting, she cannot be admitted to any public function, even if she is fully qualified. . . .

Marriage is the tomb of confidence and love. A married woman can give bastards to her husband with impunity, and even the family fortune which does not belong to them. An unmarried woman has only a feeble right: ancient and inhuman laws refuse her the right to the name and goods of her children's father; no new laws have been made in this matter. If giving my sex an honorable and just consistency is considered to be at this time paradoxical on my part and an attempt at the impossible, I leave to future men the glory of dealing with this matter; but while waiting, we can prepare the way with national education, with the restoration of morals and with conjugal agreements. . . .

Source: Olympe de Gouges, *Les Droits de la femme. À la Reine* (Paris?, 1791?)

Questions on *The Rights of Woman*

1 What special attributes and responsibilities does de Gouges assign to women?

2 Examine Article 11. How does de Gouges use the argument for free speech to make a point about women's special concerns?

3 Why does de Gouges argue that women, too, must change their ways of acting?

DOCUMENT 2.2

Robespierre and Brissot clash on the war, December 1791

Although both Maximilien Robespierre (1758–1794) and Jacques Brissot (1754–1793) were Jacobins and shared many political positions in the early years of the Revolution, they ended up fiercely opposed to one another. Their backgrounds were not all that different; both came from provincial towns, and both studied the law. True, Brissot's father was an uneducated cook whereas Robespierre's was a lawyer, but Maximilien's father deserted him and his siblings after his wife died, and Maximilien went to the prestigious secondary school Louis-le-Grand in Paris on a scholarship. Contrasting personalities may have played some role in their later differences. Before 1789 Brissot tried his hand at just about everything, from treatises advocating penal reform and writings about his travels in the new United States to pornography, blackmail and spying for the government. He was also one of the earliest French abolitionists; he founded the Society of the Friends of Blacks in February 1788. In contrast to Brissot's more flamboyant ways, Robespierre chose the straight and narrow path, returning to his hometown Arras in northern France to practice law successfully.

Two very different perspectives on war are offered in these excerpts from their speeches given in December 1791. Robespierre worried about the revival of arbitrary power within France—whether that of the king or his generals. In contrast, Brissot saw war as a way to hasten the downfall of the old order across Europe.

Robespierre at the Jacobin Club, December 18, 1791

War is always the first desire of a powerful government that wants to become still more powerful. I will not say to you that it is during war that the ministry manages to exhaust the people, squander funds and cover with an impenetrable veil its depredations and faults; I will speak to you about what touches still more directly the dearest of our interests. It is during war that the executive displays the most fearsome energy and exercises a kind of dictatorship which cannot but frighten off a nascent liberty; it is during war that people forget the deliberations that essentially concern their civil and political rights in order to occupy themselves only with external events, turning their attention away from their legislators and magistrates and attaching all their interests and hopes on their generals and ministers. . . .

It is during war that the same law [which overrides citizens' rights in the name of national security] grants [military commanders] the authority to *arbitrarily* punish soldiers. It is during war that the habit of passive obedience and the natural enthusiasm for capable leaders make the fatherland's soldiers into soldiers of the monarch or of his generals. . . . If these [heads of the army] are Caesars or Cromwells, they seize authority for themselves. But if they are courtiers without character, good-for-nothing but dangerous when they wish evil, they go back to lay their power at the feet of their master, and help him regain an arbitrary power on the condition that they will be his first valets.

Brissot at the Jacobin Club, December 20, 1791

[Austrian Emperor] Leopold should not want [war]; ten volcanoes are smoldering under his feet. One spark can set all of them ablaze in an instant.

The French court itself must fear the outcome of this war . . . it too knows that it is impossible to calculate the effects of war, the effects of a universal conflagration. It sees while trembling that at the first cannon shot, Brabant [a province in the Austrian Netherlands, present-day Belgium] can teeter and overthrow its old regime. . . . who can tell our court that the throne of Leopold will not be overthrown? Who can tell our court that the audacity of French troops will stop at its convenience? Who is going to tell it that the French will not cross the boundaries that it puts on them? . . .

Who is therefore the mortal who has been given the power to see the future and mark down for the revolution the time and the country where it must stop. Volcanoes are prepared everywhere; once again only one spark is required for a universal explosion. It is not patriotic to fear the consequences; it [universal explosion] only threatens thrones.

The courts of Europe see only too clearly the effects of the French Revolution; they see clearly that the kings are ripe [for destruction] and that their policy must be to postpone the moment when the fruit must fall. Now war would accelerate this moment; they [the kings] must therefore avoid it.

Sources: *Œuvres de Maximilien Robespierre*, 11 vols. (Paris, 2000–2011), VIII (2000): pp. 48–49; *Troisième discours de J.-P. Brissot, . . . sur la nécessité de la guerre, prononcé à la Société, le 20 janvier 1792. Société des amis de la Constitution, séante aux Jacobins, à Paris* (Paris, 1792), pp. 7–9.

Questions on the Robespierre and Brissot clash

1 Why does Robespierre fear the war and Brissot hope for it?

2 Whose vision proves the more correct in the long run?

3 As you read through the history of the revolution, consider how these two visions (fear of power and the hope for the spread of revolution) are melded and also undermined by successive governments.

TIMELINE TO CHAPTER 2

November 1789	National Assembly nationalizes the property of the Catholic Church to address financial shortfall.
January 1790	Proclamation of United Belgian States.
June 1790	Abolition of nobility.
July 1790	Civil Constitution of the Clergy restructures the Catholic Church.
June 20–21, 1791	Flight of the king and his family to Varennes.
August 1791	Beginning of the slave revolt in Saint-Domingue.
1791–1792	Thomas Paine, *Rights of Man*.
	Mary Wollstonecraft, *Vindication of the Rights of Woman*.
April 20, 1792	Revolutionary France declares war on monarchical Austria.
August 10, 1792	House arrest of Louis XVI and his family.
Sep. 2–6, 1792	September Massacres.

QUESTIONS ABOUT CHAPTER 2

1   Compare the success of the French in 1789 in making a revolution with the early failures in Western Europe. What factors made the difference?

2   France in 1789 had a social and economic system that was justified by tradition. The National Assembly replaced it with social and legal equality in the Declaration of the Rights of Man. What specific rights did it enumerate?

3   Probably the most difficult problem facing the National Assembly was the Catholic Church. Why did the National Assembly pass the Civil Constitution of the Clergy? Why was it so controversial?

4   In retrospect the September Massacres have been reviled as one of the great excesses of the revolution. Why might contemporaries have been ambivalent about this event?

5   Consider whether the revolution could have ended on August 10. What would have been necessary for that to occur?

3

A republic in constant crisis, 1792–1794

Barely two weeks after the horrific September Massacres, the newly elected deputies of the National Convention took over from the Legislative Assembly. As their first act, on September 21, 1792 they unanimously declared the abolition of royalty. Defending the motion he had put forward to this effect, Grégoire insisted, "Kings are to the moral order what monsters are to the physical order. Courts are the workshop of crime." In the fifteen months after the king's attempt to flee, public support for the monarchy had steadily eroded. Now, after a thousand years of monarchy, the French would try something most considered impossible just a year or two earlier. In a highly symbolic act, the archivist proposed replacing the king's seal with a republican one. Taking the place of the king's head in profile was a Roman-style female figure of liberty (Figure 3.1). In order to push forward, the deputies looked to the far distant, pre-Christian past for inspiration.[1]

This astonishing enterprise, with its novel language of politics and experimentation with political forms, fired the imagination of would-be republicans and revolutionaries across the globe for generations to come. At issue was not just the official constitution, which remained to be drafted, but also a titanic struggle for the hearts and minds of the French people. The deputies might see no other option available than a republic, but would a population made up largely of illiterate peasants willingly follow their lead? Or would they join the growing forces of resistance already galvanized by the schism in the clergy and the annihilation of noble privileges? For a nation at war, these were life and death questions.

Over the next two years, the French nation experienced one of the most dramatic upheavals in all of world history. Even the extraordinary events that had occurred since May 1789 could not have prepared anyone for what was to follow: the trials and executions of the king and queen, a cultural revolution designed to instill republican values, war with many if not most of the major European powers, a slave rebellion that prompted the abolition of slavery in all

FIGURE 3.1 *Seal of the Republic*
The new seal of the Republic shows a Roman goddess of liberty (known by the Roman cap of liberty on the pike she is holding in her left hand) holding the Roman-style fasces or bundle of rods that signified unity. The symbolic break with the monarchy could not have been more dramatic; a female allegory replaced the actual king, and the ideals of liberty and unity displaced the traditional notion of a king by birth and dynastic right. Etching and engraving, 1792–1794.

the French colonies, catastrophic civil wars that resulted in hundreds of thousands of deaths within France, and the development of government by terror designed to silence if not eliminate all critics. The most democratic and egalitarian regime ever seen in the world became expansionist and politically repressive, raising nagging questions about the connections between revolution and violence.

The National Convention

When the departing Legislative Assembly instituted nearly universal manhood suffrage by eliminating tax requirements and lowering the voting age from 25 to 21 (domestic servants were still excluded), expectations for change were high; the newspaper *Révolutions de Paris* exulted, "Happy France! You are going to become the motherland of the universe, the cradle of the world, the school of the human race." The French example excited enthusiasm and fear across the Western world. A group of artisans, workers, and shopkeepers had set up a London Corresponding Society to coordinate reform movements in Britain; it, too, aimed for universal manhood suffrage as well as reform of parliamentary elections. In late September 1792 it drafted a message congratulating the Convention. "The oppressed part of mankind" was praying for the French cause, they insisted, because the French had seen that the real enemy was "All-consuming aristocracy—Wisely have you acted in expelling it from France." So alarmed were the British authorities that they did everything possible over the next seven years to squash the Society and its associates, finally outlawing it altogether in 1799.

Despite or perhaps because of the extension of voting rights in France, turnout declined compared to the elections for the Legislative Assembly, from 25 percent of eligible voters to 20 percent. Some of the newly eligible had gone off to fight; in other places peasants expressed their disaffection by not voting, and royalists saw little point or were actively discouraged by Jacobin Club members from attending. Still, voting rates were higher than in the first elections of the new American republic. Since voting drew mainly the most committed, it is perhaps not surprising that many familiar names were chosen: 83 deputies, including Sieyès, Grégoire, and Robespierre, had served in the National Assembly; and 194, among them Brissot, Condorcet, and the Girondins, continued from the Legislative. Desmoulins and Marat were chosen alongside several other leading journalists. Like Robespierre, Desmoulins, and Marat, Danton was elected as one of the 24 deputies from Paris; indeed, he got more votes than any of the others, a sure sign of his popularity in the sections of the capital city. The Englishman Thomas Paine was elected by four different regions; he fled England in September 1792 to avoid being imprisoned on the charge of seditious libel for publishing the second part of his *Rights of Man*. Even though he did not speak French, Paine was named to the constitutional committee alongside Sieyès, Brissot, Condorcet, and Danton.

VICTORY AT VALMY   Writing a republican constitution took time, and the Convention faced an immediate national emergency, which had become only slightly more manageable by an unexpected turn in the war. Just as the deputies began meeting, news arrived that the French armies, with their unstable mix of volunteers and veterans, had stopped the advance of the Prussians and their Austrian and *émigré* contingents. To everyone's surprise, the French did not turn tail in the battle of Valmy on September 20; they had gone forward to the fervent patriotic cry of *Vive la Nation*, and the Prussians retreated. Within weeks, the French advanced toward the eastern and northern borders of France. Dumouriez, who had left his post as one of the Girondin ministers to take up his general's baton, led the troops to Belgium, which he believed eager for liberation from the Austrians. The great German poet and novelist Wolfgang von Goethe had accompanied the Prussian troops and immediately saw the significance of Valmy: "From this place and from this day forth commences a new era in the world's history." A citizen army was taking shape and it would transform warfare in Europe in the years to come.

Back in Paris, the deputies had to figure out how to run a provisional government and direct the war effort in the absence of a chief executive. The generals reported to the minister of war, who then informed the Convention, but the minister of war had to have the deputies' approval for changes of command or even alterations of troop deployments. The *assignats* had declined another 10 percent (to 75 percent of their face value) since the end of 1791, which made provisioning the army and supplying the cities increasingly difficult. No one was going to endorse Marat's solution of naming a dictator, but how could a body of some 750 deputies rule in any consistent or coherent fashion, especially when they disagreed about the naming of ministers? During a tempestuous session on September 29, the Convention ultimately decided to continue the Girondin ministers. Danton, who chose to be a deputy instead, used the occasion to attack Madame Roland: "you had better offer [the ministry] to Madame Roland as well," he said, since "everyone knows he [Roland] was not alone in his ministry as I was in mine."

Danton's remarks exposed the growing animosity between the Paris Jacobin deputies and the Girondins. The hard-core Jacobins became known as the Montagnards (mountaineers) because they occupied the highest seats on the left side of the hall; for the most part they represented Paris or other big cities. The Girondins tried to blame them for the September Massacres, and all during the fall the two sides exchanged increasingly heated charges of venality and even sedition in newspapers, pamphlets, and on the floor of the Convention itself. Any remaining Girondins were thrown out of the Jacobin Club, but the Girondins still rallied more support among the deputies caught in the middle, lumped together derisively as "the plain" or "the marsh." Winning over the "marsh toads" would prove crucial as neither the Girondins nor the Montagnards could prevail without them.

The trial of the king

The issue looming over all others in the fall of 1792 was the fate of the king, but at first it took a back seat to preoccupation with the war. While the ministers purged royalists and labored to get a handle on food distribution and public order, French armies moved quickly to take Mainz and Frankfurt and bottle up the Prussians. When the King of Piedmont refused to join the French against the Austrians, the French occupied Nice and Savoy, his territories on the French side of the Alps. In the north Dumouriez took Brussels in November, forcing any remaining *émigrés* to flee. Fighting alongside him was the Duke of Chartres, the son of the Duke of Orleans. The 42-year-old Venezuelan revolutionary Francisco de Miranda had been given command of part of Dumouriez's army thanks to Brissot, and with it he occupied Antwerp. Miranda demanded a huge payment from the city leaders to pay for the French occupation. His ultimate goal was the liberation of Spanish America but for the time being he fought to spread revolution outside France.

When the deputies turned to the question of the king, almost everyone seemed to agree that Louis was guilty. On all else, however, opinions scattered in different directions. Could the king be tried since by the Constitution of 1791 he was inviolable? If Louis were to be tried, what body had the authority to mount such a trial? Should a referendum be held to confirm any judgment? Should he be executed, exiled, or imprisoned? In early November the Convention decided that the nation had the right to judge the king because its sovereignty was superior to the king's executive power and that the Convention itself should try him for treason. In the midst of impassioned debate, Roland, Minister of the Interior, announced the sensational discovery of the king's secret safe in the Tuileries palace. Among the incriminating papers were letters that showed the king had been paying Mirabeau to advise him on how to manipulate the deputies; having been the first to enter the Pantheon of revolutionary heroes, Mirabeau would be the first to be disinterred. Could anyone be trusted? Had Roland kept back papers that would incriminate his fellow Girondins?[2]

Weeks of contentious discussion followed. A small group of Girondin sympathizers argued against a trial on the grounds of the king's inviolability and an equally small group of Montagnards, including Robespierre and the youngest deputy, 25-year-old Louis de Saint-Just, made the case against a trial on the grounds that such a proceeding inherently presumed innocence was even possible. Wearing shoulder-length hair and a single gold earring, Saint-Just gave his very first speech on November 13, 1792 and cut instantly to the chase: "No man can reign innocently. . . . Every king is a rebel and usurper." The king could not be tried for treason like a citizen because he was essentially an enemy alien (see Document 3.1, at the end of the chapter). Despite these arguments, a large majority voted for a trial, which began with the former king's indictment for treason on December 10. Desmoulins' father wrote begging his son not to vote guilty. "I would be inconsolable," he wrote, "to find your name on the list of those voting for the death of Louis XVI."

In a remarkable scene of political theater, Louis appeared the day after the indictment and denied all the charges. Unlike King Charles I of England, who was executed for treason in 1649, Louis did not contest the authority of his accusers to put him on trial and instead asked for legal counsel. When the trial resumed, Louis's defense team argued that the trial was illegal because the king was inviolable under the Constitution of 1791 and that the king had done nothing against the law. The appearance of the king with his modest dress and humble demeanor aroused mixed emotions, and some of the deputies now hesitated in the face of such a momentous decision. Unexpectedly, Brissot and the Girondins raised the prospect of delay by arguing for a national referendum to decide the king's fate; Brissot had earlier opposed any appeal to the people in the strongest terms. Robespierre, Saint-Just, and the Montagnards denounced the Girondins as hypocritical fomenters of civil war. Paine supported the appeal to the people and suggested exile to America. After a turbulent 12-hour session on January 14, the shouting and mutual recrimination finally ended with the decision to hold roll call votes. In the first, the next day, Louis was found guilty of treason by a vote of 693 to 0 (with 26 abstentions). In the second, which immediately followed, the idea of a national referendum was defeated by a large margin, and even some of the Girondins, such as Condorcet, voted against it because they feared the consequences of holding such a divisive vote in the midst of war and revolution.

EXECUTION OF LOUIS XVI   Now came the most wrenching decision. In a vote that dragged on for more than 24 hours, 361 deputies voted for immediate death, a majority of exactly one. Many others voted for death, but only under certain conditions. Brissot, for example, wanted a reprieve until a new constitution was accepted. Paine and Condorcet were among the 290 deputies who voted for some other punishment. The Girondins followed no one line because they were more like a caucus than a political party. Robespierre, Saint-Just, Marat, Desmoulins, and Danton voted for an immediate execution, as did the king's cousin, the Duke of Orleans, now known as Philippe Égalité. As might be expected, the next day the vote had to be verified again because it was so close, and many wanted to reopen the question of reprieve. The Montagnards insisted on another roll call vote, and a substantial majority now voted for an immediate death sentence. Most of the Girondins opted for a reprieve, opening themselves to recrimination in the months to come.

On January 21, the very next day, Louis went to the guillotine, the new instrument of capital punishment that had been in use for only nine months. A priest came to celebrate mass for the former king that morning and then accompanied him to the scaffold mounted on the Place de la Révolution (the present day Place de la Concorde). Some 80,000 armed men, soldiers and local National Guards, kept watch on the route. Braving cold rain showers, 100,000 people looked on as the king climbed the steps with courage and dignity. Louis tried to speak to the crowd, but a drumroll drowned out his words: "People, I die an innocent man." When the blade fell, the executioner picked up the severed head and showed it to the crowd (Figure 3.2) Some ran

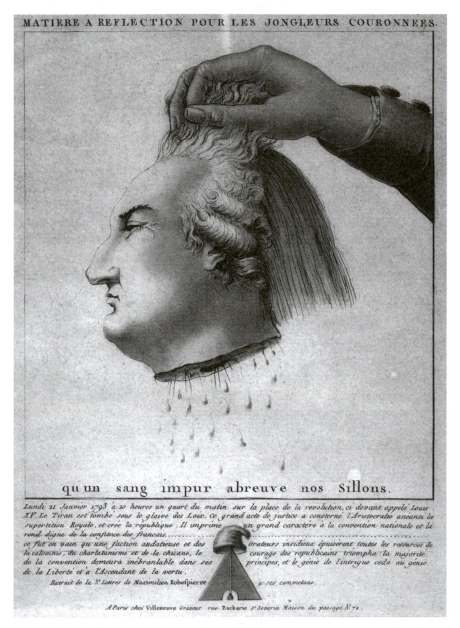

MATIERE A REFLECTION POUR LES JONGLEURS COURONNEES.

qu un sang impur abreuve nos Sillons.

Lundi 21 Janvier 1793 à 10 heures un quart du matin sur la place de la revolution, ci devant appelé Louis XV. Le Tiran est tombe sous le glaive des Loix. Ce grand acte de justice a consterné l'Aristocratie aneanti la superstition Royale, et créé la république. Il imprime un grand caractère à la convention nationale et la rend digne de la confiance des francais.............

ce fut en vain qu'une faction audatieuse et des   orateurs insidieux épuiserent toutes les resources de
la calomnie, du charlatanisme et de la chicane, le   courage des republicains triompha: la majorité
de la convention demeura inébranlable dans ses   principes, et le genie de l'intrigue ceda au genie
de la Liberté et à l'Ascendant de la vertu.

Extrait de la 5.ᵉ Lettres de Maximilien Robespierre   p. ses commetans.

A Paris chez Villeneuve Graveur rue Zacharie S.ᵗ Severin Maison du passage N.ᵒ 70.

FIGURE 3.2 *The Head of Louis XVI*
The execution of the king wrenched many hearts, so this pro-revolutionary print by the engraver Villeneuve insisted on its quality as a lesson for the other European royals. The title in French reads "Something to consider for crowned jugglers." The line just under the dripping blood comes from the Marseillaise, the revolutionary hymn: "so that the impure blood may water our fields." The rest of the text below is from a speech by Robespierre that ties the execution of the king to the creation of the republic. Etching and aquatint, Paris, 1793.

forward to dip their handkerchiefs in the blood as the crowd shouted "Long Live the Republic!" The body was buried in a common grave and covered with quicklime to hasten its decomposition.

"The blood of Louis Capet," wrote *Révolutions de Paris* newspaper, "cleanses us of a stigma of 1,300 years" of monarchy. Despite fears of a royalist uprising to save the king, only one major incident occurred; the evening before the king's execution a group of royalists murdered Michel Le Peletier de Saint-Fargeau, a former noble judge turned Montagnard who voted for death. On January 24 the artist and deputy Jacques-Louis David organized a Roman-style exhibition of Le Peletier's body on the pedestal that had once held a statue of Louis XIV. The spokesman for the Convention, Bertrand Barère, a 36-year-old lawyer from southwestern France, asked his fellow deputies to swear on the body of their martyred colleague to extinguish their personal animosities and unite to save the country. The ashes were then buried in the Pantheon.

More and more enemies

The execution of the king divided opinion almost everywhere. *The Newcastle Chronicle*, which had previously praised the French revolutionaries, now called them "inhuman butchers." The British had already begun war preparations in November 1792 when the French unilaterally declared the estuary of the Scheldt River open to international navigation. Treaties had guaranteed Dutch control since 1648; the estuary was in the Dutch Republic, an ally of Britain, but the river traversed France and Belgium before meeting the sea.

WAR ON BRITAIN AND DUTCH REPUBLIC   Britain expelled the French ambassador after the execution of Louis XVI, and in response on February 1 the Convention declared war on Britain and the Dutch Republic. Everyone now embraced war; Georges Couthon, a wheelchair-bound Montagnard, wrote to his home municipality on February 7, 1793 and assured them, "I do not doubt that if we steadfastly want it, within six months we will liberate Europe and purge the earth of all tyrants." A few months earlier he had assured them that "the happy epidemic of liberty" had already reached Spain, Prussia, and Sweden. On March 7 the Convention declared war on Spain. The United States government found itself in a quandary since it had signed an alliance with France in 1778. Secretary of the Treasury Alexander Hamilton argued that the execution rendered the treaty void since it had been signed with Louis XVI. Jefferson, who was Secretary of State, still supported the French Revolution and argued the contrary. President Washington formally declared neutrality on April 22, 1793. The debate over the French Revolution in the

United States helped coalesce the formation of two parties: the Federalists, who opposed the French Revolution, and the Republicans, following Jefferson, who generally supported it.[3]

In February and March 1793, the Convention began annexing previously conquered territories such as Nice, Monaco, some 100 communities on the left bank of the Rhine, and Belgium. Just a few months earlier, on November 19, 1792, the deputies had decreed that French armies would offer "assistance to all peoples wishing to recover their liberty." In December they decided that this would take the form of abolishing all feudal dues, noble privileges, and clerical tithes. When the French invaded, they sought out supporters like the democrats in Belgium who returned and dominated new elections set up by the French. They also set up clubs on the French model. Since the more ardent supporters of French-style reforms were almost always in the minority, as they were in Belgium, they used local assemblies and clubs to petition for annexation.

FIRST COALITION Success was short-lived. Just two days after the execution of Louis XVI, Prussia and Russia agreed to a second partition of Poland that would leave Russia effectively in control of what was left of Poland. Prussia had already regained some momentum against France and retook Frankfurt in December 1792. In March 1793 Austrian troops marched back into Belgium and defeated Dumouriez on March 18 at Neerwinden in Flemish Brabant. Dumouriez blamed Miranda and the volunteers for a panicky retreat. In the next months, the British convinced Catherine the Great and the rulers of Piedmont, Naples, and Portugal to join the growing alliance against France, known afterward as the First Coalition. In another shocking turn of events, Dumouriez asked the Austrians for an armistice and promised to march his remaining men on Paris, but when his troops refused, he defected to the Austrians on April 5. At the same time the Prussians were steadily pushing the French out of the Rhineland, thanks in no small measure to local resentment of French annexation.

Since volunteers had signed up for only one year's service in the French army, the number of men in arms had begun to decline from more than 400,000 to less than 350,000 at the beginning of 1793. When requests for new volunteers fell short, the deputies voted on February 24, 1793 to levy 300,000 additional men; all men aged 18 to 40 who were unmarried or widowed without children were considered liable to be drafted. If volunteers did not come forward, local authorities enrolled them either through drawing of lots or votes of local citizens. The rich could buy replacements.

Riots broke out in many places, but in the west of the country, especially in an area south of Nantes known as the Vendée (the name of one of the involved departments), villagers rose up in fearsome rage against the towns where recruitment was centered (see Map 3.1). They confronted National Guards mobilized to support the draft and pitilessly massacred guardsmen, officials, and constitutional priests, sometimes by the scores or even hundreds. Peasants and rural artisans focused their anger on administrators in the towns because the officials had arrested and deported their priests (rates of refusing the clerical oath reached as high as 89 percent in the region), supervised the sales of church lands to townspeople, and now organized the draft. The way to resistance had been prepared in some cases by conspiring *émigré* nobles, but rural people wanted local nobles to help them restore their priests and the monarchy. As National Guards from nearby marched to the region, a civil war took shape. Patriots promised to exterminate every last rebel and often killed women and children too. Mutual atrocities encouraged both sides to fight to the death. National Guards gained the upper hand in the area north of the Loire River but not south of it (the Vendée proper). There a spreading guerilla insurgency would bog down republican armies for years to come.[4]

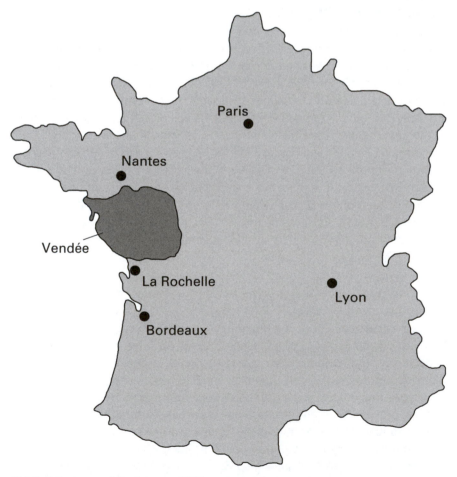

MAP 3.1 *Areas of Resistance, 1793*

The reversal of fortune in the war, increasingly organized counter-revolution in the west, and the spectacular treachery of Dumouriez enraged militants in Paris who demanded action from the deputies. In February major riots over the price of coffee, sugar, soap, and candles had brought women, in particular, back onto the streets. Colonial products such as coffee and sugar had become necessities to urban working people and as a result of the uprising in Saint-Domingue prices had risen sharply. Many militants and even most of the deputies jumped to the conclusion that food shortages, attacks on the value of the *assignats*, recruitment riots, counter-revolution, and the treachery of Dumouriez were all part of some great conspiracy fueled by English money. In fact, the English were willing to intervene wherever they could; in February they had signed a secret agreement with white colonists in Saint-Domingue to maintain slavery there if the colonists would help them take over the French colony.

The Convention had to improvise to make its authority felt. Deputies were sent out as "representatives on mission" to all of the departments to supervise recruitment and then to the armies themselves. These deputies soon became veritable war commissars with the right to requisition army supplies and replace local officials. On March 11, even before the defeat in Belgium and the defection of Dumouriez, the Convention set up an extraordinary criminal court in Paris to expeditiously try all those accused of counter-revolution or plots to re-establish royalty. The deputies supervised its operation, named the judges and jury, and drew up indictments; conviction required a simple majority with no possibility of appeal. In the debate on the revolutionary court Danton made clear that the aim was to channel the kinds of popular demands for retribution that had led to the September Massacres: "let us be terrible so that the people do not have to be; organize a court, not well, that is impossible, but the least badly that we can, so that the blade of the law hangs heavily over the heads of all our enemies."

COMMITTEE OF PUBLIC SAFETY As the situation worsened, new repressive decrees rained down. Military commissions were set up to judge counter-revolutionaries and draft resisters and execute them within 24 hours. Foreigners were required to carry passports and kept under surveillance; every municipality was asked to set up a surveillance committee, and their responsibilities quickly expanded to include denunciation of any suspicious behavior. On April 1, in a decision heavy with consequences for the future, the deputies voted to abandon parliamentary immunity, making themselves subject to arrest by their colleagues. To centralize executive functions, all the factions, including the Girondins, agreed on April 6 to set up a Committee of Public Safety, first with nine and then twelve deputies as members. It met in secret and before long gained nearly complete control over the conduct of the war and the repression of political enemies, but its membership was up for renewal every month.

Fall of the Girondins

Even as the deputies struggled to get control of an ever more alarming situation, they continued to fight amongst themselves. The Montagnards seized upon Dumouriez's links with the Girondins to accuse them all of treason, but in April and May the Girondins still had the upper hand. The Convention voted to indict Marat for having provoked through his writings pillage, murder, and the dissolution of the Convention. The maneuver backfired when the new revolutionary court acquitted Marat. When crowds of Paris militants, both male and female, began to demand the arrest of the Girondins, even brandishing lists of specific individuals, the Girondins convinced the majority of deputies to form a commission of twelve deputies to investigate. The "Commission of Twelve" ordered the arrest of leading militants in Paris. In a particularly turbulent session of the Convention, one leading Girondin threatened that if tumult in Paris continued, "Paris will be annihilated. . . . soon one would search on the banks of the Seine for any sign of Paris."

ARREST OF GIRONDINS   Delegates from the most radical sections began meeting and formed a Central Revolutionary Committee. On May 31 the Committee called on the sections and the National Guard to march to the Convention and demand the arrest of the Girondins. Confusion reigned in the hall, however, as some sections sent statements of their steadfast loyalty to the deputies and the few Girondins present demanded that the commander of the National Guard be called to account. In the end, the marchers went home after the deputies voted to abolish the Commission of Twelve.

Agitation continued in the streets of Paris and came to a head again on Sunday morning June 2. When the deputies went out to confront the marchers in person, the demonstrators, thousands of them armed, would not back down. The deputies retreated back to their assembly room and meekly voted the arrest of 29 Girondin deputies, including Brissot and two Girondin ministers, Clavière, Minister of Finances, and Pierre Lebrun, Minister of Foreign Affairs (he had been Dumouriez's chief clerk). Condorcet was left alone until July when an arrest warrant sent him into hiding. Paine was able to slip away, and British supporters of the Girondins such as Mary Wollstonecraft, who was in Paris, had to keep a low profile. Paris officials had already ordered the arrest of Roland and his wife on May 31, even though Roland had resigned his ministry in January in the face of persistent threats against him. Roland fled but his wife was imprisoned. From prison, she wrote, "the debasement of the Convention, its daily acts of weakness and slavishness, appeared to me so upsetting that I found the latest excesses almost preferable because they would serve to enlighten and bring the departments to a decision." Her words touched on a major source of conflict: did Paris speak for the whole nation?

The people of Paris had intervened before, saving the constitutional revolution on July 14, 1789, insisting on the king's return to Paris in early October of the same year, and pushing for the overthrow of the king on August 10, 1792. This intervention seemed at first to be much like the others, but in fact it marked the beginning of a new phase in the struggle for control over the revolution, this time between the deputies and the sans-culottes of Paris. Even though the Paris militants got what they wanted in the short term—the arrest of the Girondins and the supremacy of the Montagnards—their interests diverged from those of Robespierre, Danton, and the other Montagnard deputies, even Marat, who had cultivated popular support with his incessant calls for more blood to be shed.[5]

Leading the sans-culottes in May 1793 was a grab bag of militants later called by historians the *enragés* (meaning ultra-revolutionaries): Jacques Roux, an ex-priest in his early forties; Jean Varlet, an educated 29-year-old looking for a cause; Théophile Leclerc, a 22-year-old soldier who had been sent as an envoy from Lyon to Paris; and two women, 25-year-old Pauline Léon, a chocolate maker, and 28-year-old Claire Lacombe, an actress, who together founded in February 1793 the most influential women's club of the revolution, the Society of Revolutionary Republican Women. As president of the Society, Léon (who later married Leclerc) appeared at the Convention on June 2 to urge the deputies to arrest the Girondins. These five people were typical of the most committed revolutionary activists across the country; they were relatively young and educated and eager to seize upon the new opportunities afforded by rapidly evolving events. They argued for price controls, making the *assignats* the only legal tender, more severe measures against speculators and hoarders, and a direct political voice for ordinary people.[6]

The Montagnard deputies acceded to some of these demands to get sans-culottes support against the Girondins and to quiet agitation over food shortages in the capital. Despite their belief in the benefits of free markets, the Montagnards had convinced the Convention, over the objections of the Girondins, to prohibit the sale or export of gold and silver and require the acceptance of *assignats* as payment in early April 1793. In early May 1793 the Convention established price controls on grain, but peasants who produced for the market did everything they could to evade this maximum on prices and many local officials abetted their efforts.

The Montagnards resisted being pushed further or faster by the sans-culottes than they wanted to move. On June 25, just a day after the deputies had finally approved a new constitution for the republic, Jacques Roux spoke to the Convention in threatening terms: "Legislators! We declare to you that you have not done enough for the people." Despite repeated promises to strike at the "bloodsuckers" of the people, the deputies' constitution, drawn up by the Committee of Public Safety, did not explicitly condemn speculation or require the death penalty for hoarders. "The rich alone, for four years, have taken advantage of the Revolution," and it is time, Roux vowed, for "the sans-culottes" to "bring down every species of tyranny." He seemed to imply that one species of tyranny was to be found in the Convention itself.

The deputies were furious, and as laundry women in Paris commandeered shipments of soap, Robespierre denounced Roux at the Jacobin Club, and the Jacobins persuaded the Cordeliers Club, which Roux claimed to represent, to repudiate Roux. Marat devoted an entire issue of his paper to vilifying Roux, Varlet, and Leclerc as intriguers and greedy, power-hungry crooks. The influence of the *enragés* had been at least temporarily countered, but the struggle between the deputies and populist forces on their left had not ended.[7]

A summer of discontent

The Montagnards had to keep control in Paris because chaos threatened in so many other places. While voters gathered in primary assemblies to consider the proposed constitution in July, all but nine of the 29 Girondin deputies escaped from house arrest in Paris and most of them went off to foment provincial rebellions against the Convention's authority. Seventy-five of the remaining deputies in the Convention and half of the departments had officially protested the arrests of June 2. Before long, pro-Girondin armed forces were gathering to march on Paris from Caen in the north, Bordeaux in the southwest, and Marseille and Lyon in the southeast. At the same time, the Vendée rebels took several towns in the Loire valley and besieged the port city of Nantes. In late July, after a two-month standoff, the Anglo-Austrian armies took Valenciennes, a strategic French city on the Scheldt River; the Prussians reclaimed the Rhineland and the fortress city of Mainz; the Spanish had already crossed the French border; and the army of Piedmont-Sardinia stymied French armies in the Alps.

The fate of Mainz was particularly alarming because the French had tried to instigate a French-style revolution there by setting up a Society of the Friends of Liberty and Equality. A local librarian, Georg Forster, dominated the club; Forster had gained an international reputation as a 23-year-old when he published in 1777 an account of his and his father's voyage with James Cook around the world. Forster had previously traveled in Russia and lived for years in England and claimed to know 17 languages. He helped set up a Rhenish-German National Convention that declared the Rhineland a republic free of the Holy Roman Empire. He then went off to Paris to urge annexation of the region, but while he was gone the Prussians recaptured the city. With a price on his head back home, Forster stayed in Paris until his death in January 1794 of pneumonia. Until then he continued to write about the universal qualities of the French Revolution, finding in it the culmination of the Enlightenment despite the gathering tide of violence he himself witnessed. The address he and his colleagues brought to the Convention in March 1793 contained this message: "the Germans on the banks of the Rhine will never forget that the French have smashed their chains."[8]

ROBESPIERRE JOINS COMMITTEE OF PUBLIC SAFETY While Forster was waiting for news from Mainz, a 24-year-old woman from Caen named Charlotte Corday tried to help the Girondins by stabbing Marat to death in his bathtub on July 13 (Figure 3.3). She saw herself as acting to save the republic by killing a "ferocious beast." She went to the guillotine the day after Marat's state funeral, and even Jacobin newspapers had to admit that she endured the insults thrown at her with remarkable calm and courage. Galloping fears of conspiracy and demands for vengeance now greeted a reconstituted Committee of Public Safety. Danton and two other members had not been re-elected on July 10, but continuing on the Committee were Barère, the Committee's spokesman; Couthon; Saint-Just; and the 37-year-old nobleman and lawyer, Marie-Jean Hérault de Séchelles, who had presided at the Convention on the fateful day of June 2 when Couthon had proposed the arrest of the Girondins. On July 27 Robespierre was named as well, and according to Barère's recollections, "harsh measures became the order of the day." Yet it was on Barère's proposal the next day that the Girondins who had fled to raise rebellion were declared traitors. Over the next days the Committee sent some of its members to the frontiers to oversee the war effort, and it convinced the Convention to order the arrest of any foreigner from a country at war with France. As for the Vendée, on August 1 Barère assured the deputies that the Committee was preparing measures to "exterminate this rebel race, destroy their hideouts, set fire to their forests, cut down their harvests." Only the elderly, women, and children were to be spared.

This threat remained empty as long as republican forces stayed on the defensive, but an astute observer might have detected signs that the tide was turning again in the republic's favor. On June 29, the Catholic and Royal Army of the Vendée rebels managed to work its way inside Nantes, a slave-trading metropolis of some 80,000 people, but its attack fizzled for lack of coordination even though the garrison of 12,000 men had to hold off an opposing force three times as large. Republican forces eventually got the upper hand and pursued a vengeful scorched earth policy.

Gains were made on other fronts, too. "Federalism," the pejorative name given to the supporters of the Girondins, never got much popular support. The "army" sent from Caen to Paris dispersed after one minor skirmish; the other forces never left their cities. The Committee of Public Safety sent one of its members, the lawyer Robert Lindet, to organize repression in Caen, and he removed many officials and arrested some of them, but no one was executed

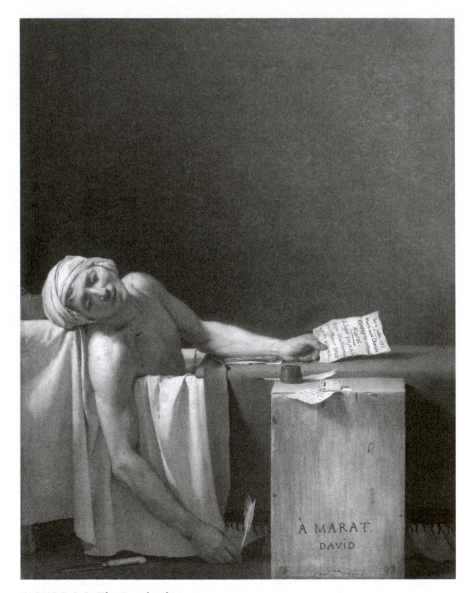

FIGURE 3.3 *The Death of Marat*
Marat became a revolutionary martyr when he was assassinated by Charlotte
Corday. The artist Jacques-Louis David depicts him here as a Christ-like figure with
clear unblemished skin. In reality, Marat had a skin disease, which is why he was
conducting business from his bathtub. He was also very controversial, and Corday
thought she was undertaking a heroic act to save the republic. David aimed to make
Marat the real hero. Oil on canvas, Paris, 1793.

in the town, in part because local officials retracted their previous statements even before republican forces arrived. Republican armies easily took Marseille at the end of August, and Bordeaux offered little armed resistance.[9]

By August, moreover, it was clear that voters had turned out in good numbers (one-third of those eligible, higher than the turnout in 1792) and overwhelmingly approved the new constitution that enfranchised servants, reaffirmed rights, and added the right to education and to government assistance in times of need. On August 10, 1793, the anniversary of the overthrow of the monarchy, the Convention held a precisely orchestrated "Festival of Unity and Indivisibility" to celebrate the acceptance of the constitution and the defeat of federalism. The organizer was the artist-deputy David, a famous painter from the 1780s who had become a kind of pageant-master for the republic. He set up four stations to commemorate the history of the revolution: a colossal figure of nature on the site of the Bastille greeted a procession of departmental delegates, deputies, military men, and ordinary people at the first station; at the second, an arch of triumph hung over the heroines of October 1789 perched on their cannon; the procession then made its way to the site of the king's execution where a statue of liberty now stood; and when they arrived at the fourth station at the Invalides square, they saw standing on a mountain (mountains now being essential props because they recalled the Montagnards), a giant papier-mâché Hercules representing the people and wielding a club against the monster of federalism. The procession finally ended at the Altar of the Fatherland on the nearby Champ de Mars; the president of the Convention, Hérault de Séchelles, laid the official tallies of votes on the constitution on the Altar, and all those present swore to defend the constitution to the death.

The Terror

The Constitution of 1793 never went into effect. Petitions flooded the Convention begging the deputies to remain in their posts. Agitation had continued in Paris over rumored food shortages, and when news arrived in Paris on September 2 that royalists had turned the southern port city of Toulon over to the British, militants in Paris organized for action again. They were led by two municipal officials who had come over to the position of the *enragés*: Jacques-René Hébert, famous as the editor of the often vulgarly populist paper, *Le Père Duchesne*, and Pierre Chaumette, one of the leaders of the August 10, 1792 insurrection and a key figure in the attack on the Girondins. They led demonstrators to the floor of the Convention on September 5 where the petitioners demanded that the deputies "make terror the order of the day." They wanted immediate judgment of the Girondins and the deployment of "revolutionary armies" (paramilitary bands) to purge the country of traitors.

Although the deputies never voted to make terror the order of the day, the Committee of Public Safety embraced the term as a way of mollifying militant demands; phrases such as "a salutary terror" and "the terror that a prompt punishment inspires" began to appear in the correspondence between the Committee and deputies on mission. The day after the September 5 demonstration, two of the most prominent supporters of the protesters were added to the Committee: the 37-year-old lawyer Jacques Billaud-Varenne and the 44-year-old actor and playwright Jean-Marie Collot d'Herbois, both of them deputies from Paris who had made their reputations in the uprising of August 10, 1792. Danton was also named but refused to take up the post. Endorsing terror afforded the Committee of Public Safety a greater sense of power when in fact its position remained precarious, as each member was up for renewal every month.[10]

The task the Committee faced was gargantuan: set the structure of the emergency government; organize the war effort; defeat the counter-revolution in the Vendée, Toulon, and anywhere else it appeared; get control of the chaotic situation in Saint-Domingue; and secure food supplies for Paris and the other big cities. To ensure the continuation of the republic, it also had to educate the population in republican values. A revolution in culture began to take shape and was accompanied by an intensified hunt for traitors. Terror came to mean not just revenge and retribution but also a general atmosphere of dread as the definition of suspects and traitors expanded inexorably.

The number of measures proposed and enforced between the end of August and the middle of December staggers the imagination. In order to bolster the effort against internal and external enemies, the Convention, on the suggestion of the Committee, ordered a *levée en masse*, a total mobilization for the war effort, on August 23. Single or married men without children aged 18 to 25 were to register for the draft and everyone else, including women and children, would have a role. All saddle horses were requisitioned along with any suitable firearms. Despite persistently high rates of desertion (20 percent of those drafted), the army had 750,000 men within a few months. Lazare Carnot, a 40-year-old former army captain, had been named to the Committee on August 14, and he immediately took charge of military affairs and the organization of the mobilization.

On September 9, the Convention created the paramilitary revolutionary army. Paid armed militants would roam the countryside searching for grain hoarders and counter-revolutionaries. Other departments soon demanded their own versions, but the Committee's proposal signaled its concerns about this force: originally designed only for Paris, it called for a maximum body of 6,000 men aged 25 to 40 who would be chosen by a commission made up of delegates from both the Commune (municipality) and the regional Department. The men would elect their immediate superiors but the upper echelon of officers would be named by the council of ministers and then vetted by the Committee itself.

The Committee had no intention of letting the *enragés* or their supporters call the shots. The Jacobin Club pressured the Paris Commune to arrest Roux on August 22 (he killed himself in prison), and on September 9 the Committee endorsed a proposal first made by Danton in the heat of events on September 5: the meetings of the sections would be limited to two days a week, and anyone needing a subsidy to attend in place of working would be offered 40 sous a session. The *enragés* opposed the move as undemocratic and contrary to the Constitution of 1793. When Varlet presented the Convention a petition of the sections to this effect, he was arrested. A campaign against Claire Lacombe and the Society of Revolutionary Republican Women culminated in the suppression of the Society at the end of October. Even while citing disorders created by the Society's demands that all women in Paris wear a red liberty cap as a symbol of adherence to revolutionary militancy, the deputies wanted to reaffirm their idea of women's proper place. The deputy Jean-Baptiste Amar explained, "women are not capable of elevated thoughts and serious meditations . . . in the French Republic do you want them to be seen coming to the bar, to the tribune, and to political assemblies as men do?"[11]

To keep the upper hand, however, the deputies had to agree to many sans-culottes demands. On September 17, the Convention voted a wide-ranging law defining as suspects to be arrested immediately anyone who by their conduct, their relations, their speech, or their writings had supported tyranny or federalism; those who could not prove the source of their income or who had been refused certificates of civic behavior by their local surveillance committees; public officials who had been suspended or removed; and any relative or agent of an *émigré* who had not demonstrated attachment to the Revolution. As many as 300,000 suspects may have been imprisoned over the next months as almost any loose talk or unrestrained behavior could be grounds for suspicion.

GENERAL MAXIMUM On September 29, the Convention decreed a general maximum, that is, a ceiling on the price of all items deemed necessities. Included in addition to grains and flours previously targeted were meats, preserved fish, oil, wine, cider, beer, salt, vinegar, candles, soap, wood, sugar, honey, virtually all metals and textiles, leather and wood for making shoes, white paper, and tobacco. Local officials had to develop tables for the maximum on each staple; the ceiling for most was the price in 1790 increased by one-third. Wages were subject to the maximum as well, but their ceiling was the level of 1790 increased by one-half, thus presumably giving some advantage to workers. Since the value of the *assignats* had fallen to 41 percent by September 1793 and inflation of the price of foodstuffs had in some places risen as high as 300 percent compared to 1790, the deputies also had to worry about enforcement. Local officials who failed to draw up the tables would be removed, and anyone buying or selling above the maximum would be subject to a fine and to designation as a suspect. By the end of October, long lines of women were forming again outside Parisian bakeries as in the short term the distribution of goods came almost to a halt.

To expedite the implementation of these far-ranging measures, the Convention approved on October 10, 1793 the emergency structure of government developed by the Committee of Public Safety. According to the first article of the decree, "the provisional government of France is revolutionary until the coming of peace." The ministers, the generals, and all the administrative bodies were to be supervised by the Committee, which would report every eight days to the Convention. A committee of twelve deputies would thus shape the fate of the republic; much would depend on the dynamics within the Committee and between committee members and the other deputies in the Convention.

The Committee appointed deputies on mission to supervise recruitment and the application of the maximum, to monitor and if necessary remove local officials, and above all to direct the war effort at the frontiers and the suppression of the counter-revolution at home. It often assigned its own members to the most difficult tasks. Although Bordeaux had quickly given up any thought of armed revolt, it was the capital of the Gironde department and hence considered the nursery of federalism. In late October, four deputies on mission marched into the city at the head of a "revolutionary army" of 3,000 bringing with them a guillotine. Between then and August 1794 a military commission presided by a young Jacobin schoolteacher condemned 300 to death.

In Lyon, Marseille, and Toulon federalists had gone further and made common cause with royalists. The siege to retake Lyon lasted two long months, and as soon as the city fell the Committee of Public Safety ordered the destruction of houses of the rich. When Couthon hesitated to put this into action, he was recalled and Collot d'Herbois sent in his place along with a "revolutionary army" from Paris; 1,900 rebels were executed. Although Marseille did not accept the British offer of aid, special courts ordered the execution of 500 people. Toulon held out until December, and when the British and Spanish retreated they burned half the French fleet caught in the harbor. As soon as the French army retook the city, 800 collaborators were executed and another 300 were condemned to death by a military commission. A particularly energetic 24-year-old captain of the artillery came to the attention of the deputies sent to supervise operations; a fervent Jacobin at the time, his name was Napoleon Bonaparte.

Violence also exploded in Saint-Domingue though there the battle lines were much less clearly drawn (see Box 3.1). Six thousand troops had been

BOX 3.1 THE WORLD'S FIRST SUCCESSFUL SLAVE REVOLT

France establishes a colony on the island of Santo Domingo

1664   Taking over from the Spanish as well as earlier buccaneers, the French establish a colony in the western part of the island.

1680   Introduced earlier to replace the native population which had been severely reduced, slaves reach 2,000 in number in French-dominated territory.

1693   Spain formally cedes the western three-eighths of the island to create the French colony of Saint-Domingue.

Saint-Domingue becomes one of the the richest colonies in the world

1700s   The economy booms, producing sugar, indigo, and cotton.

1765   So valuable was the colony that after military defeat in the Seven Years War, France cedes its vast property of Canada in order to retain Saint-Domingue.

1789   Population: 500,000 slaves, 30–40,000 white settlers, 32,000 free people of color.

The spark of the French Revolution opens the door to independence

1789–   Rebellion by free people of color suppressed, though this group
1791   does receive the right to vote along with whites.

1791   Slave rebellion begins.

1793   French commissioners in the colony declare freedom for the slaves.

1794   France abolishes slavery in France and in her colonies, but white planters organize resistance.

1794–   Led by Toussaint Louverture, slaves defeat the whites and join
1801   with French forces against the English effort to seize the colony.

1802   Napoleon sends troops to destroy Louverture's authority and reintroduce slavery.

1803   Louverture, arrested and deported to France, dies in captivity.

1804   War continues with slave victory and the creation of an independent republic called Haïti (see Chapter 5, Box 5.1).

1825   France finally agrees to recognize Haïtian independence in
           exchange for an indemnity of 150 million francs to compensate
           the dispossessed colonial owners (selling the immense Louisiana
           Territory to the United States in 1804 had brought France the
           lesser sum of 68 million francs).

---

sent to the colony to put down the slave insurrection in spring 1792, but two
of the civil commissioners that had been sent with them, Léger-Félicité
Sonthonax and Étienne Polverel, had been named on the suggestion of
Brissot and like Brissot favored the abolition of slavery. They first took the
side of the free people of color, some of whom had been granted equal
political rights in May 1791 only to have them rescinded after the eruption of
the slave revolt and then reinstated in April 1792, much to the fury of white
planters.

Sonthonax and Polverel distrusted the white planters, who talked of
demanding independence like the new United States. To make matters more
complicated, once France went to war with Britain and Spain, the most
able of the leaders of the slave insurrection, the freed slave Toussaint
Louverture, took the side of the Spanish (the other half of the island was a
Spanish colony) because they promised freedom to the slave rebels who
joined them against the French. The commissioners had originally arrived,
after all, with a mandate to suppress the insurrection. When Sonthonax
and Polverel removed the colony's governor, the governor organized the
sailors in French ships offshore for an attack on the commissioners, which
resulted in the burning again of Le Cap on June 20, 1793. The governor
then fled on ship along with most of the whites in the town, and the
commissioners changed strategy, offering emancipation to any slave who
would fight for the French. At the end of August 1793 they unilaterally
emancipated all the slaves. Back in Paris, however, the deputies were
condemning Sonthonax and Polverel as agents of Brissot, fearing that they
intended to turn the colony over to the British. It would be months before the
situation clarified.[12]

EXECUTION OF GIRONDINS Retribution against enemies was not
limited to the periphery. Brissot and 20 other Girondins went to the guillotine
on October 31, and only the intervention of Robespierre prevented the
prosecutor of the revolutionary court from going after the 75 deputies who
had protested the arrest of the Girondins (Figure 3.4). Philippe Égalité (Duke
of Orleans) followed on November 7; his son's friendship with Dumouriez had
led to the father's arrest in April. Women were not exempt. After a brief trial in

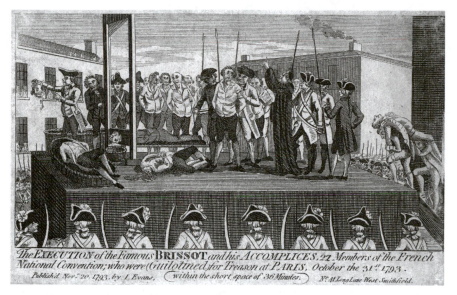

FIGURE 3.4 *Execution of Brissot and His Followers, October 31, 1793*
Events in France were followed closely around Europe. This print of the execution
of the Brissotins or Girondins was published in Britain within the month of the
event. It emphasizes the gruesomeness of the scene with decapitated bodies and
assembly-line executions. Anonymous engraving published by John Evans, London,
1793.

which she was accused of a long list of crimes, including incest with her
son, Marie-Antoinette was executed on October 16. In his capacity as
assistant prosecutor, Hébert raised the incest charge, which came as the
culmination of his vitriolic campaign against the woman he called "an old
whore" in his paper *Le Père Duchesne*. Olympe de Gouges followed
the queen to the guillotine on November 3, and Madame Roland on
November 8. Newspapers amalgamated the three women under the rubric
of "unnatural women," and the municipal official Chaumette publicly
denounced the "impudent" de Gouges and the "haughty" Roland, who had
made the mistake of thinking "herself fit to govern the republic." "It is contrary
to all the laws of nature," he insisted, "for a woman to want to make herself a
man." Roland's husband killed himself when he received word of his wife's
execution. Among the Girondins still on the run, Clavière committed suicide in
December and Condorcet in March 1794. For many European middle-class
radicals, the purge of the Girondins marked a decisive turning point; the
English writer Helen Maria Williams wrote that from their proscription "dated
all the horrors which have cast their sanguinary cloud over the glories of the
revolution."

Cultural revolution

Killing enemies of the republic, real or imagined, might tamp down resistance but adherence to a republic required educating a population of whom less than half could read and write. The deputies gave priority to breaking the Catholic Church's hold on the educational system; in May 1793 they voted to require all places of more than 400 people to set up a primary school with a lay teacher. A "republican catechism" was to replace the Catholic one taught in Old Regime schools, but it proved difficult to find the money, much less the schoolteachers, so other forms of education had to supplement formal schooling. On October 1, 1793 Gilbert Romme, a 43-year-old mathematician and deputy who had been imprisoned by the federalists in Caen for two months, explained the thinking of the Committee on Public Instruction; "in our circumstances, public instruction is the set of all the means that the government must use to make itself loved by men." "Public instruction," he explained, "speaks to the citizens in several kinds of languages: that of speech, of exterior signs, and of government action." Speech itself had to become republican: "frank without grossness, simple without stupidity, fraternal without affectation." Chief among the exterior signs were the national festivals such as the Festival of Unity of August 10; they were designed to recast the French in a republican mold by replacing monarchical and Catholic processions with republican ones filled with new republican symbols adopted from Egyptian and Roman sources.

Four days later Romme presented on behalf of the Committee of Public Instruction the outlines of a new calendar to replace the Christian one. Year one would date from the foundation of the French republic on September 22, 1792, which happily coincided with the autumn equinox. Henceforth time would be measured by the regularity of nature and reason, not religion and tradition. Twelve months with three *décades* of ten days each would get new names based on nature; late October/November, for example, was named *brumaire* because it was the month of mist (in French *la brume*). The five days left over were called *sans-culottides* and designated for special festivals. A tenth day (*décadi*) replaced the seventh day of Sunday on the Christian calendar and was to be devoted to republican festivals. Plans to decimalize the twenty-four day did not get much further than the construction of a few timepieces, but the calendar, despite deep resistance, remained in use at least officially until the end of 1805.

Even more successful, though slower to take shape, was the project of decimalizing weights and measures; from the very beginning of the Revolution authorities aimed to replace the patchwork of 250,000 different local measures with one uniform system that would apply not just to France but to the entire world. The labels "meter" and "liter" were created in 1792, but since the meter was originally defined as one ten-millionth of the distance from the North Pole to the Equator through Paris, scientific expeditions to determine this distance had to be undertaken. The system coalesced in stages in 1795 and 1799 only to be dropped by Napoleon; reinstated by France in the mid-nineteenth century, the metric system is now the official system of measurement in most countries in the world.[13]

The deputies did their best to direct a cultural revolution from above by changing the calendar; organizing festivals; ordering newspapers to be sent to soldiers at the front and giving subventions to newspapers and prints; arranging public competitions in architecture, painting, and sculpture; and putting symbols of the republic, especially the female figure of liberty, on everything from monumental statues to coins, *assignats*, and government stationery. These planned activities nonetheless risked being overtaken in the fall of 1793 by surges of anti-clerical expression that came to be known under the label de-Christianization.

DE-CHRISTIANIZATION CAMPAIGN Already in February 1792 *Révolutions de Paris* newspaper had referred to a potential "de-Catholicization" as a happy fate for France. As refractory clergy, especially in the Vendée, became increasingly associated with outright counter-revolution, local militants and deputies on mission undertook more extreme measures with the help of local "revolutionary armies." At the end of September 1793 Joseph Fouché, a deputy on mission to the town of Nevers in central France, took a series of steps that quickly drew attention. With the encouragement of the Parisian militant Chaumette, who was there visiting his home town, Fouché gave a republican sermon standing next to a bust of the Roman hero Brutus (founder of the Roman republic, not the assassin of Caesar), and he chose to deliver it at the altar of the local Catholic cathedral, suggesting that a new civil religion was going to literally take the place of Christianity. Within two weeks Fouché had not only denounced the celibacy of priests (having once studied for the priesthood himself) but also organized local "revolutionary armies" to march through nearby towns and destroy all the signs of feudalism and "superstition" and gather up the gold and jewels of churches to be sent to the Convention. He ordered the demolition of all the bell-towers of churches whose parishes had been suppressed in the reorganization of the Catholic Church and even proposed eliminating any public manifestation of Catholicism. In his most notorious gesture, he insisted that all burials be civil and not religious and that cemeteries remove any reference, such as the cross, to the resurrection of Jesus; an allegory of sleep would be sculpted on the gates of cemeteries with the words, "Death is an Eternal Sleep," thus symbolically annihilating the Catholic doctrine of the immortality of the soul.

Chaumette then enforced like-minded policies in Paris, which set the example for local militants in many other places. He and other Parisian leaders convinced the Bishop of Paris Jean-Baptiste Gobel to abdicate his position since, as one of them explained, "before long the French republic will have no other religion than that of liberty, equality and truth, a religion drawn from the breast of nature, and which, thanks to your [the Convention's] works, will soon be the universal religion." Many other priests and even Protestant pastors immediately followed his example. On November 10, 1793, just three days later, Chaumette and the municipal authorities organized a festival of reason right in the heart of Notre Dame Cathedral; a goddess of liberty, played by an actress, came out of a temple dedicated to reason that sat on a mountain hastily erected in the middle of the church. The temple was inscribed with the words "To Philosophy," which to many implied that Enlightenment philosophy, when carried to its logical conclusion, meant the destruction of Christianity. Chaumette then led the participants in the pageant to the Convention and invited the deputies to come for a repeat performance, which they agreed to do. On November 23, the municipality ordered the closing of all churches in Paris.

The movement spread rapidly through many provincial cities and towns with the resignation in total of some 20,000 priests (5,000 of whom married), confiscation of countless church valuables, and hastily arranged festivals of reason held in cathedrals and churches. Militants did not stop short of profanation. The deputy on mission in Nancy in eastern France drank publicly to the health of the republic from the chalice of the former bishop and had confessionals burnt at the foot of the guillotine in front of an audience of several thousand. At Rochefort in southwestern France, the deputy on mission converted the Catholic church into a temple of truth and gave a frankly atheistic speech. "Revolutionary armies" marched after drum majors decked out with the local bishop's miter and vestments. Similar scenes were repeated again and again. The Convention itself encouraged towns to change their names if those names evoked royalism, feudalism, or superstition, and thousands of streets, squares, villages, and towns got new names. Individual names changed, too. Fouché named his daughter, born in Nevers, after the local department, Nièvre. Chaumette changed his name from Pierre-Gaspard, both names of saints, to Anaxagoras, after a Greek philosopher exiled for impiety. In some towns and villages, half of the children born during the movement were given non-Christian names.[14]

In the name of equality, militants insisted that "citizen" should be used instead of "Monsieur" [Sir] and the informal "tu" form of "you" instead of the formal "vous," because both Monsieur and the "vous" form recalled feudal times. Everything came into question from the bindings on books, ripped off if they carried royal or aristocratic emblems, and the insignia on entryways, to historic statuary on cathedrals. The Cité section of Paris hired a contractor to take down the 28 statues of the kings of Judah on the façade of Notre

Dame Cathedral on the grounds that they were "signs of feudalism." Because they were so big and located in a gallery 52-feet high they had to be broken into chunks, and some of the heads were sold. The remaining fragments of the demolition were only located in 1977. Churches around the country suffered similar or even worse fates; some were sold off and converted into stables or warehouses. Everyday dress was not exempt. The tricolor cockade signaled patriotism, and the most ardent also sported the red liberty cap. Officials of local Jacobin Clubs often donned the red cap during meetings. White ribbons fell out of favor as hair ornaments because white was the color of the French monarchy. The wrong dress or hairstyle could make someone suspect.

The attack on the churches may have attracted militants in towns and cities, but it scandalized a large part of the French population as well as people outside France. Life in rural areas, in particular, revolved around the parish church whose priest was often the most or even the only literate person in the village. Many priests were beloved figures who provided a link to the outside world, as well as to divine grace, and in troubled times those links were especially precious. The clergy had supervised education in the past and often selected the most talented boys, among them virtually all the revolutionary leaders, to go off to church-run secondary schools. The changes introduced therefore often provoked fear, desperation, and anger and risked completely alienating large segments of the population, including those who supported the "constitutional" church. The most important republican in the constitutional church, the deputy Henri Grégoire, stood up in the Convention and refused to abjure his clerical vocation, even though he risked insults and threats for doing so. "I was chosen by the people to be bishop," he declared, "but it is neither from them nor you [the deputies] that I hold my mission."

The revolution devours its own

Although the de-Christianization movement sputtered on until the spring of 1794, Robespierre expressed his displeasure less than two weeks after the Festival of Reason. He gave a long speech at the Jacobin Club condemning atheism as "aristocratic" and insisting on freedom of religion. Hébert and Chaumette felt personally targeted. Lines were about to be drawn in the sand. In early December 1793 the Committee of Public Safety pushed through a decree centralizing power. The Committee of Public Safety would have complete command of the war effort, diplomacy, food supplies, and the operations of government. It alone named deputies on mission. All ministers answered to it. The Committee of General Security oversaw internal policing, surveillance, and revolutionary justice. The surveillance or revolutionary committees of the sections of Paris were to report directly to the Committee of General Security, bypassing the municipality. All "revolutionary armies," except the one set up by the Committee of Public Safety, were disbanded. Forbidden was any formation of so-called central revolutionary or insurrectionary committees (as in Paris in August 1792 and May–June 1793).

The tightening of the reins had two main aspects: formulating policies to consolidate the republic that would not alienate property-owners or Catholics and squashing those who questioned the authority of the Committees. The first required months of fine-tuning; the second took on such a life of its own that it ultimately brought down the government itself. Just how the two aspects—more moderate policies alongside the repression of any dissent—fit together has been a subject of controversy ever since. The role of Robespierre has been especially contentious; did he really think that the elimination of his critics was necessary to save the republic or was he just greedy for power? Was he balancing a sincere belief that he spoke for the people against the practical need to reassure rural property-owners and Catholics or did he intend to create an all-powerful state that would force the French people to conform to his own version of a republican template? In considering these questions, it is vital to keep in mind that Robespierre was a member of a committee, albeit a powerful one, and that his position was subject to approval by the deputies of the Convention.

The Convention reaffirmed freedom of religion in December, and in early January 1794 Grégoire gave the first of three major speeches against "vandalism," a term he coined. He argued that while monuments to royalism and feudalism might be legitimately destroyed, those with ancient Latin inscriptions and any that were not contrary to the spirit of equality should be safeguarded. Alexandre Lenoir, an amateur antiquarian and protégé of Barère, went further and gathered the remnants of sculpture and tombs from religious houses; in 1795 he was made director of a museum of French monuments based on his salvage. The world's first public museum of art had opened in the Louvre, a part of the king's Tuileries palace, to celebrate the Festival of Unity on August 10, 1793; it showed the collections of the king as well as paintings, sculptures, and other art objects confiscated from aristocratic houses. In this way, according to Grégoire, "the property of the people will be returned to them," but it would also be preserved for posterity.

Stepping back from the extremes of "vandalism" did not mean giving up on the project of republicanizing the people. Grégoire led the effort to ensure that all French people could speak and write French. In 1790 he sent a circular to all the departments requesting information about how many people spoke

French and how many only in *patois* [dialect]; six million, he estimated, could speak no French at all. He and many others in the revolutionary government hoped to eliminate *patois* altogether, for as Barère exclaimed in a speech on January 27, 1794, "federalism and superstition speak Lower Breton, the emigration and hatred of the Republic speak German, the counter-revolution speaks Italian, and fanaticism speaks Basque." Since "we have revolutionized the government, the laws, customs, morals, dress, commerce and even thought," we must also revolutionize language, he added. The Convention ordered the appointment of teachers of French in regions where French was not the common language.

ABOLITION OF SLAVERY   In two other areas, the deputies continued to move forward on the revolutionary project: the abolition of slavery and the redistribution of property. Black sailors had spread news of the slave revolt throughout the Caribbean and the Americas, creating intense alarm about the future of plantation slavery among slave-owners and colonial governments. A slave-owner on the British island of Jamaica captured the sentiment: "I am convinced the ideas of liberty have sunk so deep in the minds of all Negroes, that whenever the greatest precautions are not taken they will rise." Precautions were taken; the Spanish government forbade the import to Cuba of any French papers, and US President Washington advanced money to white planters in Saint-Domingue and sold them arms and ammunition. The French, however, could not retain any control without the support of the rebellious slaves against the British and Spanish. On February 3, 1794 the Convention agreed to seat three deputies, one white European, one former slave, and one of mixed race, who had been elected to represent Saint-Domingue after the abolition of slavery by the French commissioners. Although the Convention continued to suspect the motives of Sonthonax and Polverel, once faced with the favorable report from the Saint-Domingue deputies, the next day it ordered the abolition of slavery in all French colonies effective immediately and without compensation for owners. At that very moment, British forces were making progress in their invasion of the colony in collaboration with white planters, and France only secured its possession in the summer of 1794 after Toussaint defected from the Spanish and joined the French republican forces.

In a last concession to populist demands for more punishment of traitors, the Committee of Public Safety introduced legislation at the end of February 1794 to confiscate the property of those condemned by the revolutionary courts and redistribute it to needy patriots. The decision was never implemented, in part because the government had its hands full trying to enforce price and wage controls and supply food to the capital. Earlier legislation proved more successful; a law of June 1793 allowed villages to partition their common lands and divide parcels equally among residents without compensation. Many villagers also took the occasion of constant upheaval to clear forest lands for their own uses.

For the people in Paris, however, the cost of living remained the central preoccupation. In the winter of 1794 the *assignats* stabilized at about 50 percent of their face value but prices did not similarly settle, and meat, vegetables, and eggs were in short supply in Paris. The "Hébertists," followers of Hébert and Chaumette and successors to the *enragés*, threatened insurrection again. The Committee of Public Safety determined to act. It could do so because almost all the centers of resistance and rebellion in the provinces had been crushed. In the Vendée, vengeance triumphed in vicious fashion. At Nantes, the deputy on mission Jean-Baptiste Carrier allowed local militants to execute thousands of prisoners by firing squad and ordered as many as 2,000 taken on boats into the river and drowned. The military commission operating in nearby Angers condemned as many as 5,000 rebels to death. Columns of regular army soldiers marched through rebel territory and in some cases they not only burned everything in sight but also killed everyone they found. Some 200,000 people died fighting government forces in the Vendée civil war, creating bitter conflicts for the future.

In a major speech to the Convention on February 6, 1794, Robespierre appeared to justify the harsh measures that were being taken—and those about to come. "Social protection is due only to peaceful citizens," he insisted; "there are no citizens in the Republic but the republicans." In a clear embrace of terror, he argued that a revolutionary government required both virtue and terror: "virtue, without which terror is fatal; terror, without which virtue is impotent. Terror is . . . less a special principle than a consequence of the general principle of democracy applied to our country's most pressing needs." In the same speech he denounced two vaguely defined factions that were supposedly working for the ruin of the republic from the inside: those who favored too much moderation and those who pushed too far to extremes (see Document 3.2).

In a deal made with Billaud-Varenne and Collot d'Herbois, who had supported Hébert and Chaumette, Robespierre got the Committee to move against the "Hébertists" (those pushing to extremes) in exchange for sacrificing Danton and Desmoulins, his former allies and friends, who were now arguing for moderation of the Terror. Desmoulins began publishing a new journal in December 1793 called *Le Vieux Cordelier* [the old shoemaker, a play on the name of the Cordeliers Club]. In it he criticized the policies of the two committees and argued for a "committee of clemency."[15]

EXECUTION OF HÉBERTISTS   Hébert and his followers were arrested March 13–14 and executed ten days later on trumped-up charges of conspiracy with foreign powers. To make this plausible Cloots was added to the group; he and Paine had been expelled from the Convention in December and then arrested because they were foreigners (Paine spent ten months in prison but escaped death).

EXECUTION OF DANTONISTS   Danton, Desmoulins, and three of their allies were arrested on March 29 and sent to the guillotine on April 5 alongside Hérault de Séchelles, who had resigned from the Committee of Public Safety in December 1793, and several others. Once again the two committees sought to amalgamate victims, this time in order to portray the Dantonists as corrupt supporters of foreign conspiracies (Hérault had taken an Austrian mistress). Chaumette was executed on April 13 alongside ex-bishop Gobel and the widows of Desmoulins and Hébert. Lucile Desmoulins had written to Robespierre and upbraided him for letting Saint-Just with his "callousness" and "despicable jealousies" turn him against his oldest friend; she was included in the group accused of conspiring from prison to kill members of the two committees.

The citizens of Paris watched the execution of the Hébertists with little emotion, but the killing of Danton and Desmoulins profoundly shocked people. Danton, along with Mirabeau one of the greatest orators of the time, had so swayed the jurors at his trial that the proceedings had to be cut short in order to ensure conviction. When he mounted the scaffold to the guillotine, stepping through the blood of his friends, he shouted at the executioner, "Show my head to the people . . . they will not see one like it every day." A Jacobin bookseller lamented to his brother that the revolution "devours its own children; it gnaws at its intestines; it has become the cruelest and most horrible of monsters." The *London Chronicle* concluded, "Robespierre, by thus removing those whom he fears most, is paving his way to the authority of dictator."

After eight months of rule by virtual dictatorship, the Committee of Public Safety had saved the revolution from collapse, but it did so at a very high price. The Committee had tried to put the principle of equality into practice and educate the people in republicanism, but it often acted at the expense of individual liberties, not to mention lives. Even the most fervent supporters of the Committee regretted the terrible destruction of Lyon, the savagery of the drownings at Nantes, and a long list of other killings. An accurate count of the victims of the Terror is impossible to determine; it must include the 17,000 death sentences delivered by military or civilian courts, the 10–12,000 people who died in prison, and the 10–12,000 known to have been killed in summary executions without trial. The death toll in the Vendée uprising is now thought to be much higher, however, ranging from 200–250,000 on the rebel side and perhaps 200,000 on the government side. The civil war spilt much more blood than the Terror, obviously, but the deaths during the Terror made an indelible impression. The Committee would soon be called to account.

Documents

DOCUMENT 3.1
The trial of the King

As soon as the deputies in the National Convention declared a republic in September 1792, they faced a previously unimaginable question: what should be done with King Louis XVI, monarch by birthright? The Americans faced no such issue when they set up their republic; they simply separated from British King George III and went their own way. Under the Constitution of 1791 the French king was theoretically "inviolable," but the second revolution of August 10, 1792 had already deposed him. At first, the deputies debated whether the king could or should be tried and by implication punished. In the midst of their deliberations, Roland announced the discovery of a secret safe in the king's residence filled with incriminating papers. No one doubted that the king had conspired against the nation. Still to be determined, however, was whether a trial should take place, who should serve as judges, and whether the verdict should be subject to ratification by popular referendum. Some sense of the range of arguments aired can be found in two of the speeches excerpted here. The first, by the young, charismatic, and sharp-tongued Jacobin, Louis de Saint-Just, argued that the king should not be tried but rather simply executed as an enemy alien. Pierre Vergniaud, one of the great orators of the era, supported the notion of an appeal to the judgment of the people. In the end, the deputies voted to try the king and not subject their verdict to ratification by referendum.

Speech of Saint-Just, November 13, 1792

I say that the King should be judged as an enemy; even more than judge him, we must fight him. Since he was not a party to the contract that unites all French people, the judicial procedure to follow is not to be found in Civil Law, but rather in the Law of Nations . . . .

The social contract is between citizens, not between citizens and government. A contract is useless against those who are not bound by it. Consequently, Louis, who was not a party to it, cannot be judged by Civil Law. The contract was so oppressive that it bound the citizens, but not the king. Such a contract was necessarily void since nothing is legitimate that is not sanctioned by morals and nature.

Besides these reasons, which all lead you to judge Louis not as a citizen, but as a rebel, by what right does he claim our obligation to judge him by Civil Law, when it is clear that he himself betrayed the only obligation that he had undertaken towards us, that of our protection? Is this not the last act of a tyrant, to demand to be judged by the laws that he destroyed? And

Citizens, if we were to grant him a civil trial, in conformance with the laws and as a citizen, it would be him who would be trying us. He would be trying the people themselves.

For myself, I can see no middle ground. This man must reign or die. He will prove to you that all he has done, he has done to uphold the office with which he was entrusted. By engaging in this discussion with him, you cannot hold him to account for his hidden malice. He will lead you into the vicious circle created by your very accusations . . . .

I will say more: a constitution accepted by a King does not bind the citizens. They had, even before his crime, the right to banish him and send him into exile. To judge a king as a citizen; the very thought will astound a dispassionate posterity. To judge is to apply the law. A law is a relationship to justice; what relationship to justice is there between all humanity and kings? What does Louis have in common with the French people that they should treat him well after he betrayed them? . . .

It is impossible to reign innocently. The folly of that is all too evident. Every king is a rebel and usurper. Do kings themselves treat otherwise those who seek to usurp their authority? Was the recollection of Cromwell not brought to trial? And certainly Cromwell was no more usurper than Charles I, for when a people is so cowardly as to yield to the tyrant's yoke, domination is the right of the first comer, and it is no more sacred or legitimate for one than for another.

Speech of Vergniaud, December 31, 1792

What is the sovereignty of the people that is ceaselessly talked about, and that I would like to think is not simply a derisory courtesy, and to which I am certain, at least, that the National Convention renders sincere deference? It is the power to make the laws, the regulations, in a word, all the acts that concern the welfare of society. The people exercise this power, either on their own, or through their representatives. In the latter case, and that is our case, the decisions of the representatives of the people are executed as laws. But why? Because they are presumed to be the expression of the general will. From this presumption alone they draw their force; from this presumption alone is derived the character that makes them respected.

From this it follows that the people conserve, as an inherent right of their sovereignty, the right to approve or disapprove; thus it follows that if the presumed will does not conform to the general will, the people retains, as a right inherent to its sovereignty, the right to express their view. And the instant that this expression has taken place, the presumed will must disappear—that is to say the decision by the national representatives. To rob the people of this right would be to strip away its sovereignty; the very representatives that the people chose would have transformed the people's sovereignty by a criminal usurpation. It would in effect transform the people's representatives into kings or tyrants . . . .

Any act emanating from the representatives of the people is an attempt on the people's sovereignty if it is not submitted for formal or tacit ratification. The people who promised inviolability to Louis can alone declare that it wishes to use the right to punish, to do what it had renounced. Powerful considerations prescribe that you [the Convention] conform to principles: if you are faithful to them, you risk no reproach; if the people wish the death of Louis XVI, they will order it. If, on the contrary, you violate these principles, you risk at least the reproach of deviating from your duty: and this deviation will make a dreadful responsibility weigh on your heads.

Sources: *Archives Parlementaires*, "Séance du mardi 13 novembre 1792," vol. 53: 390–392; *Archives Parlementaires*, "Séance du 31 décembre 1792," vol. 56: 90, 95.

Questions on Saint-Just and Vergniaud

1   Consider the perspective and attitudes of the Jacobins and Girondins from the excerpts of the speeches by Saint-Just and Vergniaud. How are they different?

2   Both speakers invoke Rousseauian notions—the general will and the social contract. How do they employ these concepts?

3   Which one of the two revolutionaries appears on the defensive?

DOCUMENT 3.2
Robespierre explains the need for terror

By early 1794, the revolutionary government had subdued its enemies: the Vendée, foreign armies, federalist cities, and more. Yet the Terror continued, and its advocates grew bolder, in part because of the perceived need to quickly mold a republican citizenry and in part because differences over policy still divided the revolutionary leadership. In this speech Robespierre explained the principles animating the Committee of Public Safety's position.

Maximilien Robespierre, Report on the Principles of Political Morality, given at the National Convention, February 6, 1794

What is the goal toward which we aim? The tranquil enjoyment of liberty and equality; the reign of that eternal justice, the laws of which are graven, not on marble or stone, but in the hearts of all men, even in the heart of the slave who has forgotten them, and in that of the tyrant who denies them.

We want an order of things where all the low and cruel passions are enchained, all the beneficent and generous passions awakened by the laws; where ambition is but the desire to merit glory and serve the fatherland; where distinctions only grow out of equality itself; where the citizen submits to the magistrate, the magistrate submits to the people, and the people submit to justice; where the fatherland assures the well-being of every individual, and where each individual prides himself on the prosperity and glory of the fatherland; where every soul expands through the continual communication of republican sentiments and by the need to merit the esteem of a great people; where the arts embellish the liberty that ennobles them, and commerce is a source of public wealth and not merely of the monstrous opulence of a few families . . . .

Hence all that tends to excite a love of the fatherland, to purify morals, to elevate minds, to direct the passions of the human heart towards the public good, should be adopted and established by you. All that tends to focus them in an abjection of selfish egotism, to awaken an infatuation for little things and a disdain for greatness, must be rejected or repressed by you. In the system of the French revolution that which is immoral is impolitic, and what tends to corrupt is counter-revolutionary. Weakness, vices, prejudices are the road to monarchy . . . .

Therefore continually wind up the sacred spring of republican government, instead of letting it run down. I need not say that I am not here to justify any excess. The most sacred principles are being abused; the wisdom of government consists in consulting circumstances, seizing the right moments, choosing the means; for the manner of bringing about great things is an essential part of the talent of producing them, just as wisdom is an essential attribute of virtue . . . .

If virtue be the spring of popular government in peacetime, the spring of popular government during a revolution is *virtue combined with terror*: virtue, without which terror is destructive; terror, without which virtue is impotent. Terror is nothing other than prompt, severe and inflexible justice; it is therefore an emanation of virtue; it is less a distinct principle than a consequence of the general principle of democracy applied to the most pressing needs of the country.

Source: Convention Nationale. Rapport sur les principes de morale politique qui doivent guider la Convention Nationale dans l'administration intérieure de la République, fait au nom du comité de salut public, le 18 pluviose, l'an 2e. de la République, par Maximilien Robespierre, imprimé par ordre de la Convention Nationale (Paris, 1794), pp. 3–4, 8, 13.

Questions on Robespierre's speech

1   Given that direct threats to the government are winding down, how does Robespierre justify terror?

2 Think about the situation in which Robespierre gives this speech. Why would he mention excess and abuses?

3 What echoes of the Enlightenment and the Declaration of the Rights of Man and Citizen occur in this document?

TIMELINE TO CHAPTER 3

Sep. 20, 1792	Victory at Valmy over the Austro-Prussian army.
January 1793	The Convention tries and executes Louis XVI.
February 1793	France declares war on Britain and the Dutch Republic and initiates a draft.
March–Sep.	First Coalition forms to fight France: includes Britain, Dutch Republic, Russia, Piedmont, Naples, Prussia, Austria, Spain, and Portugal.
April 6, 1793	Executive Power mainly entrusted to the Committee of Public Safety.
May 31–June 2	Parisian sections invade the Convention and demand the arrest of the Girondins.
July 27, 1793	Robespierre appointed to the Committee of Public Safety.
September 29	Law of the General Maximum.
Fall, 1793	De-Christianization campaign.
October 31, 1793	Girondin leaders executed.
February 4, 1794	Slavery abolished.
March, 1794	Arrest, trial and execution of Hébertists.
April, 1794	Arrest, trial and execution of Dantonists.

QUESTIONS ABOUT CHAPTER 3

1 The Convention chose to govern through a series of committees, with great powers granted to the Committee of Public Safety. Why did they choose to disperse power in this way?

2 The relatively moderate Girondins had been Jacobins. What drove the two groups so far apart?

3 Why were the forces of the Convention able to defeat so many internal revolts and at the same time keep the armies of Europe away from France?

4 The Committee of Public Safety not only saved the government, but also extended many of the goals of the revolution of 1789. What were these revolutionary successes?

5 How did the opposition grow in 1793 and 1794, in spite of the successes and power of the Committee of Public Safety?

4

The power of the military, 1794–1799

Even as government by terror was racing headlong over a cliff, French armies were positioning themselves for success. Carnot's reforms and the *levée en masse* produced the largest army ever seen in European history; 800,000 French soldiers, commanded by officers who had been promoted because of their battlefield successes, now confronted the coalition's combined forces of 430,000 men. In the years that stretched from the fall of Robespierre in the summer of 1794 to the rise of Bonaparte in fall 1799, the world consequently witnessed yet another string of unexpected and transformative developments. The French swept through Europe, remaking governments in their own image, but at the same time, the focus on war steadily reshaped the republic back home. The young and ambitious generals promoted by Carnot became the arbiters of the republic's destiny. One of the youngest of them, Napoleon Bonaparte, took over the republic in 1799 at the age of 30 and proceeded to install an authoritarian regime that would inspire countless imitators in the centuries that followed.

The fall of Robespierre

The executions of the Hébertists and Dantonists left many deputies unsettled. The Committee proceeded to claim more police powers for itself, elbowing aside the Committee on General Security, and forced the closure of popular clubs in the Paris sections and the replacement of the Commune's (municipal) leadership. It also recalled those deputies on mission, such as Fouché and Carrier, known for their violent reprisals. These actions spread fear and resentment that would soon be focused on Robespierre and his closest followers. Two attempts to assassinate Robespierre in late May only succeeded in deepening the paranoia gripping government leaders; in the first of these the perpetrator actually shot at Collot d'Herbois after lying in wait all day for Robespierre.

FESTIVAL OF THE SUPREME BEING Two events finally tipped the balance. The artist-deputy David put together a lavish Festival of the Supreme Being on June 8, 1794 (Figure 4.1) to present Robespierre's vision of deism as an alternative to the atheism of the de-Christianization movement.[1] Although the festival and its central idea attracted popular support across the country, the effort boomeranged; Robespierre officiated because he had been elected president of the Convention a few days before, and his seeming to take the role of high priest of a new civic religion offended many. "It is not enough that he is the master, now he has to become a god," complained one critic.

LAW OF 22 PRAIRIAL Two days later Couthon presented in the name of the Committee a law (known as the law of 22 Prairial after the date on the revolutionary calendar) that dramatically increased the number of death sentences from the revolutionary court: the accused lost any right to legal counsel and only two judgments were allowed, acquittal or death (see Document 4.1, at the end of the chapter). The category of political crimes

FIGURE 4.1 *Festival of the Supreme Being, June 8, 1794*
This anonymous print of the Festival of the Supreme Being tries to convey the Supreme Being's approval with sun breaking through the clouds. On the mountain in the center stands a column with the figure of Hercules, the symbol of popular force. Young women in white often formed distinct groups in festivals as a way of showing that everyone had a role to play in the festival and in the revolution. Hand-colored etching, 1794?

expanded even further to include those who sought to "inspire discouragement," "mislead opinion," or "disparage" the National Convention. The rate of executions in Paris jumped from six a day in spring 1794 to 26 a day in June and July. Sixty deputies so feared for their lives that they no longer slept at home.

9 THERMIDOR   As dissension intensified, even among members of the Committee of Public Safety, Robespierre made the mistake of staying away from the Committee and the Convention for six weeks, appearing only at the Jacobin Club where he denounced Fouché and forced his expulsion. On July 26 Robespierre returned to the Convention and rambled through a speech in which he condemned unnamed members of both the Committee of Public Safety and Committee of General Security. That night he got Collot d'Herbois and Billaud-Varenne excluded from the Jacobin Club. Those under threat wasted no time in organizing. The next day (9 Thermidor on the revolutionary calendar), when Robespierre tried to follow up, he was shouted down by calls of "Down with the tryant!" Sitting as president of the Convention, Collot d'Herbois allowed only accusers to speak. The deputies ordered the arrest of Robespierre, Saint-Just, and Couthon and their known followers in Paris. But since the commander of the Paris National Guard and many of those in the Commune and the sections were Robespierrists, would the will of the Convention hold?

That night could not have been more confusing or chaotic. The stakes must have terrified everyone involved in this conflict. Robespierre, his brother Augustin, Saint-Just, and Couthon (in a wheelchair since 1789) all escaped their jailors and gathered at city hall. Outside, some of the sections had mobilized for another popular uprising against the Convention like the movement that brought down the Girondin deputies on June 2, 1793. But in the end the Convention managed to arrest the inebriated commander of the National Guard, declare the Robespierrists outlaws (thus bypassing the need for a trial), and rally the majority of the sections to their defense. The sections supporting Robespierre melted away, allowing the Convention's forces to take city hall without resistance (Figure 4.2). Robespierre tried to commit suicide by shooting himself; the next evening the executioner ripped the bandage off his jaw to fit his head in the guillotine. His brother, Saint-Just, Couthon, the commander of the Paris National Guard, and leaders of the Commune were executed with him; the following day 71 of their supporters met the same fate. Robespierre had made too many enemies within the Convention and the two major Committees, and the common people of Paris trusted the Convention as a body more than any one faction or leader within it, even Robespierre.[2]

Thus ended the life of the one of the French Revolution's most powerful and most enigmatic figures, loved by few, hated by many, and still a subject of

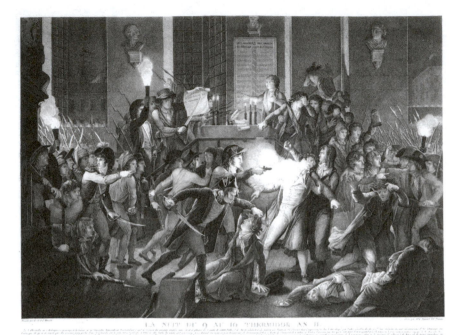

FIGURE 4.2 *The Fall of Robespierre, July 27, 1794*
Like many prints from this period, this one is impossible to date precisely. The engraver, Jean-Joseph Tassaert based it on a painting that no longer exists by Fulchran Harriet. It shows the scene when National Guards came to arrest Robespierre and his followers at city hall. In this rendition, someone shoots Robespierre, but in other versions of the event, Robespierre tried to kill himself. Stipple engraving.

fascination today. Was Robespierre's fall predictable, as one German lady-in-waiting wrote to a friend, because it was "preordained that these monsters should gobble each other up"? Or was it the product of cynical maneuvering by a handful of deputies who feared they would pay for their own bloody misdeeds? Robespierre repeatedly invoked his own likely martyrdom as "slave to the fatherland." A rather fussy provincial lawyer who had attracted only modest notice before 1789, Robespierre had gradually assumed the mantle of spokesman for revolutionary purity. He supported democracy from the very beginning, yet he also insisted that nothing must stand in the path of revolution, not even regard for the people. The "incorruptible," as he was known to his admirers, was not a great orator like Mirabeau or Danton; he read out every carefully crafted word. He was, however, a superb political tactician, who knew how to put his followers in positions of power and how to play rivals off against each other. By 1794 he had so identified himself with the revolution that he could tolerate no dissent. Still, he was after all only one of twelve members of the Committee of Public Safety.

The Thermidorian reaction

Even though Robespierre's overthrow had been engineered by some of the most zealous proponents of terror such as Fouché, Collot d'Herbois, and Billaud-Varenne, it nevertheless triggered a seismic shift against the policies associated with terror. Within the next days and weeks, the Convention received more than 700 addresses of congratulation from local authorities, popular clubs, and the armies. Everyone now rejoiced at the defeat of the "despicable conspiracy" of the "new Cromwell" and his "cowardly accomplices." Although the chief conspirators against Robespierre wanted to argue that he was single-handedly responsible for the "system of terror," most people did not believe that Robespierre could "do all that evil alone." Within a month Billaud-Varenne, Collot d'Herbois, and Barère of the Committee of Public Safety had been denounced as accomplices alongside four members of the Committee of General Security including David. The deputies left the first three alone for a time but ordered the arrest and imprisonment of David. He was released a few months later, arrested again in 1795, but finally let go to resume his artistic career in Paris.

Billaud-Varenne, Collot d'Herbois, and Barère resigned from the Committee of Public Safety, and in April 1795 the Convention ordered their deportation to French Guiana (on the northeastern coast of South America). Barère went into hiding, Collot d'Herbois died of yellow fever in Guiana, and Billaud-Varenne eventually escaped and went first to New York City and then to Haïti (Saint-Domingue) where he died in 1819. Once foreign enthusiasts had come to Paris to join the forces of revolution; now the revolutionaries themselves were being dispersed to the four corners of the world. European opponents of the republic felt relief. A German physics professor wrote to a colleague, "The fall of Robespierre improves the credit of the Convention. Perhaps we could take soundings for peace."

REPEAL OF 22 PRAIRIAL LAW   Even before the trials of other "terrorists" got underway, the Convention dismantled the system of terror step-by-step. On August 1, 1794 the Convention repealed the law of 22 Prairial, which it had approved not long before, and ordered the arrest of the chief prosecutor of the revolutionary court, Antoine Fouquier-Tinville. A cousin of Desmoulins, Fouquier-Tinville nonetheless had prosecuted him and the Dantonists and after 9 Thermidor turned around and loyally supervised the executions of the outlawed Robespierrists. His association with death was too overpowering, however, and after a lengthy trial he was executed.

Within a week of Fouquier-Tinville's arrest, suspects were being released en masse from the Paris prisons. The Convention ordered the shutdown of all the special commissions and revolutionary courts of the provinces, but kept the revolutionary court in Paris for crimes against national security; they restored protections for the accused. The Committee of Public Safety lost its wide-ranging powers and new rules guaranteed regular changes in its membership. The commander of the Paris National Guard was replaced by a committee of five. The Paris Commune was stripped of much of its authority. Sectional assemblies were limited to meeting once every 10 days and then forbidden altogether. Revolutionary committees were allowed only in big towns and cities and their numbers and responsibilities were reduced.

By autumn the move against the "bloodsuckers" and "cannibals" of the Terror was accelerating. Bands of young dandies known as "the gilded youth" sang anti-Jacobin songs in the theaters, complained loudly about their mistreatment during the Terror, and even attacked the Jacobin Club in Paris. The Convention took the occasion to close down the club in November. It ordered the trial of Carrier and of members of the revolutionary committee in Nantes for the atrocities committed there. The trials revealed the horrific details of the mass drownings and shootings, of innocent people crammed in stinking cells, and of all manner of harassment, bullying, corruption, and theft by revolutionary committees. Carrier was executed in December 1794. In the same month, the Convention officially recalled the deputies who had protested the arrest of the Girondins in June 1793 and declared the abolition of the maximum on prices and wages.[3]

The Convention had no intention of seeking peace, however. While keeping the rebels in the Vendée contained, the French defeated the coalition's armies and occupied Belgium while also invading northern Spain and the Italian states. By early 1795 the French had also gained control of the Dutch Republic and the left bank of the Rhine. The stadholder fled to England, and the revived Dutch patriot movement declared a "Batavian Republic" that was forced to sign onerous peace terms with the French. The Dutch gave up territory to the French in the south, agreed to pay the French 100 million guilders reparations and also garrison at their own expense 25,000 French soldiers. This first "sister republic" set the pattern for those that followed: the French encouraged reforms such as rights for religious minorities and the abolition of torture but also demanded subservience to their national aims. Dutch colonial possessions soon felt the reverberations. Dutch colonists in South Africa revolted against the control of the Dutch East India Company and put on tricolor cockades, but they quickly faced a different challenge when the British defeated a Dutch fleet and occupied Cape Town with a force of 5,000 soldiers. The British also invaded and occupied the Dutch colony of Ceylon in order to protect India against any French incursion.

As the political atmosphere in France relaxed and signs of ostentatious wealth reappeared, the popular classes faced yet another harrowing winter of rising prices and food shortages. The inflation cannot be blamed entirely on the abolition of the maximum because the maximum had never been very strictly enforced. Still, the *assignats*, which had fallen to 40 percent of their face value in August 1793 and then stabilized until August 1794, now began to fall precipitously once again and collapsed by June 1795 to 5 percent of their nominal value. Harsh winter weather had frozen the Seine, disrupting grain shipments, and prices skyrocketed. The British novelist and poet Helen Maria Williams described the situation in May:

> Whilst all Europe is probably watching with solicitude the progress of the French arms, and the variations of their government, the French themselves, almost indifferent to war and politics, think only of averting the horrors of famine. . . . The same paper that announces the surrender of towns, and the success of battles, tells us that the poor die in the streets of Paris, or are driven to commit suicide through want.[4]

Women suffered the most; they were the ones who waited in endless lines for bread and watched their children go hungry as bread rations in Paris shrank from four ounces a day to two and then to one ounce. Women began again to intercept carts carrying provisions into the city.

BREAD AND THE CONSTITUTION   In desperation and fury, marchers invaded the Convention on April 1 and 2, 1795 and demanded "bread and the constitution of 1793." The National Guard enforced martial law, and the Convention chose this moment to order the deportation without trial of Billaud-Varenne, Collot d'Herbois, and Barère. Another series of demonstrations led by women on May 20–23 made similar demands but this time led to the killing of a deputy in the meeting room by the rioters. When the Convention got control, it took draconian measures to prevent any future popular uprising.

MILITARY SUPPRESSION   It set up a military commission that ordered the immediate execution of 36 insurgents and heard charges against 11 Montagnard deputies for supporting the insurrection; two deputies killed themselves on hearing of their impending arrest, and six others tried to stab themselves upon being sentenced. Three succeeded in killing themselves, including Gilbert Romme, the architect of the revolutionary calendar. More than a thousand local militants were arrested. The Parisian popular classes never again marched into the assembly hall to enforce their demands.

Outside of Paris revenge against revolutionary excesses turned into a kind of anti-terrorist rage. Crowds smashed busts of Le Peletier and Marat and tore out liberty trees. Street names were changed back again. Refractory priests and *émigrés* began to return. Lists circulated of local "terrorists," "denouncers," and "drinkers of blood," that is, members of local Jacobin clubs or revolutionary committees and prosecutors or presiders of revolutionary courts. When the Convention ordered the disarmament of all former terrorists after the repression of the demonstrations in Paris of April and May 1795, many communities proceeded to arrest those on the lists, sometimes with the encouragement of deputies on mission. Countless scores were settled by beatings, individual assassinations, and in the southeast of the country, in particular, by organized murders with horrific mutilations of those unlucky enough to find themselves gathered together in prison. Some two thousand Jacobins died in this way in the southeast alone, many of them killed by gangs such as the royalist Company of Jesus operating in the Lyon region.[5]

Political stalemate: The Directory government

The Convention tried to set up a government that would maintain a centrist line and avoid the very different pitfalls of royalism and populism. The deputies scrapped the Constitution of 1793; after lengthy debate a new one was approved by the Convention in August 1795 and ratified by the voters the next month. Citing the example of the new United States, the deputies set up a two-house legislature, with a Council of Five Hundred as the lower house to propose legislation and a 250-member Council of Ancients with the responsibility of passing legislation. Members of the Five Hundred had to be at least 30 (until 1797, the requirement was 25 years old), and to sit in the Ancients at least 40 years old. Wanting to keep any one figure from becoming dominant, the deputies came up with a five-man Executive Directory to carry out the laws. The Councils chose the Directors who served with staggered terms so that no fixed group might consolidate power.

The Constitution of 1795 gave the Directors wide-ranging powers. They named the ministers and even the generals. They supervised local administrations, could order arrests, and shaped policies, both domestic and foreign. Still, with the replacement of one Director a year and inevitable conflicts for dominance, the Directory faced great difficulty in setting a single course. One of the first and most influential of the Directors, the ex-nobleman Paul Barras, described their meetings as veritable "gladiatorial combats." (Figure 4.3). Policies and ministerial appointments shifted with each change in the political winds. In four years, six men came and went as minister of war; nine men went through the revolving doors of the new ministry of police.[6]

The Convention intended to install a republic dominated by property-owners that would maintain legal equality and resist any return to the Old Regime. The new declaration of rights and duties emphasized security and property alongside liberty and equality and placed a premium on obedience to

FIGURE 4.3 *Paul Barras in His Director's Costume*
The one figure of continuity in the Directory regime was the ex-noble Paul Barras.
Before 1789, like many young nobles he served in the army and was sent twice
to India. He supported the Revolution, was elected a deputy to the Convention
and voted for the death of the king. Shifting position with every change in the
political winds, he developed a reputation for corruption. Here he is shown in his
Director's Costume. Etching and engraving by Pierre Tardieu after a drawing by
Hilaire Ledru, 1799.

the law and the state. About two-thirds of adult men met the requirements for voting, but they chose electors to make the final choices and only 8 percent qualified to be electors. The deputies and Directors wore special costumes whose references to Greek and Roman precedents were designed to give them a greater sense of dignity. One foreign visitor to Paris complained that the costume of the legislators was "too far removed from ordinary dress," and its "theatrical air" kept it from being "seriously dignified and truly imposing." Even worse, the Directors with their plumed hats looked like the kings on playing cards.

ROYALIST UPRISING   To guarantee continuity, the Convention decreed that two-thirds of deputies in the "new" legislature had to come from the Convention itself. Most of the sections in Paris rejected this decree and some 5,000 insurgents, including many royalists, tried to mount an insurrection on October 5. Called the Vendémiaire revolt because it took place in that month of the revolutionary calendar, it forced the Convention to call in the army. Named to lead the troops in Paris was the deputy Barras, known for his pitiless repression of Marseille and Toulon and for his role in defending the Convention on 9 Thermidor. He chose Bonaparte as his second-in-command because they had worked together at Toulon in 1793. Bonaparte got hold of cannon parked six miles away and used them to disperse the insurgents, killing hundreds. Barras was then chosen as one of the first five Directors alongside Carnot; all five Directors had voted for the death of the king.

Barras would continue as Director until the end of the regime, all the while cultivating relations with the regime's eventual gravedigger, Bonaparte. He introduced Bonaparte to his future wife Joséphine de Beauharnais, a creole from Martinique, whose husband, an aristocrat and general, had been guillotined during the Terror. Barras had protected her and perhaps been her lover during her most vulnerable moments, before handing her on to the young Bonaparte. Described by one of his colleagues as the "leavening agent of corruption," in retrospect Barras stood for all that was wrong with the Directory; a relentless intriguer, he paid Fouché to spy on his colleagues and was widely reputed to be willing to sell himself to the highest bidder.

FRUCTIDOR COUP   The two-thirds decree could only hold back the torrent of dissatisfaction for a while because the new constitution called for annual elections to replace one-third of the deputies. In March of 1797 royalists won the majority of seats up for election. In September Barras joined with two of his colleagues to order the arrest of Carnot and another Director along with 53 supposedly royalist deputies. Bonaparte had encouraged them to undertake this Fructidor coup (so-called after the month of the revolutionary calendar) and sent an aide, General Pierre Augereau, to lead his troops into the Council rooms and carry out the arrests. Carnot fled but the others were deported to Guyana. The rump Councils then annulled the election results in many departments, purged local officials suspected of royalism, and closed royalist newspapers.

CONSPIRACY OF EQUALS   Not surprisingly, the next threat came from the Jacobin left, even though the government had successfully dismantled one left-wing group called the Conspiracy of Equals. Led by Gracchus Babeuf, a newspaper editor in Paris, the group supposedly planned an insurrection to redistribute property and institute direct democracy. Having agitated on behalf of peasants in the early revolutionary years, Babeuf developed positions that seemed to later observers to be a first step toward communism (a term not yet invented); he apparently hoped that a secret cell of dedicated revolutionaries could take power, establish a temporary dictatorship, and set up collective farms. None of these proto-Leninist ideas appeared in his newspaper, which appealed mainly to Jacobins such as Fouché and David. Infiltrated by a police spy, some 50 alleged conspirators were arrested in May 1796. After a lengthy trial that failed to tarnish Jacobinism as a whole, Babeuf and one of his colleagues were executed for the crime of having advocated the adoption of the Constitution of 1793, a position that they had only taken as a strategic concession to attract wider support.[7]

FLORÉAL COUP   In the aftermath of the suppression of the Babeuvists and the purge of royalists, Jacobins began to reorganize in "constitutional circles" that supported the Directory but wanted to push it leftward. When they did well in the elections of March 1798, the Directors organized what became known as the Floréal coup of May 11, 1798 (again named after the month in the revolutionary calendar) when the Councils annulled the results in 29 departments, eliminating 127 newly elected deputies. After something similar happened the next year, however, the deputies refused to support further purges and insisted that two Directors resign and be replaced. By then only one in nine of eligible voters participated in the elections. The high rate of abstention should not be considered surprising. Although more voters had participated in 1797 and 1798, the rate in 1799 was the same as 1795, about one-third less than in 1792.

Sieyès had been elected Director just before this mini-coup against the executive, and he would go on to play a major role in Bonaparte's ascension. For the moment, however, the two new Directors leaned toward the Jacobins. The Jacobin Club re-opened in Paris and 150 deputies joined alongside three generals known as Jacobin sympathizers: Jean-Baptiste Bernadotte, the war minister; Jean-Baptiste Jourdan; and Augereau, the strong man of the anti-royalist coup of 1797.

Although the constant intervention to shape and even overturn election results ultimately proved fatal to the Directory regime, the four years of its existence allowed several important initiatives to take root. Despite the continuing failure of efforts to provide secular education to all boys because of a lack of teachers, the regime developed the kind of elite scientific and technical education that would soon be emulated everywhere else. The students admitted to the new *Ecole polytechnique* (1795) were taught by the most eminent scientists of the day, and like students in the new or reorganized schools of artillery, cavalry, mines, bridges and roads, and geography, they were trained to be servants of the state.

Artistic and intellectual life recovered their vigor in the relaxed political atmosphere. The number of new novels published increased ten-fold between 1794 and 1799, and despite the regime's efforts to install censorship of the theater, plays continued to attract big audiences, especially for the new genre of melodrama. With its thunder and lightning, dark caves, and orphans facing fearsome tribulations, melodrama gave audiences a moment in which to relive the terrors of the past years and overcome them. After David's release from prison in the fall of 1795, he regained his position as undisputed master of French painting, but he and his students now produced more portraits. Public exhibitions at the Louvre drew more and more visitors, and they saw more portraits and family scenes. The proportion of paintings devoted to family scenes doubled between 1793 and 1799. Everyone seemed to be looking for a return to something like normal life. At the same time, however, the display of paintings and statues confiscated from newly conquered territories aroused fierce criticism across Europe.

The Directory put into practice the Thermidorian Convention's plan to set up a National Institute to organize the various disciplines, award prizes in the place of the Old Regime academies, and to disseminate knowledge to the public. The section of moral and political sciences included many of the leading philosophers and social theorists of the day, including Sieyès and the physician and hospital reformer Pierre Cabanis. Many of the men in that section had been associates of Condorcet; they supported a moderate republic and would go on to play key roles in the elaboration of the social sciences, or as Cabanis called them, "the science of man and society." As supporters of a moderate republic, they believed in freedom of opinion but not necessarily for newspapers. One of the organizers of the Institute explained, the government could not grant "impunity to Marat out of gratitude for Bacon and Montesquieu."

Although Cabanis argued in print that women had weaker brains than men and so were unsuited to "long and profound meditations," one of the leading intellectuals of the age was a woman, Germaine de Staël. Only 29 years old in 1795, de Staël had already made a name for herself with a book on Rousseau. She would go on to write novels, essays about literature, and one of the first comprehensive studies of the French Revolution as a phenomenon. As the daughter of Necker, wife of a Swedish diplomat, and lover of various political figures, she was no stranger to politics, and her salon in Paris attracted the leading moderate republicans including Sieyès and Barras. Her most famous liaison was with Benjamin Constant, a fellow Swiss republican and novelist known for his writings in support of political liberalism. Suspected of royalist sympathies because of her father, de Staël found herself ordered out of France on more than one occasion, but she remained like Constant a steadfast supporter of a centrist republic.

Unfortunately, the economic policies of the Directory regime reflected none of the luster created in other areas of intellectual life. Despite the Directors' support for the idea of creating a national bank, the Councils rejected the plan out of fear of the power it would give to bankers. Instead the government tried to replace the *assignats* with a new paper money called *mandats territoriaux* ["territorial money orders," that is, paper based on the value of nationalized properties], but they collapsed within a year. Deflation accelerated when the government converted two-thirds of the national debt into bonds in 1797; they were supposed to be valid for the purchase of national lands but a year later the government decreed that national lands could only be bought with metal currency, effectively repudiating two-thirds of the debt and creating hardship and resentment among its bondholders. In 1795 the regime had introduced a new metal currency as part of the metric system; the *franc*, divided into 10 *décimes* of 10 *centimes* each, was supposed to replace the *livre* and be composed of a set amount of silver, but in fact the government had trouble keeping up with demand so various different kinds of hard currency (specie) remained in circulation.

Although the government took steps to improve the collection of taxes, it never succeeded in making up its shortfalls. An attempt to levy forced loans on the better-off citizens, payable in specie or grain, failed to bring in the expected sums, so the government instituted a new direct tax on doors and windows (which remained on the books until 1925) and revived some of the hated indirect taxes of the Old Regime such as tolls on goods entering local markets, stamp taxes on newspapers, and duties for the registration of legal documents. Even though revenues increased in 1798 and 1799, the government still depended on private bankers for the credit to keep it going; they were demanding the astounding level of 2–4 percent per month (not year) for loans in the late 1790s.

The success of French arms

In this precarious financial situation, military conquest ultimately proved essential to the regime's survival. Armies learned to finance themselves from local resources and demanded payments from every city they conquered. They sent back to Paris not only art treasures but also cold cash, sometimes in the form of church silver and gold melted down to bars that could be shipped to France. Bonaparte sent 15,000,000 francs worth back from Italy by August

1796 and another 35 million by March 1797. The hauls from Belgium and the Rhine were smaller but still substantial.

This stripping of assets was made possible by the success of French arms. The five Directors developed clashing positions about the objectives to be pursued: should France focus above all else on protecting its "natural" frontiers—the Rhine, the Alps, and the Pyrenees—or should France's armies republicanize the rest of Europe? Even the first choice meant taking over new territories, especially control of the left bank of the Rhine. Ironically, the second choice followed from an attempt to guarantee the first. In 1796 the Directory named the 26-year-old Bonaparte as commander of a new campaign in Italy because they wanted to draw Austrian forces away from the Rhineland and simultaneously replenish the coffers with Italian riches. Before leaving for his new post, the young Corsican married Joséphine, who was six years older and already the mother of two children. The Italian campaign soon exceeded everyone's expectations and set the Directory on a new expansionist course.[8]

With 45,000 men that he found "naked and ill-fed" Bonaparte brilliantly maneuvered to drive a wedge between the 25,000 Piedmontese and 35,000 Austrian soldiers arrayed against him. After defeating each in turn in a swift series of battles in the mountain passes of the Ligurian Alps, he swept into the plains of Austrian-ruled Lombardy. At the battle of Lodi, he personally led one of the critical bayonet charges. Upon taking Milan he congratulated his men: "You have won battles without cannons, crossed rivers without bridges, you have made forced marches without shoes, bivouacked without brandy and often without bread." The Kingdom of Sardinia-Piedmont sued for peace and gave up Nice and Savoy to France. Austria was next.

Bonaparte had to move quickly before Austria could bring in reinforcements. He deployed once again his signature strategy: moving with speed—at one point marching his men 30 miles in less than two days—he positioned himself between the enemy contingents and then massed his men to defeat each one in turn. He took on the Austrians again and again in the fall and winter, and kept winning, often using his personal charisma to urge his men on when defeat seemed all but certain. In February 1797 the French captured the fortress of Mantua in northern Italy with its garrison of 30,000 men and promptly prepared to invade Austria itself. By April the Austrians had agreed to preliminary peace terms.

As Bonaparte moved from west to east across Italy, he replaced local governments, finally merging many of them together in a Cisalpine Republic headquartered in Milan. Local "patriots" agreed to a constitution modeled on the French one of 1795 with Directors and a two-house legislature and departments with uniform administrations. Equality under the law including equal inheritance for girls, religious toleration, the abolition of Catholic religious orders, and the confiscation of church lands all followed. But so too did the expenses to maintain a French army of 25,000 men and constant interference from the French in the new republic's affairs. Barras got Fouché named as French ambassador, a post that required constant negotiation with the general whom Bonaparte had left in charge. A separate Ligurian Republic on the same model was set up in Genoa for the far western regions of northern Italy.

TREATY OF CAMPOFORMIO   After months of personal negotiation with the Austrians, which began before and ended after the arrest of the royalists in the Paris government, Bonaparte signed the Treaty of Campoformio in October 1797. Despite their grumbling about his personal role, the Directors had little choice but to accept it, especially since Bonaparte's rapid-fire victories had made him a hero in Paris. The Paris police reported that his "praises are sung by everybody." When he returned to Paris in December the Institute elected him a member. A grand banquet was held in his honor in the Louvre Museum, which now began displaying captured enemy arms and battle standards in the galleries that housed the artistic booty sent back from Italy. The militarization of society was well underway.

Bonaparte captured the popular imagination despite, or perhaps because of, several obvious impediments. First of all, he was not exactly French. Napoleone di Buonaparte was born on the island of Corsica to parents with Italian origins. The year of Napoleon's birth, 1769, France had conquered and incorporated Corsica, but Napoleon always spoke French with an accent. He hated being called "the Corsican," and as he ascended the military ranks he changed the spelling of his name. The second son in a family of nine surviving children, he was born noble. This meant that though his parents were far from rich, he could be admitted as a scholarship boy to a military school at Brienne, east of Paris in the Champagne region of France. It also meant, however, that he was a potentially suspect noble as France became a republic. He made up for it by embracing republicanism.

Coming from a modest noble family Bonaparte avoided the cavalry with its expensive outlays and chose the artillery where his skill at mathematics and talent for surveying the field of battle enabled him to advance rapidly. A man of average height for his time, Bonaparte primarily wielded the power of personality. Separated from his family at the age of ten and surrounded by schoolmates who mocked him for his origins, he learned to count on himself, and he soon grasped that he could lead. Later on, the sheer force of his charisma would fling men into battle, even against daunting odds. But Bonaparte also knew how to make the most of his success; he mastered the social media of his time, including the bulletin hastily penned from the front, and used it to spotlight his every move, making himself central to the action, even when he was not. In this respect, the Italian campaign proved decisive;

during it, Bonaparte honed the public relations techniques that would ultimately bring him to power and enable him to change the course of so many destinies.

Bonaparte had been eager to make peace because the Austrians had the winter to regroup and also because he worried about the increasing prominence of Augereau, who took command of the bigger Army of the Rhine after helping the government purge the royalists. By the treaty, the Austrians recognized the Cisalpine Republic, the French annexation of Belgium, and by secret articles, the extension of French borders to the Rhine. In exchange Bonaparte handed the Venetian Republic, independent for more than a thousand years, over to the Austrians, but not before shipping the four bronze horses on the façade of Saint Mark's basilica in Venice back to Paris. The payment of a huge bribe to Barras could not save the Venetians.[9]

With the peace, the First Coalition against France collapsed. Patiently cobbled together once Great Britain entered the war in 1793, it had already suffered several blows. Prussia had agreed to neutrality in April 1795 because it wanted time to consolidate its gains from the third partition of Poland carried out with Austria and Russia in January of that year. In August 1796 Spain consented to ally with France in exchange for the guaranteed possession of its colonies. Russia shelved its plan to arm an expeditionary force of 50,000 men when Catherine the Great died in November 1796. Although French armies made only intermittent headway across the Rhine, getting as far as Munich but then retreating, Bonaparte had managed much in Italy. He even invaded the Pope's lands and demanded a huge indemnity. After he left Italy, Bonaparte's successors occupied Rome and supervised the creation of a Roman Republic, and when forces of the kingdom of Naples attacked them, they pushed further south and set up a Parthenopean Republic in Naples. By March 1799 the French had also occupied the two remaining independent states in Italy: Piedmont and Tuscany (see Map 4.1).

Peace with Austria enabled the French to annex Geneva, making it into a French department, and to supervise the installation of a Helvetic Republic in March 1798 that brought together the diverse Swiss cantons under a constitution written in Paris by Swiss republicans. It too followed the model of the French constitution of 1795. The French oversaw the same changes they introduced elsewhere: abolition of guilds, rationalization of tolls and tariffs, religious toleration, closure of convents and monasteries and confiscation of their lands, abolition of torture and reform of the courts, and authorization of newspapers. Everywhere the French prevailed, despite their penchant for interference and exploitation, the number of newspapers and periodicals increased.

Only one major enemy remained: Great Britain. In July 1795 British ships had carried 3,000 French *émigrés* to Quiberon Bay in Brittany where the royalists hoped to rally locals to their side. Republican troops under General Lazare

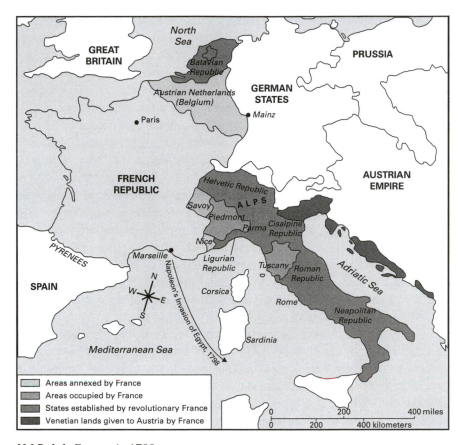

MAP 4.1 *Europe in 1799*

Hoche routed them, and nearly 800 were executed as traitors. Hoche tamped down resistance in the Vendée by deploying roving columns to surround insurgent villages, and the two most important leaders of the revolt were executed in early 1796, but this did not stop the British from looking for occasions to foment resistance to the French republic. British superiority at sea allowed Britain to blockade French ports on the English Channel, threaten French control of their colonies in the Caribbean, and hold the Dutch and Spanish fleets at bay. The British had to be taken on and Ireland seemed a prime spot for invasion with its oppressed Catholic population waiting for deliverance.

IRISH REBELLION   Having failed to land an expeditionary force in 1796, the Directory tried again in 1798. It expected support from the United Irishmen, an organization set up by the young Protestant lawyer Wolfe Tone to unite Catholic and Protestants in demanding independence for Ireland. Tone had gone to France in early 1796 and met with various politicians and generals including Bonaparte to urge them to act. Outlawed by the British, militants of the United Irishmen nonetheless rose up in the spring of 1798. The French sent only a small contingent because French war aims had shifted elsewhere by then. With the Irish leadership on the run, the British crushed the uprising, killing as many as 30,000 Irish. Tone killed himself in prison to avoid hanging. Britain had deployed 73,000 regular soldiers, more than twice as many as saw action in any of the major engagements of the wars on the continent.[10]

Although the French found allies throughout Europe among local "Jacobins" and "patriots," they also faced ferocious resistance to their relentless expansionism. Supporters of the French and the new republics were to be found almost exclusively in the towns and cities; resistance had its heart in the countryside where the French occupiers demanded supplies. In the Rhineland, those who joined pro-French clubs and administrations urged the formation of a Cisrhenane [Rhine] Republic, but French occupiers rejected this idea. The French were more interested in getting the 150,000,000 francs in cash they demanded from Rhineland cities between 1794 and 1799. Five-sixths of local tax revenue was going to the French army, not to mention enormous quantities of grain and meat.

Even though Rhineland peasants theoretically benefited from the French abolition of serfdom, in practice, the disruption of trade, the flight of aristocrats and princes, and the loss of local welfare provided by churches created the kind of misery that encouraged banditry. Peasants sheltered bandit gangs that attacked French patrols, preyed on travelers, and in some cases, singled out the Jews because the French had insisted on granting them rights. Bandit gangs also roamed through the annexed Belgian territories but proved even more disruptive in southern Italy. A Catholic cardinal commanded the *Santa fede* or Most Christian Armada of the Holy Faith that organized Calabrian peasants to resist the new republic headquartered in Naples. The royalists paraded their local religious relics as they attacked known "Jacobins" or sympathizers with the French. This violence would reach its zenith during the overthrow of the republic in Naples, but similar kinds of banditry and collective violence also agitated northern Italy where Viva Maria gangs rampaged against Jacobins and Jews. They pillaged houses, desecrated synagogues, and in Siena, for example, killed several Jews and publicly burned their bodies.

Explaining French success

French soldiers had raced across Europe with a speed unprecedented in modern European history and in the process they upended all the usual expectations about warfare. How had this astounding reversal come about? In early September 1792 the revolution seemed on the verge of destruction as the Austrian, Prussian, and French *émigré* armies approached Paris. By March 1799 France directly or indirectly controlled large swaths of territories in Belgium, Holland, the Rhineland, Italy, and Switzerland and was busily remaking them all in the French image (see Map 4.1). The First Coalition against France collapsed in part because it was a coalition; the different states had separate armies and command structures and conflicting interests. Yet that same disparate coalition worked well at the beginning of the war. What had changed was the French army itself. Despite political turmoil at home, the French won great victories because their officers developed unrivaled organizational and tactical skills and their ordinary soldiers felt a patriotic bond with each other and therefore with an army that they saw as their own. This success had its downside, however; popular generals soon would be called on to involve themselves far more in those very Parisian politics that officers and their men traditionally ignored.

Intense factional struggles under the Directory regime never undermined the war effort in part because the armies had imbibed the revolutionary ethos and could promote such goals independently. The military had become a formidable freestanding school of patriotism that promoted social advancement as well as nationalism. The contrast with the Old Regime was stark. The Old Regime army had recruited rank and file soldiers from society's misfits, and public opinion contemptuously regarded them as robbers and miscreants. Edmond Dubois-Crancé, who rose to the rank of general when he was not serving as a deputy, said of the Old Regime army in December 1789, "Is there a father who does not tremble to abandon his son, not to the hazards of war, but to a mob of unknown brigands, a thousand times more dangerous?" National conscription, for which Dubois-Crancé was arguing, changed that view, as service became a sign of patriotism, not social failure.

If anything, the officer corps changed even more. Under the Old Regime high-ranking officers had nothing in common with their men; they were nobles or aspiring to become such. Nobles from traditional military families had grumbled that the buying of commissions undercut the quality of the leadership by bringing in men with money and no background in the military, and some of the old nobility supported greater attention to merit after 1789. The massive defections of noble officers between 1789 and 1792 changed the basis of the argument. Although some nobles, like Bonaparte, remained, officers had to be found in the middle and even lower classes. The revolutionary generals came from every walk of life, from old aristocratic military families on down. Bonaparte's second-in-command in Italy, Alexandre Berthier, came from a family ennobled under Louis XV; Augereau was the son either of a worker or a servant.

It is nonetheless true that some reforms had been undertaken before 1789 that bore fruit in the 1790s. Influenced by the Enlightenment, military thinkers sought a more humane approach that would limit war to the fewest casualties possible; strategy and tactics were to be valued more than brute force or attrition. Officers should be taught to discipline their men with respect. To this end, they were encouraged to abandon the demeaning punishment of striking a soldier on the back with the flat side of the sword. Even the notion of an armed force representative of the nation had earlier antecedents in the image of the American citizen army of the War of Independence. One French volunteer described meeting George Washington for the first time: "He dressed in the most simple manner, without any of the marks distinctive of a commanding officer." This young aristocrat could see the virtue of a different approach to military authority.

New reforms combined with older ones in an endeavor to inspire troops, especially improving the relationship between the commanders and the commanded. In the first years of the Revolution the deputies hoped that a volunteer force could be integrated into the army while maintaining its civilian roots and newly proclaimed political rights including voting. Old Regime troops enjoyed few rights; until 1793 a soldier had to seek the permission of his commanding officer to marry. Soldiers were now to be judged by the same principles as civilians if they committed crimes, and military courts even had juries for a time. Most important, soldiers had a right to elect their officers and also to advance through seniority. Ironically, given the universal goals of the revolution, the army maintained internal borders as troops from other parts of Europe and Africa remained poorly integrated into the service.[11]

Nevertheless, as Carnot famously affirmed (though the remark is often attributed to Bonaparte), "every French soldier carries a field-marshal's baton in his knapsack." The youth and rapid ascension of French generals proves the saying right; in 1795 Bonaparte was 26 and Hoche just 27 years old. Hoche was a corporal in 1789 with little hope of advancement yet by early 1796 he had been named sole commander of all forces fighting the Vendée rebels, an army of at least 100,000 men. Being a general in the French republican army held its risks. Generals, too, faced political dangers, especially during the Terror. In 1793–1794 no less than 84 generals were executed as traitors, often only for losing a battle. Hoche was arrested and imprisoned during the Terror; after the fall of Robespierre, Bonaparte spent a brief time under arrest as a suspected Robespierrist. He had worked closely with Robespierre's brother when Augustin served as deputy on mission to the army of Italy.

After 1793, and especially after 1795, facing a series of military setbacks, the government moved away from the initial attempts to "civilianize" and democratize the army and placed more emphasis on discipline. Over the course of 1793 the army organized new "demi-brigades" by amalgamating two battalions of volunteers with a battalion of the regular army. Although intended to inject republican ideals into the royal army, the amalgamation also served the purpose of removing the volunteers from their local affinities and incorporating them more fully into an army controlled by the national government. In 1794 and 1795 the government steadily whittled away at the principle of election of officers in order to give the central government and superior officers more control.

When the Directory came to power in 1795, it ordered a further rationalization, cutting the number of demi-brigades in half in order to fill the ranks of depleted units and to slim down the officer corps that had grown bloated with elections and seniority. By then, the importance of the Old Regime army had been much reduced, since soldiers from it accounted for only 18 percent of the men under arms. Combined with growing draft evasion and desertion, the Directorial consolidation reduced the size of the active force to under 400,000 in 1798 but at the same time fostered a weeding out of officers, leaving behind, as Dubois-Crancé pithily noted, a "corps of chosen and purified officers," that is, committed professionals.

Officers chosen for their skills and technical knowledge could rely on the solidarity of soldiers who were organized in mess groups or squads of 16 men. Sharing meals, sleeping arrangements (such as they were), and the fears of battle in these squads, the rank and file experienced fraternity in life and death fashion. But the sense of belonging to a unit and a nation with the mission to bring liberty to the benighted had its downside, too. As the French successfully invaded Belgium, the Dutch Republic, the Rhineland, and the Italian states, they moved ever farther from home and regular sources of supplies. They requisitioned what they needed unit by unit, and that requisitioning sometimes turned into pillage, rape, and murder. The French were soon viewed as occupiers, not liberators.[12]

The attitudes of ordinary soldiers to these changes are difficult to pin down. Many wrote home with proud professions of patriotism. One peasant from eastern France shared his emotion with his parents: "either you will see me return bathed in glory, or you will have a son who is a worthy citizen of France who knows how to die for the defense of his country." Others, as might be expected, expressed boredom, disappointment with military life, and grief over the loss of friends in battle. They longed to go home and also wished to be reassured that home was still the same familiar spot they had left. In fact, the revolutionary wars mark the first time that "homesickness" became a widespread concern. Draft evasion and desertion were continuing problems; the rate of desertion rose from 4 percent in 1794 to 8 percent in 1796 and 1797.[13]

As the generals experimented with new forms of attack made possible by mass armies, they turned away from eighteenth-century ideals of limited casualties toward a kind of total war, in which the ideology of republicanism— or simply French superiority—justified crushing the enemy. The impulse to exterminate the opposing side took its most catastrophic form in fighting the Vendée rebels. Fighting would turn equally horrific whenever French forces confronted guerilla warfare, as they did in southern Italy and would in the next years in Spain.

Regular battles, too, changed character. The huge number of new soldiers and the lack of time to train them dictated crucial changes in French strategy and tactics. Conscripts inevitably lacked the training to fire quickly in turn in the customary three lines, so officers had to improvise. They sent forward clouds of skirmishers to hide in ambush and disrupt enemy lines; the skirmishers and snipers need only follow the officer in charge whose own initiative determined the course of the action. Officers ordered their men to fire in line sometimes, but they always emphasized bayonet charges in huge columns as a way of turning the tide. Hoche explained, "no maneuvering, nothing elaborate, just cold steel, passion and patriotism."

The French often won when they could concentrate a higher number of men for battle (hence the importance of dividing the enemy's forces), and they lost when they could not. But France's enemies had a hard time coming to terms with these "innumerable hordes." Austrian Chancellor Thugut complained in November 1796, "When one realizes that Bonaparte, a young man of twenty-seven years, with no experience, with an army that is only a heap of brigands and volunteers, with half the strength of ours, defeats all of our generals, one must naturally bemoan our decadence and debasement."

Bonaparte comes to power by way of Egypt

When Bonaparte triumphantly returned to Paris at the end of 1797, he had a new goal in mind: the conquest of Egypt. During his last months in Italy, he eagerly discussed the idea of an invasion with his subordinates. He had written to the Directors from Italy with his plan: "The time is not far when we will think that in order truly to destroy England, we have to take Egypt." Egypt would give the French an overland route to India, Britain's most important colony; moreover, it seemed ripe for the picking because of the weakness of its Ottoman overlords. In contrast, an invasion of England itself, though long in the planning, seemed much more difficult. Bonaparte's fascination with Alexander the Great and reading of travel accounts convinced him that Egypt was part of his destiny.

The new foreign minister, Talleyrand, supported the idea of an invasion, having come to it himself quite separately. An aristocrat, Catholic bishop, and deputy in the National Assembly of 1789, Talleyrand had left France after the August 10, 1792 uprising against the monarchy. Unwelcome in England because he had supported the Revolution until then, he sailed to the United

States in 1794 and stayed two years. While there he advised foreign investors, such as Dutch bankers fleeing the 1795 French invasion, and witnessed the desperation of white planters ruined by the insurrection in Saint-Domingue. He renewed acquaintance with Moreau de Saint-Méry, who arrived about the same time and set up a bookshop in Philadelphia that became a center for the French exiles including Louis Philippe, now the Duke of Orleans after the execution of his father. The American Philosophical Society, established by Franklin, elected Talleyrand and Moreau as members.

When Talleyrand got his name removed from the *émigré* list (he had left on a valid passport) and was allowed to return to Paris, he gave two papers at the Institute, arguing that France needed to pursue a new colonial policy that would replace the losses in the Caribbean with colonies closer to home, such as Egypt. Thanks to the personal intervention of his longtime friend Germaine de Staël with Barras, Talleyrand was named foreign minister in July 1797. Bonaparte began corresponding with him about the prospect of an invasion.

INVASION OF EGYPT Finally, in April 1798 the Directors named Bonaparte commander of a new Army of the Orient. He immediately set about organizing a secret invasion force that would depart from Toulon and carry with it 167 scientists and hundreds of artists and engravers in addition to 40,000 sailors and soldiers. Leading the scientific part of the expedition were the mathematician Gaspard Monge and the chemist Claude Berthollet, both founding members of the Institute in Paris. Bonaparte wanted to be seen as a philosopher and scientist and not just a conquering general.

At first, all went as planned. A huge French flotilla left Toulon on May 19 and took the island of Malta, ruled ineffectively by the remnants of the Order of St. John of Malta. Managing to avoid a British fleet, which was looking for them, the French arrived at Alexandria on July 1, 1798. Because the port was too shallow, the French disembarked at Aboukir Bay, a 4-hour march away. The French overwhelmed the defenders in Alexandria, and Bonaparte promptly issued a proclamation in Arabic asserting that the French only intended to restore Ottoman authority and guarantee Egyptian independence from the local Mameluke rulers (see Document 4.2). Since the Mamelukes were descended from slaves taken by the Ottomans in central Asia, they could be portrayed as foreign to both Egyptians and Ottomans.[14]

Things started to go wrong as soon as the French set off for Cairo, which required a 72-hour march across the desert to reach the Nile. Having trekked without much food or water, the soldiers vented their frustration after the first inconclusive battle by pillaging and massacring villagers. After winning what he described as a major battle on July 21 outside Cairo (later dubbed the Battle of the Pyramids, though the pyramids were more than 20 kilometers away), Bonaparte entered the city. He tried to win over local notables but alienated many by requisitioning all the horses, raising new taxes, and requiring every

Egyptian to wear the tricolor cockade. He set up the Egyptian Institute with Monge as president and himself as vice-president (all but one of the members were French) and asked them to study a variety of questions ranging from whether army ovens for baking bread could be improved to an analysis of the present state of Egyptian jurisprudence and education. The scientists eventually published more than 20 volumes of their *Description of Egypt* (1809–1828). Undermining this thirst for knowledge about Egypt was a developing policy of repression; when a group of engineers sent to build ovens was sodomized, murdered, and mutilated, the French burnt down the village in reprisal. Similar revenge was exacted wherever resistance turned deadly.

BATTLE OF THE NILE   The situation took an even more dramatic turn for the worse when the British fleet sailed into Aboukir Bay at five o'clock in the evening on August 1. Despite the late hour, the British commander, 40-year-old Admiral Horatio Nelson, immediately engaged the French. He had already lost an eye and an arm in previous battles and was soon temporarily blinded by shrapnel, yet by nightfall Bonaparte's flagship *Orient* had gone down with 600,000 francs worth of gold and diamonds taken from Malta. After another day of fighting, only two French ships of the line and two frigates managed to escape from the Battle of the Nile; eleven warships and two frigates had been sunk. The bay was littered with scorched bodies. The French lost 3,200 men, either killed or wounded, the British less than 1,000. The British lost no ships. The victors then blockaded the coast, stranding Bonaparte and his army.

Despite the improbability of attacking India by an overland route—the chief British posts were more than 3,500 miles from Cairo—Bonaparte had no choice but to continue on land. France did have potential allies in India, in particular Tipu Sultan, the ruler of the kingdom of Mysore, who had been actively seeking French aid in fighting the British since the late 1780s. French soldiers in his capital city of Seringapatam had even set up a Jacobin Club and planted a liberty tree, but only a few such men had managed to make their way from Île de France (present-day Mauritius), the nearest French outpost by sea, 2,500 miles away.

In early September 1798, the Ottoman Sultan declared war on the French, having maintained neutrality until then and even having tried to negotiate an alliance with the French republic. On October 21 the people of Cairo rose in revolt and began sacking French and Christian houses; they killed 300 French. In retaliation Bonaparte ordered the bombardment of rebel areas; soldiers desecrated the Grand Mosque, stomping on the Koran while plundering valuables. After ferreting out and executing the revolt's ringleaders, Bonaparte offered a full pardon and compared himself to a prophet: "the day shall come when all men shall see beyond all doubt that I am guided by orders from above and that all human efforts avail naught against me." He then prepared to invade "Syria" (present-day Israel) with 13,000 men to take on a joint Mameluke–Ottoman force.

The French army's suffering and brutality now knew no bounds. Harassed constantly by Bedouins, the army slogged alternately through burning sands and torrential downpours and eventually reached Jaffa (near modern day Tel-Aviv) in early March 1799. After a 4-day siege, the French took the walled coastal city and massacred thousands of its inhabitants, including civilians and enemy soldiers who surrendered. Revenge came in the form of the plague, killing 700–800 soldiers and striking fear in everyone's heart, except Bonaparte, who went to visit the sick in a show of bravado (Figure 4.4). He then tried to take Acre, but after two months of fruitless assaults, he had to withdraw in May as British ships brought up Ottoman reinforcements. His army retreated back to Cairo razing villages and abandoning plague victims all along the way. Only 8,000 men were still fit to fight by mid-June, yet Bonaparte managed to repulse an attempted Ottoman invasion at the Battle of Aboukir in July. Just a few days before, a soldier made the most important discovery of the entire expedition: the Rosetta Stone, named after the village where it was found, was a hefty 4-foot piece of black basalt that displayed Greek alongside Egyptian hieroglyphs, making possible the eventual decipherment of the long mysterious ancient Egyptian language.

On the night of August 22, 1799 Bonaparte secretly abandoned his army in Egypt and slipped back into France. In May, unbeknownst to Bonaparte, the Indian leader Tipu Sultan had been killed fighting the British, who had used an intercepted letter from the French general to the Mysore ruler to justify attacking Tipu. More concerned with events closer to home, Bonaparte had learned of French reverses in Italy, and his brothers urged him to seize the moment, which had been created in large measure by his Egyptian campaign. The devastation of the French fleet at Aboukir Bay had turned the tide once again; Russia had joined a Second Coalition against France alongside the Ottoman Empire, Britain, and Austria because Russia feared that Bonaparte's conquest of Malta and invasion of Egypt would displace Russian interests in the eastern Mediterranean. A combined Austro-Russian army soon drove the French back across the Rhine and out of much of Switzerland and northern Italy.

Russian and Turkish forces helped the *Santa Fede* bring down the republic in Naples after most of the French left to fight in the north. Royalist mobs proceeded to murder known Jacobins. Admiral Nelson arrived with the King of the Two Sicilies (King of Naples) in tow and rejected the armistice that granted remaining republicans safe passage out of the city; 99 republican leaders were executed, among them the reforming jurist and freemason Mario Pagano, author of the republican constitution of Naples, and Eleonora Fonseca Pimentel, a poet and the editor of the republic's official newspaper. Thousands more

PEINT PAR GROS.

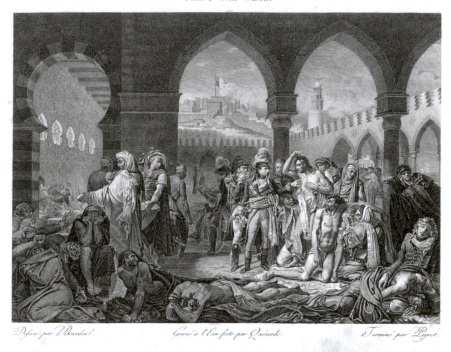

Défessé par Bourbon?   Gravé à l'Eau forte par Quévertis: Terminé par Pigeot:

BUONAPARTE VISITANT L'HÔPITAL DE JAFFA.

FIGURE 4.4 *Bonaparte Visiting Victims of the Plague in Jaffa*
In a gesture of bravado, Bonaparte did not hesitate to visit his soldiers sick with the plague at the hospital set up for them in Jaffa in 1799. At the same time, he also did not think twice about massacring enemy soldiers and hapless civilians. For some, he was a figure of almost superhuman bravery; for others, especially his enemies, a callous and cruel monster. He was certainly a consummate propagandist, encouraging artists like Antoine-Jean Gros, who painted the picture on which this print is based, to draw attention to his bravery and concern for his men. Etching and engraving, ca 1804.

were imprisoned or exiled. Nelson's role has been debated ever since. He had to defend himself against critics such as Helen Maria Williams who complained of his refusal to protect "the illustrious martyrs of liberty."

On October 11 rumors reached Paris that Bonaparte had landed in southern France. Spontaneous expressions of "universal joy" broke out in theaters and cafés. All along his route up to Paris huge crowds greeted him as a conquering hero and potential savior, thanks in part to his own propaganda efforts. His dispatches from the front, published in all the newspapers, talked only of victories, never setbacks; he had conquered Malta, Alexandria and Cairo, and the British win at the Battle of the Nile, which he minimized, could hardly offset these achievements. He even portrayed his return as a sacrifice for the good of the nation.

When Bonaparte reached Paris, the military situation had actually stabilized. A new conscription law required all French men aged 20 to 24 to be registered so that they could be called up by birth years. Republican forces put down a royalist uprising in the southwest of France, killing 1,000 rebels, many of whom were army deserters and draft-evaders. Attempts to reignite fighting in the Vendée eventually fizzled, and most important, French armies counter-attacked and drove the Russians out of Zurich and pushed back an attempted British invasion of Holland.[15]

Still, many longed for an end to the constant political upheavals of the Directory regime, whose greatest defect was the inability of its leaders to create a viable party of the center. Like all eighteenth-century people in the Atlantic world, Directorial republicans rejected organized political parties in principle. Parties, as the word suggests, represented partial interests, not the common good. Only the Jacobins had moved toward organizing as a national party, combining legislative caucusing with local affiliates and circulated electoral lists, but those efforts only made them more suspect. Moreover, they were hardly seeking to represent the center.

In 1799 both royalists and Jacobins seemed to be making yet another comeback, but the former Jacobin Fouché, named Minister of Police in July 1799 with the support of Barras and Sieyès, closed down the revived Jacobin Club and relentlessly pursued both royalist and Jacobin journalists. Fouché, Barras, Sieyès, and Talleyrand now made common cause; they wanted a much stronger executive and looked for a general to fill the role. Hoche had died of tuberculosis in 1797, and Barthelemy Joubert, commander of the army of Italy, died fighting the Russians in Italy in August 1799. With Bonaparte's return, and the people's wildly enthusiastic reception of him, the choice became obvious, and it got support as well from leading members of the Institute such as Cabanis. The timing was perfect since Lucien Bonaparte had been elected president of the Council of Five Hundred on October 23, a week after his older brother's arrival.

18 BRUMAIRE COUP   On November 9, 1799 the plotters set into motion the last *coup d'état* of the Directory era, known as the coup of 18 Brumaire (the date according to the revolutionary calendar). This time, however, the goal was to change the regime itself. Barras, who preferred another general, simply resigned and stood aside; some said he took a massive bribe. The Council of Ancients voted to move the meetings of the two councils out of Paris to guard against a fictitious Jacobin plot. The next day at a former royal chateau in the suburb of Saint-Cloud, Bonaparte nearly bungled the plan by marching right into the Council of Five Hundred where he was greeted with outraged cries of "Down with the dictator!" from Jacobin deputies who now realized a coup was in the making. He fled the room and may even have fainted, but after a few moments of upheaval Lucien went outside and convinced the soldiers guarding the councils to intervene to save Bonaparte from "assassination" and disperse the deputies.

Over the next hours Lucien gathered together a rump of some 100 deputies to hastily and illegally approve a new regime led by three "consuls": Bonaparte, Sieyès, and one of the other former Directors and close colleague of Sieyès, Pierre-Roger Ducos. The move promised some continuity with the Directory regime, but a month later Bonaparte made clear his desire for sole authority; the new constitution named Bonaparte First Consul and he got new, more pliable, second and third consuls who essentially served as advisers. Lucien, now Minister of the Interior, falsified the ratification results to claim popular support for the new regime; in fact, fewer voted for it than had approved the never-implemented Constitution of 1793. Still, Bonaparte promised to continue the republic and make it stronger. He could count on popular support as long as France kept winning on the battlefield.

The first military coup in modern history had taken place, though few understood its significance at the time. The military had helped purge the legislature in 1797 but only by enforcing a government decision rather than displacing it altogether. France was about to embark on yet another adventure: an authoritarian government ruled by a general still active in the field. Bonaparte came to power by using military force and his military reputation. He did not, however, install a military dictatorship. He would maintain the trappings of a civilian government even while favoring his military comrades and his own family members. Ultimately, like his rise, his fall would be determined by the fortunes of France's armed forces.

Documents

DOCUMENT 4.1

The Law of 22 Prairial Year II (10 June 1794) Limiting Rights of Defendants

One of the great mysteries and controversies of the French Revolution was created by the Law of 22 Prairial that severely limited the rights of defendants. Since the government had defeated most of its enemies, both internal and external, why did the Committee of Public Safety continue to enlarge its definition of suspect behavior and demand even more draconian punishments? More than half of all those condemned to death by the revolutionary court in Paris were sentenced in June and July 1794. The law

*created such broad categories for treason that many believed that no one
could be safe under such circumstances.*

Article 4. The revolutionary court is instituted to punish the enemies of
the people.

Article 5. The enemies of the people are those who seek to destroy public
liberty, either by force or by cunning.

Article 6. The following are deemed enemies of the people: those who
would instigate the re-establishment of royalty, or have sought to disparage
or dissolve the National Convention and the revolutionary and republican
government of which it is the center; those who have betrayed the Republic
in the command of places and armies, or in any other military function,
provided intelligence to the enemies of the Republic, [or] labored to disrupt
the provisioning or servicing of the armies; those who have sought to impede
the provisioning of Paris or to create scarcity within the Republic; those who
have supported the designs of the enemies of France, either by shielding the
hideaways and impunity of conspirators and aristocrats, by persecuting and
insulting patriotism, by corrupting the authorized representatives of the
people, or by abusing the principles of the Revolution or the laws or measures
of the government by false and perfidious applications of them; . . . those
who have sought to inspire discouragement in order to favor the enterprises
of the tyrants leagued against the Republic; those who have disseminated
false news in order to divide or upset the people; those who have sought to
mislead opinion and to prevent the instruction of the people, to deprave
morals and corrupt the public conscience, to undermine the energy and the
purity of revolutionary and republican principles, or to stop the progress
thereof either by counter-revolutionary or insidious writings, or any other
machination; . . . those who, charged with public office, take advantage of it
in order to serve the enemies of the Revolution, to harass patriots, or to
oppress the people; finally, all who are designated in previous laws relative
to the punishment of conspirators and counterrevolutionaries, and who, by
whatever means or with whatever outward appearances they disguise
themselves, have made an attempt against the liberty, unity, and security of
the Republic, or worked to prevent its strengthening.

Article 7. The penalty provided for all offenses under the jurisdiction of the
revolutionary tribunal is death . . . .

Article 13. If either material or moral proofs exist, apart from proof from
witnesses, there shall be no hearing of witnesses, unless such formality
appears necessary, either to discover accomplices or for other important
considerations of public interest . . . .

Article 16. The law provides patriotic jurors as the counsel for unjustly
accused patriots; it accords none at all to conspirators.

Source: *Archives Parlementaires*, vol. 91 (Paris, 1976): 483–485.

Questions on the law of 22 Prairial

1   Consider Robespierre's speech on public morality (Chapter 3, Document 3.2). Does it provide the blueprint for this law?

2   Consider Article 16, which lays out in very ambiguous terms why no counsel for the defense was allowed. Why would this article be especially troubling?

DOCUMENT 4.2

The invasion of Egypt

As is the case with all memoirs, the likelihood of bias or self-serving motives must be considered and the memoirs of Louis Fauvelet de Bourrienne, an intimate of Bonaparte from childhood on, is certainly no exception. The memoirs were only published in 1829, long after the events in question. Because he served as Bonaparte's private secretary at the time of the invasion, his account nonetheless affords rare access to the motives and perceptions of the general. These excerpts come from the first few months after the landing in Egypt in 1798 and explain French hopes and disillusionment as the latter arose.

First excerpt:
HEADQUARTERS ON BOARD THE "ORIENT," The 4th Messidor, Year VI. [June 22, 1798]

BONAPARTE, MEMBER OF THE NATIONAL INSTITUTE, GENERAL-IN-CHIEF.

SOLDIERS—
    You are about to undertake a conquest the effects of which on civilization and commerce are incalculable. The blow you are about to give to England will be the best aimed, and the most sensibly felt, she can receive until the time arrives when you can give her her deathblow.
    We must make some fatiguing marches; we must fight several battles; we shall succeed in all we undertake. The destinies are with us. The Mameluke Beys who favour exclusively English commerce, whose extortions oppress our merchants, and who tyrannise over the unfortunate inhabitants of the Nile, a few days after our arrival will no longer exist.
    The people amongst whom we are going to live are Mahometans. The first article of their faith is this: "There is no God but God, and Mahomet is his prophet." Do not contradict them. Behave to them as you have behaved to the Jews—to the Italians. Pay respect to their muftis, and their Imaums, as you did to the rabbis and the bishops. Extend to the ceremonies prescribed by the Koran and to the mosques the same toleration which you showed to the synagogues, to the religion of Moses and of Jesus Christ.

The Roman legions protected all religions. You will find here customs different from those of Europe. You must accommodate yourselves to them. The people amongst whom we are to mix differ from us in the treatment of women; but in all countries he who violates is a monster. Pillage enriches only a small number of men; it dishonours us; it destroys our resources; it converts into enemies the people whom it is our interest to have for friends.

The first town we shall come to was built by Alexander. At every step we shall meet with grand recollections, worthy of exciting the emulation of Frenchmen.

BONAPARTE.

Second excerpt: July 1798

The march of the French army to Cairo was attended by an uninterrupted succession of combats and victories. . . . The Mamelukes were defeated, and their chief, Mourad Bey, was obliged to fly into Upper Egypt. Bonaparte found no obstacle to oppose his entrance into the capital of Egypt, after a campaign of only twenty days.

No conqueror, perhaps, ever enjoyed a victory so much as Bonaparte, and yet no one was ever less inclined to abuse his triumphs.

We entered Cairo on the 24th of July, and the General-in-Chief immediately directed his attention to the civil and military organization of the country. Only those who saw him in the vigour of his youth can form an idea of his extraordinary intelligence and activity. Nothing escaped his observation. Egypt had long been the object of his study; and in a few weeks he was as well acquainted with the country as if he had lived in it ten years. He issued orders for observing the strictest discipline, and these orders were punctually obeyed.

The mosques, the civil and religious institutions, the harems, the women, the customs of the country—all were scrupulously respected. A few days after they entered Cairo the French were freely admitted into the shops, and were seen sociably smoking their pipes with the inhabitants, assisting them in their occupations, and playing with their children.

The day after his arrival in Cairo Bonaparte addressed to his brother Joseph the following letter, which was intercepted and printed. Its authenticity has been doubted, but I saw Napoleon write it, and he read it to me before he sent it off.

CAIRO,
7th. Thermidor (25 July 1798)
You will see in the public papers the bulletins of the battles and conquest of Egypt, which were sufficiently contested to add another wreath to the laurels of this army. Egypt is richer than any country in the world in coin, rice, vegetables, and cattle. But the people are in a state of utter barbarism. We cannot procure money, even to pay the troops. I may be in France in two months.

Engage a country-house, to be ready for me on my arrival, either near Paris or in Burgundy, where I mean to pass the winter. . . .

(Signed) BONAPARTE

When alone with me he gave free vent to his emotion. I observed to him that the disaster [of the loss of the French fleet at Aboukir Bay] was doubtless great . . . "Let us then wait patiently to see what the Directory will do for us."—"The Directory!" exclaimed he angrily, "the Directory is composed of a set of scoundrels! they envy and hate me, and would gladly let me perish here. Besides, you see how dissatisfied the whole army is: not a man is willing to stay."

The pleasing illusions which were cherished at the outset of the expedition vanished long before our arrival in Cairo. Egypt was no longer the empire of the Ptolemies, covered with populous and wealthy cities; it now presented one unvaried scene of devastation and misery. Instead of being aided by the inhabitants, whom we had ruined, for the sake of delivering them from the yoke of the beys, we found all against us: Mamelukes, Arabs, and fellahs. No Frenchman was secure of his life who happened to stray half a mile from any inhabited place, or the corps to which he belonged. The hostility which prevailed against us and the discontent of the army were clearly developed in the numerous letters which were written to France at the time, and intercepted.

Source: Louis Antoine Fauvelet de Bourrienne, *Memoirs of Napoleon Bonaparte*, ed. R.W. Phipps, 4 vols. (New York, 1891), available at http://www.gutenberg.org/files/3567/3567-h/3567-h.htm#linklink2HCH0013, vol. I: chapters 13, 14.

Questions on the invasion of Egypt

1   How did the invasion fit Bonaparte's overall plan for conquest?

2   Using this document and the text chapter, what reasons can you suggest for his abrupt change of heart toward the Egyptians?

3   Are there specific aspects of this document that encourage a belief that these descriptions accurately reflect Bonaparte's views?

TIMELINE TO CHAPTER 4

| June 8, 1794 | Festival of the Supreme Being presided over by Robespierre. |
| June 10, 1794 | Law of 22 Prairial limiting rights of defendants. |

July 27, 1794	9 Thermidor; the fall and execution of Robespierre, Saint-Just, Couthon, and allies on the city council.
August 1, 1794	Repeal of Law of 22 Prairial.
April 1–2, 1795	March on the Convention demanding "bread and the Constitution of 1793."
May 20–23, 1795	Deputies order the military to suppress populist demonstrations.
October 5, 1795	Royalist uprising in Paris smashed by the military.
May 1796	Arrest of radical Gracchus Babeuf and members of the Conspiracy of Equals.
September 1797	Fructidor coup; two royalist directors purged.
October 1797	Treaty of Campoformio between France and Austria recognizes new Cisalpine Republic, one of many new sister republics.
May 1798	Floréal coup against newly elected Jacobins to the Convention.
May–October, 1798	Irish rebellion against British fails.
July 1798	Bonaparte invades Egypt.
August 1–3, 1798	Defeat of the French at the Battle of the Nile.
November 9, 1799	18 Brumaire; Bonaparte comes to power in the final coup of the Directory regime.

QUESTIONS ABOUT CHAPTER 4

1   Compare the governing system of the Directory to that of the Committee of Public Safety. How did the Directors seek to change political direction? What were the major problems—even as it came into existence—that this system would face?

2   The Directory was a government with no desire to return to the Old Regime. How was this reflected in its policies?

3   Scholars have long asserted that it was the revolutionary ethos that made the French armies so strong. Argue for or against this premise.

4   Was the creation of satellite states and the desire to control Egypt part of one policy or two disconnected policies?

5

From Bonapartist republic to Napoleonic empire, 1800–1807

Napoleon Bonaparte cuts such an extraordinary figure on the stage of world history that it is hard to fathom that he had no script in mind for taking or exercising power. The evidence for improvisation is nonetheless compelling. Between 1799 and 1804, Bonaparte, First Consul, made himself First Consul for life, then Napoleon I, Emperor of the French with a right of dynastic succession. In the beginning he ruled from the center, then he moved to the right by creating a new nobility and entourage of courtiers, yet he also guaranteed certain revolutionary achievements including equality under the law, careers open to talent, and the transfer of the Catholic Church's properties to lay buyers. Although he refused to allow any organized opposition, Napoleon carefully calibrated every move; he made sure that he retained the support of landed and financial elites as well as popular interest in his exploits at home and abroad.

Consolidating executive authority at home enabled Napoleon to pursue his global ambitions, but even here he improvised. As the Egyptian expedition had shown in 1799, Napoleon dreamed of creating a global empire, but the failures of the same expedition also foretold its limits; British naval superiority would force him to concentrate on Continental Europe. And concentrate he did. Napoleon took personal charge of the French military and led it to almost unimaginable conquests in Europe. By 1808 he had remodeled Europe by introducing dramatic changes in laws and governments, even while transforming the sister republics into kingdoms run by members of his own family or personal favorites. The world had not experienced such a whirlwind for centuries, and it was therefore fitting that the nineteenth-century German philosopher of history G. W. F. Hegel called him "world-historical" and compared him to Alexander the Great and Julius Caesar.

Improvising authoritarianism

The new regime got off to a promising start. In contrast to previous legislative upheavals, no executions of deputies and remarkably few purges of political personnel took place; many of those in office decided to support the new government in the hopes that it would ensure greater stability. The nature of this regime was far from certain, however. Bonaparte had easily out-maneuvered Sieyès, who had hoped the general would be willing to assume a largely ceremonial post as "Elector." Bonaparte had no intention of becoming "a disembodied shadow of a do-nothing king," and the new hastily written constitution reflected his views. It had no declaration of rights, and in the proclamation that accompanied its publication, the three consuls emphasized above all else the need to "end uncertainty" and institute powers that would be "strong and stable." "Citizens," they proclaimed, "the Revolution has stabilized on the principles that started it: it is completed." The Revolution had ended but not been rejected.

BONAPARTE'S CONSTITUTION   The complex structure mandated by the constitution fooled no one as to its basic principles: Bonaparte exercised sole authority, the legislature served as a rubber stamp, and the voters were limited to naming lists of men considered capable from which the government handpicked its officials. The republic was now a republic in name only; Bonaparte was effectively the sole representative of the nation. The constitution explicitly named him First Consul for a 10-year repeatable term with the power to appoint the members of a Council of State and all the ministers, ambassadors, government officials, civil and criminal judges and officers in the armed forces. It granted Bonaparte the fabulous salary of 500,000 francs a year; the pay for the rank he held in 1793 of artillery captain was 3,500 francs. The other two consuls earned 150,000 francs each; members (not "deputies," which implied popular representation) of the legislature earned 10–15,000 francs.

As a consolation prize for Sieyès and Roger Ducos, a Senate of lifetime members was formed; the two former consuls were named to it and given charge of co-opting the other 58 members. The meetings of the Senate were closed to the public. From the lists sent up by the voters, the Senate chose the members of the Tribunate and Legislative Body and the Supreme Court judges. In principle the senators would appoint future consuls. They also decided on the constitutionality of laws that the Tribunate might question. In fact, however, the Senators knew what they owed to Bonaparte; they had a lifetime annual sinecure of 25,000 francs. To seal the deal, Bonaparte handed Sieyès a landed estate near Paris worth 480,000 francs.

Laws could be proposed only by the central government; ministers suggested laws, the Council of State drew them up, a Tribunate of 100 members discussed them, and then a Legislative Body of 300 members voted on them without further discussion. Limited seating for spectators prevented public participation, and the press was muzzled; the government immediately shut down 60 of 73 newspapers in Paris. "If I give it free reign," Bonaparte admitted, "I shall not remain in power for three months."

The legislature was reduced to an advisory role, and in any case, its members were appointed through a convoluted system. All adult males except servants could vote but sent only 10 percent of their number to the communal assembly. By the time candidates were listed for the highest offices, only 0.1 percent of adult males were eligible. Moreover, the government soon drew up lists of the 600 highest taxpayers in each department, known as "notables," and it was from those lists that the government inevitably chose the highest officials and members of the legislatures. In this way, Bonaparte aimed to attract the rich and prominent to his regime and minimize any political pressure from the voters.[1]

Enforcing peace

It is one thing to rule from the top and quite another to make authority present on the local level. Upon taking power, Bonaparte moved quickly to reverse the flow of authority from the local level upward; it would now run downward from his person. A law of February 1800 established a new cadre of officials to run the affairs of each department and report directly to the government. Every department would be assigned a prefect (*préfet*, still the top departmental official in France), and each district (*arrondissement*) in the department would have a deputy prefect. With the help of his brother Lucien, now Minister of the Interior, Bonaparte selected the prefects within two weeks' time. The First Consul also appointed the deputy prefects and the mayors of all cities of more than 5,000 people; the prefects named the mayors of smaller towns. The government almost immediately ordered the prefects to provide comprehensive reports on the state of affairs in their departments, in part to gauge public opinion on the change of regime, and in part to take preventive measures wherever necessary. To maintain order the new government increased by 50 percent the size of the national police force (*gendarmerie*) created in 1791.

Bonaparte relied on an astutely timed alternation of accommodation and repression to maintain his authority. He met personally with leaders of the Vendée rebellion, promised amnesty to those who would lay down arms, and at the same time showed no mercy to those who continued to resist. Columns of gendarmes, national guards, and regular soldiers swept through areas of royalist and Catholic rebellion in the west and southeast killing rebels who took them on, arresting suspected brigands, and carrying out some 2,300 executions ordered by military courts between 1800 and 1802. When Count

Louis de Frotté, the leader of royalist bands wreaking havoc in Normandy, gave himself up in February 1800, he was executed by firing squad along with his staff. Some whispered that Bonaparte wanted revenge for Frotté telling tales about Bonaparte fainting when his coup threatened to unravel.

Bonaparte wanted to suppress rebellion as soon as possible because he needed troops for the resumption of war with Austria. As he secretly formed a new Army of the Reserve out of troops freed up from internal pacification, he made his position clear: "Our task is not to defend our own frontiers but to invade the territory of our foes." The Russian tsar had withdrawn from the Second Coalition, and the French leader saw his chance to regain territories recently lost in Italy and southern Germany; the British refused Bonaparte's disingenuous offer of peace, but they had no intention of engaging at that point in a costly land war. They would use their two to one superiority over the French in fighting ships to blockade some French ports and bombard any coastal towns that the French controlled on the Italian coast.

VICTORY OVER THE SECOND COALITION   While the Army of the Rhine under General Jean Moreau moved into Bavaria in order to cut off one of the Austrian armies, Bonaparte audaciously marched his 35,000 men of the Army of the Reserve right over the 8,000-foot high Great Saint Bernard Pass in the Alps in mid-May 1800. The cannon had to be dragged through the snow inside tree trunks. With the Austrians caught unaware, the French easily seized Milan on the other side of the mountains and re-established the Cisalpine Republic. In June Bonaparte nonetheless nearly lost a major battle at the village of Marengo because he divided his troops in an effort to find the enemy and ended up fighting with only half his men. The others came up just in time and pushed the Austrians back, but one of Bonaparte's closest comrades from Egypt, 31-year-old General Louis Desaix, was shot dead at the beginning of the counter-attack.

PEACE WITH AUSTRIA   Bonaparte returned to Paris and left other generals to occupy much of northern Italy. Moreau continued his march eastward, defeating the Austrians in December 1800 in the forests near Hohenlinden, 16 miles east of Munich. With the road to Vienna now open, the Austrians finally sought peace. By the treaty of 1801 the Austrians confirmed all the French gains of the 1797 Treaty of Campoformio: the annexation of Belgium and territories along the left (west) bank of the Rhine and the existence of the Batavian, Helvetic, Ligurian, and Cisalpine Republics.[2]

PEACE WITH BRITAIN   Bonaparte wanted a broader peace in order to consolidate his regime. When William Pitt was forced to resign as British prime minister after 17 years in office, the British came to terms; in 1802 they agreed to give back most of the colonial territories they had occupied in exchange for the French leaving Egypt, the Papal States, and territories of the Kingdom of Naples. Britain controlled India, but France now dominated Continental Europe.

Spain had already ceded the eastern half of Hispaniola (the western half was French Saint-Domingue) to France in 1795 and by a secret treaty in 1800 gave back to France Louisiana, a massive territory west of the United States that was more than twice the size of metropolitan France. Taking back Louisiana, lost during the Seven Years' War, became possible when the First Consul's older brother Joseph negotiated a convention with the United States in 1800 ending a "quasi-war" in which French privateers seized American ships and the United States embargoed all trade with France. The French also signed agreements with Russia, Prussia, and even the Ottoman Empire, which now feared British influence in Egypt. Looking back on this period, Talleyrand, Bonaparte's foreign minister, boasted that France in only two and a half years had gained "a power, a glory, and an influence beyond any an ambitious mind could have desired for her."

Building support at home

Despite all his success abroad, Bonaparte knew he still had enemies at home. He kept on Fouché as Minister of Police, and the cunning former de-Christianizer unraveled several plots. One attempt nearly succeeded, however. The evening of December 24, 1800, a street vendor's cart blew up just as the coaches carrying Bonaparte and members of his family to the opera passed by. Bonaparte escaped injury and continued on to a rapturous welcome at the opera, but the blast killed several bystanders and wounded dozens. Although Fouché eventually ferreted out the royalists who set the bomb, Bonaparte used the occasion to get rid of his most prominent Jacobin opponents; he had the Senate condemn 130 Jacobins to deportation without trial.

In contrast, the First Consul bent over backwards to reconcile former nobles and Catholic clergy. Although the constitution expressly forbade the return of émigrés, he had the official list of émigrés closed in March 1800 and encouraged requests for removal from the list. Lafayette was one of the first beneficiaries; he returned and recovered most of his lands but refused Bonaparte's offer of a position in the Senate. In April 1802 a general amnesty was offered to any émigré who returned to France by September of that year and swore an oath of loyalty to the constitution; the only exceptions were those who led insurrections. The returning émigrés were kept under police surveillance, and the regime guaranteed the sales of legally confiscated lands.

CONCORDAT WITH POPE In 1801 Bonaparte oversaw negotiations of a Concordat that regularized relations with the Pope (see Box 5.1). The First Consul wanted to reconcile French Catholics to his regime, and the Pope, whose predecessor had died in French captivity, wanted to bring France back into the Catholic fold. Bonaparte's own attitude was utilitarian: "There must be

BOX 5.1 CHURCH–STATE RELATIONS DURING THE FRENCH REVOLUTION

Eighteenth-century background

	Catholic Church, state church of France, with monarch as leader of the church.
	On the eve of the revolution, some toleration for Protestants and Jews.
Aug. 26, 1789	Declaration of the Rights of Man and Citizen grants freedom of religion.

Remaking the Church to accommodate the Revolution

November 2, 1789	Church lands seized to provide funds for the Revolution.
July 12, 1790	Civil Constitution of the Clergy reforms Catholic Church, including more equitable pay for clergy, a reduction in the number of parish priests and bishops, and most controversially, the election of clergy.
November 27, 1790	Clergy, to qualify for positions in the Constitutional Church, must take an oath to support the revolution.

Resistance and repression

1791	Almost half of the clerics refuse to take oath.
March–April 1791	Pope rejects the civil constitution, threatening to excommunicate those who take the oath.
May 27, 1792	Refractory priests may be deported: after Oct. 1792 may be executed (estimated 30–40,000 deported and 2,000 or more executed in coming months).
1793	Armed rebellion intensified significantly in response to revolutionary challenges to Catholic Church.
September 1793	De-Christianization begins: the government of the Terror recognizes only morality not religion, movement winds down gradually in spring 1794.
1794–1799	Thermidorians and Directory retract many repressive measures, but after a royalist uprising (Oct. 5, 1795) the government restores previous legislation regarding clerics, though in coming years gradually loosens it.

Napoleonic intervention to effect compromise

| 1801 | Concordat. |
| | Catholicism recognized as the religion of most French people, but not the official state religion. |

	Selection of clergy restored to the bishops but Napoleon picks the bishops.
	State would pay clergy, but confirm ownership of former church lands to those who purchased them when the church was nationalized.
1804	Coronation of Emperor.
	Pope in attendance but Napoleon usurps Pope's role by crowning himself.

a religion for the people, but this religion must be in the hands of the government." He had already allowed people to choose between Sunday and the *décadi* of the revolutionary calendar for their day off.

The Pope agreed to recognize officially the French republic and renounce any effort to reclaim church lands that had been nationalized. In exchange, the Civil Constitution of the Clergy and the required clerical oath of allegiance to it were suppressed. All previous bishops, those who took the oath and those who did not, were removed. In line with the general drift of the regime, voters no longer elected bishops and parish priests. Bonaparte got the right to name bishops, though they only held office once invested by the Pope, and the bishops chose the parish priests. The First Consul deliberately selected a mixture of Old Regime, revolutionary, and new centrist bishops. The document said nothing about the monasteries and convents that had been shuttered. Bonaparte and his advisors remained hostile to the revival of male religious orders unless they were devoted to overseas missionary work, but they allowed the gradual revival of female orders to provide education, nursing, and care of the poor.

Catholicism did not become the official state religion; it was simply the religion of the great majority of French people. Jews and Protestants could continue to practice openly. After a brief experiment with the separation of church and state initiated in 1795, the government returned to paying the Catholic clergy's salaries (it also paid those of Protestant ministers), and Bonaparte had no intention of giving Rome the upper hand over the French church. When the legislature finally accepted the Concordat in time for Easter services in 1802, and after the Pope had publicly promulgated his half of the bargain, the First Consul unilaterally released a series of "Organic Articles" that asserted the primacy of the French state over the French church; no papal bulls, briefs, or legates could be received in France without permission of the government. The Pope had no choice but to swallow his fury at this sleight of hand. After a decade of upheaval France's overwhelmingly Catholic population breathed a collective sigh of relief; under the Directory parishioners, often led by women, had even resorted to breaking down the doors of boarded-up churches to hold impromptu masses, sometimes with a lay person officiating.[3]

From Easter 1802 onward Bonaparte used Catholic services alongside government festivals to underline his legitimacy. He kept only two revolutionary festivals, July 14 and the commemoration of the foundation of the republic on September 22, but he turned them into celebrations of his regime. He returned from his campaign in Italy in time for the festivities on July 14, 1800, significantly calling it the Festival of Concord, and used the occasion to officially mourn the battlefield death of his comrade Desaix, all the while keeping the focus on himself as the miraculous victor of Marengo. He ordered portraits of himself from all the major artists, especially David, and had them placed prominently in public buildings where previously only allegories of the Republic served as decoration. The cult of personality had begun.

Pursuing the same objective of melding together Old Regime and revolutionary elements in new institutions, Bonaparte began to break through the economic logjams left by a decade of revolution. In early 1800 he announced himself as the first shareholder and official protector of a new Bank of France with a capitalization of 30,000,000 francs. Necker's dream of turning the *Caisse d'Escompte* into a truly national bank was gradually realized. Two of the regents of the new bank were Old Regime bankers who had managed to survive the Terror and even create new banks during the Directory that foreshadowed this one: the Swiss banker Jean Perregaux and Jean-Barthelemy Le Couteulx de Canteleu, a deputy in the National Assembly, ardent supporter of Necker, deputy in the Council of Ancients, and member of one of France's most influential banking and manufacturing families. In 1803 the Bank got the exclusive right to circulate paper money in Paris, which became legal tender all over France in 1808.

For the most part, however, the regime relied on metallic currency, and to do so more successfully it standardized coinage: in 1803 the government set the 5 gram silver one franc piece as the basis for all currency exchange, including gold. Gold would henceforth trade at 15.5 times the value of silver, and the one franc piece would be 9/10ths silver. In this way, the face value of coins was tied directly to the value of metal in them. Coins were decimalized, that is, they followed the metric system. Over time the new one franc coin served as the US dollar of its day for international trade. Coinage could reinforce the regime in even more direct ways; the same decree of 1803 ordered that all coins be stamped on one side with the head of Bonaparte and the legend "First Consul," and that the reverse side have two olive branches with the legend "French Republic."

With the help of his Minister of Finance, Martin Gaudin, who had been a financial official under the Old Regime and during the revolutionary decade,

Bonaparte established firm central control of state finances, including drawing up honest budgets. Peace enabled him to balance a budget that devoted 60 percent of revenues to the military in wartime. In the early years of the regime, moreover, many segments of the population prospered; the values of land and wages were all increasing, and the return to metallic currency kept inflation in check. The government initially relied on direct taxes, most of them introduced in the early 1790s, but to meet mounting war expenses after 1803 it revived the Old Regime tax on salt and monopoly of tobacco and introduced a tax on alcohol. Continuing policies developed under the Directory, the government turned to resources from conquered territories to make ends meet and did so increasingly in the last years of the regime.

First Consul for Life

Having made peace and set in motion an amalgamation of the Old Regime and the republic, Bonaparte now took the next step. In May 1802 the Second Consul, Jean-Jacques Cambacérès, previously a deputy to the Convention and the Council of Five Hundred, officially requested a plebiscite to ask the voters whether Napoleon Bonaparte should be made First Consul for Life. Forty percent of eligible men voted, a high number compared to previous regimes, and almost all of them registered a public "yes" vote.[4]

CONSUL FOR LIFE   As soon as the Senate officially named him Consul for Life, Bonaparte demanded a new constitution, which cut the size of the Tribunate in half and closed its meetings to the public and gave the First Consul the right to draw up treaties without legislative approval and to name his own successor. The Senate got new powers, too: it governed the colonies, could suspend trial by jury, overturn judicial verdicts, and dissolve the Tribunate and Legislative Body. These theoretical powers ran up against the reality that Bonaparte could name anyone he wanted to the Senate. Elections now lost meaning; voters chose members of electoral colleges at the local level, but at the departmental level members had to be selected from the list of the 600 highest taxpayers, and those chosen served for life. The First Consul named the presidents of the colleges, even at the local level.

From the very beginning, Bonaparte had aimed to reorganize French society by putting social elites in charge, but after 1802, he began to distinguish those elites in new ways, eventually creating a new kind of nobility based on service to the state. Nearly a quarter of the prefects he named in 1800 were former nobles and that proportion only rose over time. As he said in May 1802, when proposing the establishment of a Legion of Honor, the nation was "so many grains of sand." What it needed was the erection of "a few great granite blocks on the sands of France." The Legion of Honor would recognize service, rather than wealth, but most of the decorations went to men who had distinguished themselves in battle. By the end of 1805 nearly 12,000 legionnaires had been named, a number that reached to more than 38,000 in 1814; less than 5 percent of them were civilians, and virtually all the civilians were high-ranking state or church officials. The Legion of Honor, with many more civilians, still exists today.

Even as the regime moved in a more aristocratic direction, it continued to offer promotion through merit. In 1802 the government introduced the *lycée*, which is still the cornerstone of French secondary education today (though now co-educational and without military trappings). The *lycée* was designed to combine the best elements of the Old Regime colleges run by religious orders with the central schools set up during the revolutionary decade. They offered a more up-to-date scientific and mathematics curriculum and competitive scholarships, but only 37 of them had been established by 1808. More than a third of the scholarships were reserved for the sons of soldiers or civilian administrators, and students wore uniforms and followed strictly regulated programs of instruction. Bonaparte did not believe in education for the lower classes or for women. He left primary schooling in the hands of the Catholic Church and local officials until 1808, when he tried to exert more state control, but he basically believed that the peasants and workers should learn only to remain politically passive. As for girls, he said that "public education does not suit them . . .; marriage is their whole destination."

Re-establishing slavery

Bonaparte's improvisational governing style was nowhere more on view than in his colonial policy. Having recovered colonies lost to Britain and regained Louisiana, he hoped to get back French control of Saint-Domingue and make the Caribbean and Louisiana the centerpieces of a revived world wide French empire. Officially, he announced the continuance of slavery in colonies where it had never been abolished (Martinique, Réunion) and emancipation where it had already occurred (Saint-Domingue, Guadeloupe); he also brought back the slave trade. He nonetheless hoped to eventually restore slavery everywhere. He sent 20,000 soldiers under the command of his brother-in-law Charles Leclerc with secret instructions to arrest Toussaint Louverture, the most successful of many black generals emerging from the slave revolt in Saint-Domingue.

REINTRODUCTION OF SLAVERY Leclerc was to disarm the black rebels, force the ex-slaves back onto the plantations and eventually re-establish plantation slavery. The First Consul ordered General Antoine Richepanse to reintroduce slavery in Guadeloupe, and though French forces quickly defeated a revolt against this decision, news of French intentions made its way to Saint-Domingue where it fueled a much more determined resistance.

Toussaint's decision to join the French in 1794 had changed the balance of forces on Saint-Domingue. Sonthonax and Polverel were recalled to France to explain their decision to offer emancipation, leaving the island with little in the way of republican leadership. Toussaint by then had 4,000 men under his command, and as the son of an African slave, he offered something to his men that the mixed-race commanders could not: a personal understanding of bondage. Moreover, since Toussaint had gained his freedom in 1776 and could read and write, he could stand up to any of the other free men of color. As the armies massed by Toussaint and the other commanders successfully pushed back the British and the Spanish invaders, Toussaint gradually established his dominance. Faced with the collapse of the plantation system, he endeavored to militarize labor, essentially forcing freed slaves to continue working.

Although Toussaint had an army of about 20,000 men by 1802, his efforts to centralize power in his own hands antagonized his many rivals. They stood by when Leclerc managed to capture the rebel leader and send him back to France. Toussaint died in prison in 1803, a martyr in the eyes of British and American abolitionists (he was recognized as a hero of the French Republic in 1998). The "war of extermination," as Leclerc described it, nevertheless proved much more difficult than anyone imagined; the French sent 10,000 more soldiers to Saint-Domingue to reinforce Leclerc, including thousands of Poles who hoped the French would reward them by supporting their demands for independence.

SAINT-DOMINGUE BECOMES HAÏTI   The freed slaves of Saint-Domingue had the last word. By the time of Toussaint's death, both Richepanse and Leclerc had died of yellow fever alongside thousands of their soldiers; 70 percent of the original expeditionary force died of disease. Seeing the futility of the even more murderous campaign undertaken by Leclerc's successor, which included gassing black prisoners in the holds of ships, Bonaparte withdrew his forces, sold Louisiana to the United States, and gave up on his dream of an empire spanning the entire globe. "Damn sugar, damn coffee, damn colonies!" was Bonaparte's response to the unexpected turn of events. The success of the slave revolt in Saint-Domingue thus paved the way to the westward expansion of the United States, including, ironically, the extension of slavery in the southern part of the Louisiana Territory. The rebels in Saint-Domingue declared the independence of Haïti in 1804 and before long served as a haven for other Latin American independence fighters (see Document 5.1). Slavery would not be finally abolished in the other French colonies until 1848.

The turn toward paternalism

Since Bonaparte believed that authority should flow downward and obedience upward, he favored bosses over workers, fathers over children, and husbands over wives. Laws passed in 1803 reaffirmed the 1791 injunction against worker's associations and strikes, especially those aimed at raising wages or decreasing hours, and revived the Old Regime worker's passbook (*livret*), issued by the local police. To change jobs, a worker had to give the new employer his passbook signed by his previous employer to attest that he had completed all his obligations. In 1806 the government set up arbitration councils in the major manufacturing cities, but by law the owners always had a majority and simple workers had to be represented by their foremen. Workers nonetheless kept their underground networks called *compagnonnages* alive; wherever they traveled workers in the same trade would know where to go to find a place to stay or information about possible employment.[5]

CODE NAPOLEON The regime's emphasis on the authority of social superiors got its clearest expression in new legal codes. Bonaparte brought to fruition the revolutionary effort to unify more than 300 different local codes. He did it by personally presiding over more than half of the 102 sessions of the Council of State devoted to the task; Cambacérès, who had been actively involved in the discussions of the Convention and the Directory in this area, supervised the others. The new civil code was completed in March 1804 and known after 1807 as the Code Napoleon. It reaffirmed legal equality, freedom of religion, the abolition of feudalism and hereditary privilege, and the secularization of the state.

In the domain of family law, however, the Code moved decisively backward by restoring the powers of fathers, many of which had been curtailed during the revolutionary decade. Although it carried forward the revolutionary insistence on equal inheritance, even for girls, it now allowed property-owners the free disposition of a quarter of their property. Illegitimate children could no longer inherit or seek recognition of paternity. "Society," Bonaparte maintained, "has no interest in having these bastards recognized." A father could even order his children aged 16 to 21 years old to be imprisoned up to six months. Minors had to have their fathers' permission to marry.

Bonaparte personally intervened in discussions of the code when the status of women was at issue, and the final product reflected his traditional Corsican belief in male superiority. When Germaine de Staël had challenged him at dinner at Talleyrand's in 1797 to name the greatest woman, past or present, he replied, "the one who has the most children." According to the new code, a husband owed his wife protection but a wife could not acquire property, contract a debt, work, or make a will without the husband's consent. Divorce was retained, perhaps because Bonaparte, though anything but loyal himself, was fed up with his wife's infidelities as well as her inability to give him an heir, but the grounds for divorce were now limited and introduced a double standard regarding adultery. A woman could only divorce her husband if he brought his mistress to live in the family house. A man could divorce his wife for adultery under any circumstances and even have her imprisoned. Divorce rates plummeted.

Emperor Napoleon I

Another foiled royalist attempt to assassinate Bonaparte prompted the First Consul to take the next step and have himself declared Emperor Napoleon I with the right of hereditary succession. A plebiscite on the question in May 1804 once again gained the overwhelming support of the voters, even though some staunch republicans, such as Carnot, opposed the move. Carnot, a member of the Tribunate, had also opposed making Bonaparte Consul for Life, but such dissent was relatively rare. "The time has come," explained a more pliable member of the Tribunate, "to leave the sea of dreams and approach the empire of reality. . . . The crown of Charlemagne is the just heritage for one who has known how to imitate him." The quote captured the essence of the move; Napoleon became emperor of the French, not France, by popular will that recognized his merit, not his birth.

Hereditary succession was introduced in order to give stability to a regime that depended on one person, but at the same time the emperor resolutely rejected any attempt to bring back the Bourbon monarchy. He had even given a pension to Robespierre's sister and a scholarship to the son of Desmoulins. He used the occasion of the British-financed conspiracy against him to kidnap and execute as a co-conspirator Louis Antoine de Bourbon, Duke of Enghien, tenth in line to the succession of Louis XVI. General Moreau, the victor of Hohenlinden, was also implicated, but Napoleon pardoned him since he was only too happy to have one of his military rivals banished to Pennsylvania (see Document 5.2).

The kidnapping and execution of Enghien scandalized many aristocrats who had been willing to accept Bonaparte. One of the most influential of them was the returned *émigré* Viscount François de Chateaubriand, who with his friend Germaine de Staël helped initiate the European-wide literary movement known as romanticism. Chateaubriand had embraced Bonaparte and even dedicated the second edition of his pro-Catholic work *The Genius of Christianity* to the First Consul. After the execution he resolutely opposed the emperor and was ordered not to live anywhere near Paris. De Staël had already been sent into exile in 1803, and Napoleon had been so irritated by her novel *Delphine* (1802) that he took the trouble to write a review attacking its "wrong-headed, antisocial, dangerous principles." What he really disliked was her influence; as he said, every time people saw her they liked him less.

EMPEROR NAPOLEON On Sunday December 2, 1804, Napoleon took a gold Roman-style crown of laurel wreath from the Pope's hands and crowned himself in front of 20,000 spectators at Notre Dame Cathedral in Paris, which in 1793 had notoriously served as a Temple of Reason (Figure 5.1). He then crowned his wife Joséphine as empress. Napoleon wore an ermine-lined cloak like the French kings and carried a medieval scepter for the ceremony that took place almost exactly 1,000 years after Charlemagne had been crowned emperor by the Pope in Rome (in December 800). This Pope came to Paris and watched while the emperor crowned himself in front of courtiers who dressed much like Old Regime nobles.

The coronation foreshadowed Napoleon's turn in an aristocratic direction. Between 1804 and 1814 his court expanded three-fold from 83 to 217 courtiers with official titles such as Grand Chamberlain and Grand Master of Ceremonies and special uniforms for every function. More than half of the courtiers came from the Old Regime nobility. The 150-page palace etiquette manual that Napoleon had drawn up laid out the various offices and even the kinds of chairs and tables appropriate for each room in the Tuileries, the former royal palace that had been originally assigned to all three consuls but which Napoleon took over in 1802 and made his imperial palace in 1804. Although he dressed most often in simple military uniform, Napoleon insisted that courtiers dress and act the parts he wrote for them.

FIGURE 5.1 *The Coronation of Emperor Napoleon I*
David's magnificent and monumental painting of the coronation scene was not finished until 1807. It captures the moment when Napoleon is about to crown his wife Joséphine, having already crowned himself with a golden laurel wreath, the laurel wreath being the crown of Roman emperors. Oil on canvas.

At the center of the imperial court was Napoleon's own family: his 54-year-old widowed mother Letizia, his one older and three younger brothers, his three sisters, and Joséphine's two children from her previous marriage, Hortense and Eugene Beauharnais. Even though his younger brother Lucien had helped bring him to power and was eventually named Senator, Napoleon excluded him from the line of succession when he refused to agree to an arranged marriage. After 1804 Lucien lived in exile in Italy and then Britain. The brothers Joseph and Louis (the latter married Joséphine's daughter Hortense in 1802) were named Imperial Highnesses with the right of succession and given 1,000,000 francs a year and households of their own. Napoleon's sister Caroline married one of his right-hand men, Joachim Murat, in 1800; the son of a farmer who rose rapidly through the ranks, Murat had helped Bonaparte put down the uprising in Paris against the Convention in 1796, served with him in Egypt, and was named Marshal of France in 1804. Like most of the family members, he would go on to hold even more exalted titles in the years to come. Napoleon's brothers, Murat, Fouché, and Cambacérès were all freemasons; Joseph became Grand Master the month before the coronation. Napoleon could have suppressed the network, but instead he allowed it to continue as a base of his support. Not surprisingly, this perpetuation gave added support to the idea that the freemasons formed a conspiratorial network with outsized political influence.

Once war resumed and France made further conquests, Napoleon set up a system of donations in 1806 by which he gave loyal followers grants of lands confiscated in enemy territories. By 1815 he had handed over 30 million francs worth of land to 6,000 individuals. The final step toward re-establishing an aristocracy was taken in 1808 when Cambacérès, Arch-Chancellor since 1804 with an annual salary of 333,333 francs, proposed that the Senate set up a series of new titles for those who had given the nation exceptional service. Never explicitly called a nobility, the titles of prince, duke, count, baron, and chevalier of the empire certainly recalled it, especially once those named gained the right to pass their titles on to their heirs, which they did if they could guarantee a certain level of wealth. Between 1808 and 1814, Napoleon gave out 3,263 titles; 59 percent went to the military, 22 percent to high state functionaries, and 17 percent to other notables. Nearly a quarter came from Old Regime noble families because Napoleon hoped to integrate them with his new regime. The highest-ranking princes and dukes (there were only 34 of them in total) came from the family (Joseph, Louis, Murat) or high state office (Cambacérès, Third Consul Charles Lebrun, Talleyrand, Fouché, and Gaudin). The number of imperial nobles was much smaller than the number of nobles under the Old Regime, and they enjoyed no legal privileges, only status and honor.[6]

After 1804 Napoleon took various measures he could not implement earlier for fear of antagonizing republicans. In September 1805 the government announced the suppression of the revolutionary calendar. The emperor insisted on eliminating the Tribunate in 1807 because it had been the one place where members like Carnot had spoken against the Concordat, the Legion of Honor, and Bonaparte's elevation to emperor. Although the government had already eliminated the Class of Moral and Political Sciences of the National Institute in 1803 because its subject matter encouraged criticism, it was only in 1807 that its preferred news outlet, *La Décade philosophique*, was suppressed. The government reduced the number of printers allowed in Paris by two-thirds. In a less official but no less significant fashion, Napoleon encouraged the return of "Monsieur" [Mister, Sir] to daily speech, displacing the more egalitarian "citizen."

To reinforce his image, already widely seen in paintings, prints, and on coins and described daily in the largely official press, the emperor intended to make Paris into the capital of an empire modeled on ancient Rome and filled with monuments to his military triumphs and glory. It was no longer enough to bring back Italy's treasures to display in the Louvre Museum; Roman-style triumphal columns and arches now dotted Paris. Using Trajan's Column of 113 A.D. as a model, construction began in 1805 on a column in the Place Vendôme dedicated to the victories of Napoleon's armies. The first stone of the massive Arc de Triomphe at the end of the Champs-Elysées was laid on the emperor's birthday, August 15, 1806. At the same time construction started on a smaller, but still 63-foot high triumphal arch, the Arc du Carrousel, in front of the Tuileries palace. The four bronze horses from Saint Mark's basilica in Venice, the only surviving example in Europe of an ancient quadriga (triumphal chariot drawn by four horses abreast), sat on top. Because the arch was quickly finished, Napoleon regularly used it for public processions celebrating his victories. Like the Arc de Triomphe, two neo-classical buildings begun in 1807 and 1808—the church of the Madeleine and the Bourse (Stock Exchange)— were only completed after Napoleon's fall from power. They nonetheless testify, even today, to the emperor's grandiose vision of his regime.[7]

War again

The resumption of war in 1803 had made the question of succession even more urgent for Napoleon and his inner circle. Neither the British nor the French really wanted peace. The British had no intention of letting Napoleon dictate to Europe, which was clearly his goal, especially now that British ships and the loss of Saint-Domingue threatened his plans for a more global reach. In early 1803, even as the French were losing control of Saint-Domingue, Napoleon supervised the consolidation of 268 separate German states, some only cities, into 82 larger ones that would be less dependent on the protection of the Holy Roman Emperor. He had already annexed Piedmont in northern Italy and had himself elected President of the Italian Republic, which under his tutelage replaced the Cisalpine Republic. He also named himself "mediator" (essentially protector) for what was now called the Helvetic Confederation of Swiss states. In other words, Napoleon continued to extend his dominance over Europe even in peacetime. After the British refused to evacuate Malta as promised in the peace terms and put an embargo on all trade with France and the Batavian Republic, both sides went to war in May 1803. With brief interruptions, it continued until 1815, pulled in most of Europe's powers at one time or another, and had repercussions around the world.

RESUMPTION OF WAR Britain had naval superiority but could not mount a large army to fight in Europe because so many of its forces were needed in Ireland, the Caribbean, and India to protect its far-flung colonial and commercial empire; three-quarters of the British army of 114,000 was stationed overseas with no less than 20,000 of them in Ireland alone. Two major consequences followed: Britain had to seek alliances in Europe; and Napoleon set out to crush his nemesis before they could succeed. The British press had been reviling and ridiculing the emperor and spreading stories of atrocities he had encouraged in Egypt, his wife's infidelities, his religious hypocrisy, and his Corsican sadistic streak. British caricatures now showed him as "little Boney," a diminutive figure dwarfed by his own hat (Figure 5.2).

As soon as war was declared, Napoleon ordered the arrest of all British subjects in France and sent troops to occupy Hanover, the German home territory of the Hanoverian king of Britain, George III. In preparation for invasion of England, he started construction of a flotilla of boats and by January 1804 had assembled 70,000 troops near Boulogne. On August 15, his birthday, he reviewed the troops, now 80,000 strong, and handed out crosses of the Legion of Honor in an elaborate pageant. If Britain could be defeated at home, Napoleon's dream of global empire might be attained after all.

"Everyone's imagination was drawn to the idea of the conquest of England," enthused Claire de Rémusat, lady-in-waiting to Joséphine, but the logistics of the operation proved intractable. Even the festivities in August 1804 turned sour; several of the hundreds of boats newly constructed in France and Holland sank in view of British telescopes across the Channel. As dinner was served in the evening, a heavy rain pounded the tents, reminding all present of the difficulties awaiting the fleet. By the end of 1804 more than 2,000 vessels waited to transport 127,000 troops, still some 40,000 less than planned. *The Times* of London used a parody of the famous soliloquy in Shakespeare's *Hamlet* to deride Napoleon's inability to close the deal:

T'invade, or not t'invade—that is the question—
Whether 'tis nobler in my soul, to suffer

FIGURE 5.2 *British Anti-Napoleon Cartoon*
This caricature published by William Holland with the title "General Monkey and General Wolfe!!" is typical of British anti-Napoleon propaganda from the time of the projected French invasion. Napoleon, in his over-sized hat, says in bad English, "Begar [*sic*], what a dam Giant, me wish I was safe away from him." Hand-colored etching, 1803.

> Those haughty Islanders to check my power
> Or to send forth my troops upon their coast
> And by attacking crush them. . . .
> To fight—perchance to fail: Aye, there's the rub . . .[8]

In January 1805 Napoleon secretly assured the Council of State that he had only spent such huge sums on the invasion in order to have his armies ready to attack on the continent.

He had not dropped the idea, however. Sensing the prospects offered by Spain declaring war on Britain the month before, Napoleon quickly revised his plan for the invasion; the French fleet in Toulon would join with the Spanish fleet and sail to the Caribbean in order to draw the British away from the Channel and then rapidly return to support an invasion in early June 1805. The Toulon fleet managed to escape British Vice-Admiral Nelson's detection, arrived in Cadiz in April, and proceeded as planned to the Caribbean. Nelson chased after them. At the same time Napoleon tried to divert attention by journeying to Milan and having himself crowned King of Italy, having turned the Italian Republic into a kingdom. He made his stepson Eugene vice-king, annexed Genoa and the Ligurian Republic to France, and made Lucca into a principality ruled by his sister Elisa, who was married to a Corsican general in his army. He explained his intentions to his closest associates: "Europe cannot be at rest," he claimed, "except under the rule of a single head who will have kings for his officers, who will distribute his kingdoms to his lieutenants."

Faced with the inevitable delays of travel at sea, Napoleon put off the invasion of England until August 1805. The Toulon fleet returned to Europe but rather than proceeding as ordered to meeting another French fleet at Brest, it retreated back to Cadiz to avoid the British. Furious upon learning this news in late August, Napoleon finally abandoned the invasion plan and redirected the troops to the east for an expected confrontation with Austria, which had joined the Third Coalition with Britain, Russia, and Sweden. They each had their own reasons for opposing Napoleon, but the British brought them together by offering massive subsidies; the Russians were promised £1.25 million annually for every 100,000 soldiers they put in the field. The alliance is called the Third Coalition because it was the third attempt to ally against France since 1789. Prussia stayed neutral at first, even though the British had offered them even bigger subsidies, but signed a secret agreement with the Russians in November promising to send an army to their aid in December.

Napoleon consolidated his armies under the name *Grande Armée* [great army] to signal his overall command and with nearly 200,000 soldiers he raced across the Rhine. Before the Russians could arrive with their 100,000 men, the French encircled the Austrian army at Ulm on the Danube River in Bavaria, an electorate whose ruler would soon ally with France and be allowed by Napoleon to call himself king. On October 20, 50,000 Austrian prisoners taken in the campaign filed in front of Napoleon. As the French proudly displayed the hundreds of cannon and thousands of horses captured at Ulm, the joint French and Spanish fleets prepared to sally forth against the British blocking their passage out of Cadiz. Eighteen French and 15 Spanish vessels faced off against 27 British ships on October 21 and were decimated in the Battle of Trafalgar, even though a sniper killed British commander Nelson. The French lost 13 ships, the Spanish nine, the British none. Some 450 British sailors died as compared to 3,400 French and 1,000 Spanish. Superior British tactics and gunnery had prevailed. The French navy never recovered from this crushing defeat, even though the government embarked on an ambitious program to build 150 new ships of the line.

Napoleon did not learn of the naval debacle at Trafalgar until November 17, and by then the *Grande Armée* had forced the Russians to retreat and taken Vienna. The army did not march as one unit, in large part because it had to forage for supplies, but the seven infantry corps had to remain close enough to provide support once contact was made with enemy forces. Murat commanded the 23,000 strong cavalry, and the seven infantry corps were led by generals of great talent including Augereau; Jean Bernadotte, who married a sister-in-law of Joseph Bonaparte; and Michel Ney, the son of a barrel maker. Napoleon headed farther east, leaving 20,000 troops in Vienna. The 27-year-old Russian Tsar Alexander I, who had taken personal command of his army, ordered his generals to attack the French because he believed that Napoleon's suggestion of an armistice reflected the weakness of the French position. This was the first of Napoleon's traps.

BATTLE OF AUSTERLITZ   Since the Austro-Russian force outnumbered his, Napoleon had to rely on deception, and his careful study of the potential battlefield outside the village of Austerlitz gave him two ideas, one that almost backfired and one that in the end resulted in an astonishing victory. First, he deliberately overextended his right flank in order to draw the enemy forces there; he intended to bring up reinforcements and catch them in a pincer movement. The ruse worked but the Austro-Russian army attacked further south than expected, so Napoleon decided to break through the center using his second idea. When surveying the terrain on horseback, he had seen that the morning fog would hide his men below the heights that he allowed the enemy to occupy.

As the sun rose on the first anniversary of his coronation on December 2, the French stormed the heights and after many wild swings of momentum back-and-forth, they divided the Austro-Russian forces and chased the Russians down across a frozen lake, where French artillery fire broke the ice swallowing men, horses, and cannon. The French cavalry pursued the enemy, but for the most part let them retreat because the rout was complete. The Austro-Russian forces suffered 15,000 casualties (dead or wounded) and gave up 12,000 prisoners. The French lost 1,300 dead and about 7,000 wounded. The cannon captured were melted down to form the Vendôme column in Paris.

On December 4, the Austrian emperor Francis II came to Napoleon in person to request an armistice, while the Russian tsar took his troops back home hoping to fight another day. Much to Tsar Alexander's dismay, the Prussians signed an agreement with France on December 15 to cede some small territories in exchange for Hanover and an official alliance with France that would eventually include closing their ports to British shipping. By the peace agreement signed on December 26, Austria gave Venice to the Kingdom of Italy, various Venetian possessions to France, and other territories to France's new German allies Bavaria, Württemberg, and Baden. Francis II lost 3 million subjects and one-sixth of his revenue and agreed to pay reparations of 50 million francs.

Napoleon was just getting started. Early in 1806 French troops once again occupied Naples, which had joined the enemy's coalition, and from there took over the south of Italy, chasing out Russian and British troops. Napoleon named his brother Joseph as King of Naples. At the same time, he transformed the Batavian Republic into a Kingdom and made his brother Louis King of Holland. The Senate was not even consulted. In July, Bavaria, Baden, Württemberg, and a gaggle of smaller German states consented to join a Confederation of the Rhine that had been drawn up by Talleyrand after he negotiated the peace treaty with Austria. The states of the Confederation promptly withdrew from the Holy Roman Empire, and Napoleon announced that France no longer recognized the 1,000-year-old Empire. Francis II had no choice but to dissolve the Holy Roman Empire and retrench as Austrian Emperor, if only to prevent Napoleon from taking the title of Holy Roman Emperor himself.

Napoleon thus set in motion a transformation of Europe; Italy was now more unified than it had been since the Roman Empire had collapsed 1,400 years before, and the German Confederation laid the foundations for future German unification. These changes were not just alterations of names. The Grand Empire, as Napoleon called it, had three major components: annexed territories, satellite kingdoms, and client states. Annexed territories were divided into departments, just like the rest of France, and got prefects, some of them local men, who gathered information, restored order, and sought local collaborators in establishing religious toleration and equality under the law. The kingdoms of Italy, Naples, and Holland were satellite kingdoms whose rulers, for obvious reasons, took the lead from Napoleon who wanted them to introduce French-style reforms. In 1806 the Napoleonic Code became the law in the Kingdom of Italy, and Joseph abolished the remnants of feudalism in the Kingdom of Naples. Although Napoleon sent the satellite kingdoms French advisers and gave them French rulers, local people manned the administrations. Napoleon did not hesitate, however, to carve out large chunks of land to give out as duchies or fiefs called donations to his inner circle. The German Confederation was the prime example of what would become over time an even more important element in the Napoleonic array, the client state. Like the annexed territories and satellite kingdoms, client states were expected to provide money and men to the Napoleonic war machine, which became increasingly dependent on them. The Confederation signed on to provide 65,000 soldiers (see Map 5.1).[9]

Defeating Prussia and Russia, but not Britain

Napoleon returned to Paris in January 1806 and stayed there eight months resolving domestic issues while keeping a close eye on developments in Europe. He replaced the festivals celebrating the fall of the Bastille and the

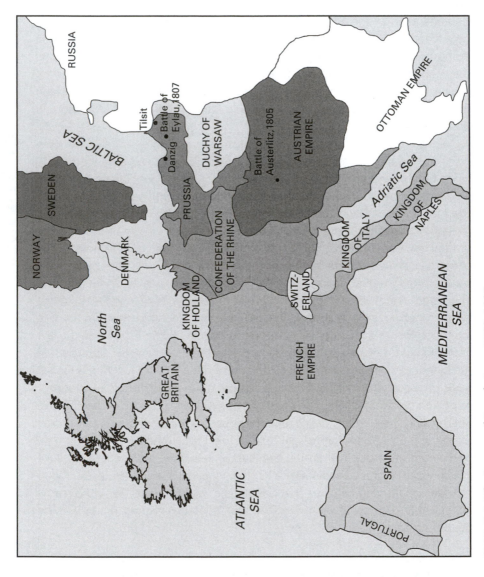

MAP 5.1 *The Success of French Arms, 1799–1807*

declaration of the republic with two imperial festivals: August 15 to celebrate his birthday and the return to Catholicism (August 15 is the Feast of the Assumption); and the first Sunday in December to commemorate the anniversary of his coronation and the victory at Austerlitz. To sort out French finances, made more problematic by the huge war costs, he arrogated to himself the power to name a governor of the Bank of France, replacing the regents. Seeking greater control over Jewish institutions, he convoked a Sanhedrin (traditional court) of rabbis and other notables and on the model of Protestant organization set up a system of consistories to supervise Jewish communities. The prefects chose many members; the consistories collected the funds to pay rabbis, who unlike Protestant and Catholic clergy were not paid state salaries. Even Napoleon's own family had to incline to his absolute will; he drew up an official family pact that required his approval for any marriage contract and that forbade divorce.

Discontent was brewing in Prussia where Louise, the wife of Prussian King Frederick William III, supported French royalists and pressured her vacillating husband to react more aggressively to Napoleon's continuing insults. The French had violated Prussian neutral territory without a second thought in the Ulm campaign, and now rumors circulated that the French emperor was thinking of giving Hanover back to Great Britain in exchange for peace. At the end of September 1806 the Prussian king sent an ultimatum to Napoleon demanding that he withdraw his troops back across the Rhine. By the time Napoleon received it, he had rejoined the army, now 180,000 strong. He had every intention of dispensing with the Prussians before the Russians, still officially at war with France, could join them in this Fourth Coalition.

With their slow-moving columns and ponderous strategy, the Prussians were no match for the French, and on October 14 they suffered major defeats at the twin battles of Jena and Auerstedt in eastern Germany. Half the Prussian soldiers were killed or wounded; the French lost 6 percent of their men. By the end of October the French had taken Berlin, the capital of Prussia. As this lightning 33-day war was coming to an end, Napoleon sent proclamations to the Poles urging them to join him to fight the Russians, even though he had no intention of promoting their independence. By the end of November French armies had taken Warsaw, more than 300 miles from Berlin. The Elector of Saxony, who had joined the Prussians, sued for peace, became King of Saxony with Napoleon's approval, and joined the German Confederation.

The Russians moved south as winter set in. One of the bloodiest battles of the entire era took place during a driving snowstorm in early February 1807 at Eylau, east of the major port city of Danzig (present-day Gdańsk in Poland), in east Prussia. Napoleon barely pulled out a victory, but at enormous cost; both sides lost one-third of their men, about 25,000 each. Augereau's corps alone lost 5,200 men, including every single general and colonel. Surveying the carnage, Marshal Ney lamented, "What a slaughter, and what did we achieve? Nothing." Napoleon agreed but composed bulletins that masked the extent of the damage. When Napoleon viewed the painting by David's student, Antoine Gros, of the battlefield the next year, he took off his own Legion of Honor medal to pin it on the artist. Gros, who functioned almost like an official war painter to the regime, captured the devastation of the scene while still highlighting Napoleon's concern with the welfare of his men.

As both sides prepared for more fighting in the spring, the French besieged Danzig in order to get its supplies. The Prussian garrison capitulated at the end of May. In response to Prussian complaints that they had not tried hard enough to save the city, the Russians decided to attack despite being heavily outnumbered by the *Grande Armée* that now included Saxon, Dutch, Italian, and Polish regiments. On June 14, 1807, the seventh anniversary of the Battle of Marengo as Napoleon reminded his men, the Russians suffered a catastrophic defeat, losing 20,000 killed and wounded compared to 8,000 on the French side. With the war against the Ottoman Turks going badly in the south and the Austrians unwilling to join the Fourth Coalition, the tsar had little choice. His commanding general lamented, "This is no longer warfare, it is a veritable blood bath. There must be peace at last."[10]

Negotiations began almost immediately, and Napoleon determined on a charm offensive to win over Tsar Alexander as an ally. They met first on a raft in the middle of the Niemen River that was constructed by the French for the occasion (Figure 5.3). Napoleon beguiled the taller, younger Russian and wrote to Joséphine, "If Alexander were a woman, I would make him my mistress." On the tsar's insistence, the Prussian king was invited the second day, but his coldness to Napoleon ended any chance of reconciliation between them. In a letter to his wife Louise, Frederick William referred to the French emperor as "that monster, choked out of hell." The peace treaties, drawn up on land at nearby Tilsit, would reduce Prussia to a kind of vassalage, thus creating a dangerous enemy for the future.

PEACE WITH RUSSIA AND PRUSSIA The first treaty signed on July 7 between Russia and France left Russia most of its territory in exchange for an official alliance with France and a promise to declare war on Great Britain if mediation failed. France would not stop Russia from conquering Finland, which belonged to Sweden, still at war with France, and promised to eventually aid the Russians against the Turks, their erstwhile allies. The treaty with Prussia signed two days later eviscerated Frederick William's kingdom; Danzig became a free city, and Prussia had to give up one-half of its territory and population. Its Polish possessions, taken in the three partitions, became the Grand Duchy of Warsaw under the personal control of the King of Saxony, thus giving the Poles some recompense for their loyalty, though the Duchy was in reality another satellite state. Other Prussian territories in the north and west,

ENTREVUE DES DEUX EMPEREURS (*)
LE 25 JUIN 1807, À UNE HEURE APRÈS-MIDI.
Dédiée à la Grande Armée.

FIGURE 5.3 *Napoleon Meets Alexander I*
This etching and engraving celebrates the famous meeting of the two emperors in 1807. Both artists, the draughtsman Jacques Swebach-Desontfaines and the engraver François Couché, were known for their illustration of the Napoleonic legend in the making. Paris, sometime after 1807.

including Hanover, were grouped together in a new Kingdom of Westphalia. Napoleon named his brother Jerome king; Jerome promptly promulgated a new constitution, abolished serfdom, gave rights to the Jews, and instituted the Napoleonic Code while also agreeing to provide money and men to the French empire. The Swedes finally accepted an armistice in September, after the French took one of their major fortresses in Pomerania, a German-speaking territory on the Baltic just south of Sweden. That left Great Britain.

CONTINENTAL SYSTEM To force Britain to seek peace, Napoleon issued a decree from his military headquarters in Berlin on November 21, 1806 ordering a complete blockade of the British Isles. All commerce, including mail, with "perfidious Albion," an insult the French had been brandishing since 1793, was forbidden, and all the satellite states and allies were expected to comply. Both Britain and France had been trying for years to impose blockades against each other, but this "Continental System" seemed more likely to succeed now that Napoleon had control of much of Europe. In fact, however, though the export to Europe of British-made goods declined between 1806 and 1809, British exports to the rest of the world increased. French attempts to encourage manufacturing at home had a positive short-term effect but no one on the continent caught up with British mechanization of textile production. Moreover, the price of raw cotton on the continent rose precipitously compared to the relatively stability of prices in Britain. Neutral nations, such as the United States, found their vessels subject to confiscation by both sides. Smuggling soon flourished, and Napoleon eventually had to accept it; he even allowed the sale of Dutch gin to the English, for instance, as long as they got hard currency in exchange.[11]

The reasons for success

At the end of July 1807 Napoleon returned to Paris after a ten-month absence. His Minister of Police Fouché organized a special performance of a new opera written for the occasion, *The Triumph of Trajan*, that included triumphal arches like the ones being built in Paris, horse-drawn chariots, and hundreds of special costumes. Trajan was the soldier-emperor who pushed the boundaries of the Roman Empire to their furthest extent and rebuilt Rome. The comparison was not far-fetched; the French emperor had stretched French influence to the farthest reaches of Europe and in record time had defeated almost all the major powers of Europe. He had accomplished military goals that the French kings could not have dared to imagine. Napoleon had begun rebuilding Paris too, and despite his wandering away from many of the central principles of the French Revolution, he had brought a considerable measure of internal peace to France while continuing to reward exceptional talent and service.

What accounts for this extraordinary record of success? There is little consensus about Napoleon's strategic and tactical skills on the battlefield. Detractors portray him as a gambler who often blundered his way to victory; many of his initial plans went awry. His defenders focus instead on his uncanny ability to sense the right move and his courage and decisiveness in making it; he repeatedly snatched victory from the jaws of defeat by keeping his reserves at the ready and bringing them up at just the right moment. The personal psychological element should not be discounted. Napoleon was a charismatic figure on the battlefield. He repeatedly demonstrated bravery, had 19 horses shot from underneath him, and his favorite horse, an Arabian named Marengo after the battle, was wounded several times. Napoleon too was wounded at least two times seriously and other times more superficially but he always kept his wounds secret. In contrast, he talked extensively about officers who had sacrificed themselves to take bullets meant for him. Napoleon could urge his men on to feats that were almost superhuman. In the 1805–1807 campaign the *Grande Armée* marched more than 1,000 miles at a pace never before seen: 15 miles a day for weeks on end and much faster when required. One of his opponents estimated that Napoleon's presence on the battlefield could be counted as the equivalent of 40,000 men.[12]

By 1807 Napoleon was getting fat, though this did not stop him from having affairs all along the way of the army's progress, and he spoke more harshly and refused to countenance any criticism. He was at the height of his power at home, having had the Senate abolish the only body that criticized him, the Tribunate. The police reported declining enthusiasm for war; in 1806 the Senate had sent a delegation to Napoleon in Berlin begging him not to continue, but the plea fell on deaf ears. Napoleon's victories simply whetted his appetite for more. His drive to colonize Europe would lead him to further battles that would stretch his supply lines and finances even thinner. His addiction to conquest thus ultimately proved his undoing. The defeated learned how to reform themselves in order to be better prepared, and the various annexed, satellite, and allied states came to resent the constantly increasing demands for more money and men. Napoleon would try to train Europe like a dog on a leash, but Europe turned snarly and bared its teeth. Dividing and conquering worked for many years, but in the end Napoleon would lose when the powers of Europe formed a coalition that actually fought as one.

Documents

DOCUMENT 5.1

The leading general of the new state of Haïti explains his goals, January 1, 1804

Jean-Jacques Dessalines was a former slave who became the first emperor of Haïti (a name taken from an indigenous language). He emerged as the military leader of the resistance to the French after Toussaint Louverture was captured and sent back to France in 1802. In fighting the French, Dessalines did not hesitate to match their atrocities with his own, and after achieving the liberation of the country, he ordered massacres of the remaining whites. He had himself named Emperor because Napoleon had done the same. In this document he announces his intention to break with the past of colonization and slavery. In 1806 Dessalines was assassinated by a group of his generals. Unpopular at the time of his death, many now credit Dessalines with saving Haïti from Bonaparte's plan to re-enslave its people.

The General-in-Chief to the people of Haïti,

Citizens,

It is not enough to have expelled from our country the barbarians who bloodied it for two centuries; it is not enough to have put a stop to the always resurgent factions who took turns making light of the phantom of liberty that France held up before our eyes. By a last act of national authority we must assure forever the empire of liberty in this country where you have been born; we must rip away every hope of re-enslaving us from the inhuman government that kept our spirits for so long in the most humiliating torpor; we must finally live independent or die.

Everything here recalls the cruelties of this barbarous people; our laws, our customs, our cities all still carry the French imprint. What am I saying? There are still French people on our island and you think you are free and independent of this republic that fought every nation, it is true, but which never vanquished those who wanted to be free?

And what! We have been the victims for fourteen years of our own credulity and indulgence; we were vanquished, not by French armies but by the deceptive eloquence of their agents' proclamations. When will we tire of breathing the same air as them? What do we have in common with this people of executioners? Its cruelty compared to our patient moderation; its color to ours; the extent of the seas that separate us, our vengeful climate—they tell us clearly enough that they are not our brothers, that they will never be our brothers, and that if they find asylum among us, they will still be the fomenters of our discords and our divisions. . . .

Indigenous people of Haïti! My happy destiny called me to be one day the sentinel who watches over the idol to which you have sacrificed yourselves. I have watched, fought, sometimes alone, and if I have been happy enough just to put into your hands the sacred object that you entrusted to me, think how it is up to you now to preserve it. In fighting for your liberty, I have worked for my own happiness. Before consolidating it with laws that assure our free individuality, your chiefs whom I have assembled here, and myself, we owe you a final proof of our devotion.

Generals, and you chiefs, united here with me for the happiness of our country, the day has come, this day that will immortalize our glory and our independence. . . .

Swear to the entire universe, to posterity, to ourselves, that you forever renounce France and will die rather than live under its domination, to fight to the last breath for the independence of our country.

And you, a people that has been miserable for too long, witness the oath that we are taking and remember that I have counted on your constancy and your courage when I threw myself into the career of liberty in order to fight despotism and tyranny, against which I have struggled fourteen years. Recall that I have sacrificed everything to rush to your defense and that of your relatives, your children, and your fortune, and that now I have only the riches of your liberty. My name has become a horror to all peoples who want slavery; despots and tyrants only utter it when cursing the day I was born. If ever you refuse or murmur against the laws that the genius of your destinies dictates to me for your happiness, you will deserve the fate of ungrateful peoples.

1 January 1804

Signed: J.- J. Dessalines

Source: Louis Boisrond-Tonnerre, *Mémoires pour servir à l'histoire d'Haïti* (Paris, 1851), pp. 2–7. Boisrond-Tonnerre was a mixed-race Haïtian who served as Dessalines' secretary.

Questions on the leading general of the new state of Haïti

1 How does Dessalines depict the French?
2 What image of himself does Dessalines try to convey?

DOCUMENT 5.2
Napoleon's reasons for making himself Emperor

In a statement to the Legislative Body on December 31, 1804, Napoleon laid out the situation of the country and used the occasion to explain his motives in making himself Emperor. The plot cited in the first sentence was an elaborate scheme, actively inspired by officials in the British government, to assassinate Bonaparte and bring the Bourbons back to power. Fouché unraveled the conspiracy, and several royalists were arrested and executed. General Charles Pichegru, who had escaped Guiana, where he had been deported after the Fructidor coup against royalists in 1797, was found strangled in his prison cell. General Moreau, a hero of the French armies, insisted that he had refused to join in the conspiracy so Napoleon allowed him to be exiled to Pennsylvania. In the most shocking development, Napoleon took the occasion to abduct and arrest the Duke of Enghien and then have him executed as a co-conspirator.

A plot hatched by an implacable government [he is referring to British financing of an assassination attempt on him] was about to plunge France back into the abyss of civil wars and anarchy. The discovery of this horrible plot profoundly stirred all France, and anxieties that had scarcely been calmed awoke again. . . .

Experience has taught us that shared power is impotent and at odds with itself. It was generally felt that if power was delegated for a time, it was so unstable as to discourage any prolonged undertakings or far-reaching plans. If vested in an individual for life, it would lapse with him, and after him would prove a source of discord and anarchy. It was finally recognized that for great nations the only salvation lies in hereditary power, which alone can assure their political life and make it endure for generations, even for centuries.

The Senate, as was proper, gave voice to this common concern. . . . The necessity of hereditary power in a state as vast as France had long been perceived by the First Consul. He had endeavored in vain to avoid this conclusion and he tried to establish a system of election that could perpetuate the state's authority and transfer it without danger and disorder.

Public concern and the hopes of our enemies emphasized the importance of his task; his death would have wrecked his hard work. . . . Under such circumstances, and with such a pressure of public opinion, there was no alternative left to the First Consul. He resolved, therefore, to accept for himself, and for two of his brothers after him, the burden imposed by the exigencies of the situation. . . .

From this moment Napoleon was, by the most just of titles, Emperor of the French. No other act was necessary to sanction his rights and consecrate his authority.

But he wished to restore in France the ancient forms and recall those of our institutions that divinity seems to have inspired. He wished to impress the seal of religion itself upon the opening of his reign. The head of the Church, in order to give the French a striking proof of his paternal affection, wanted to officiate at this august ceremony.

What deep and enduring impressions did this ceremony leave on the mind of the Emperor and in the memory of the nation! What thoughts for future races! What a subject of admiration for all Europe! . . .

The oath of Napoleon shall be forever the terror of the enemies and the protection of the French. If our borders are attacked, it will be repeated at the head of our armies, and our frontiers shall never more fear foreign invasion.

Source: Exposé de la situation de l'empire français (10 nivôse an XIII) (Paris, 1806), pp. 4–6, 8, 9.

Questions on Napoleon's reasons for making himself Emperor

1   Does Napoleon present himself as a dictator? What is the image of himself that he is trying to portray?

2   How convincing would French people find his explanations? Why did they accept them?

TIMELINE TO CHAPTER 5

December 1799	Bonaparte's Constitution.
June 1800	Victory over the Second Coalition.
February 1801	Peace treaty with Austria.
March 1802	Peace treaty with Great Britain and other European powers.
April 18, 1802	Concordat announced between France and the Pope.
May 1802	French attempt to reintroduce slavery in Saint-Domingue.
August 2, 1802	Napoleon becomes Consul for Life.
May 1803	War with Europe resumes.
January 1, 1804	Saint-Domingue declares independence as new state of Haïti.
March 1804	Code Napoleon issued.
December 2, 1804	Napoleon crowns himself Emperor Napoleon I.
December 2, 1805	Decisive defeat of Austria at Battle of Austerlitz.
November 1806	Continental System (economic blockade of Great Britain).
July 1807	Peace treaties with Russia and Prussia.

QUESTIONS ABOUT CHAPTER 5

1 How did Napoleon combine authoritarian practices with a revolutionary veneer? What did he do to encourage French assent?

2 How did defeating the Second Coalition lead to the recovery of French global power?

3 What methods did Napoleon use to achieve stability in state finances?

4 What did Napoleon do in order to create a social hierarchy compatible with his rule? Did he employ different approaches before and after the establishment of the Empire?

5 Did Napoleon depart from revolutionary practices in his treatment of women?

6

The Napoleonic eagle soars and finally plummets, 1808–1815

The eagle was Napoleon's favorite symbol because it identified him with Roman imperial glory. He personally gave a bronze eagle to every regiment to adorn its standard or colors. The loss of that eagle could destroy a regiment's morale in battle. Yet Napoleon himself could not always be present in battle, and after 1807, it became harder and harder for him to be there given the dispersion of his forces across Europe. Racing as he did habitually between Paris and the latest crucial battle, even Napoleon was stretched thin trying to be emperor of France, king of Italy, and commander-in-chief of the *Grande Armée*. Ultimately, his absences from Paris would prove as fatal to his regime as his military losses.

In 1808, however, the eagle was soaring. The impoverished Corsican noble had made himself the equal not just of any contemporary king but of the greatest conquerors in the past. Having made sure of his authority at home, when he returned from his victories in eastern Europe he began preparing even more audacious military adventures, this time in Portugal and Spain. At the same time, the new alliance with Russia revived French dreams of global empire. Napoleon proposed to Russian Tsar Alexander that they divide up the European territories of the Ottoman Empire and send a joint expeditionary force to India via Persia, and he revived plans to attack Britain directly. These plans fizzled when ferocious resistance in Spain, as well as British landings in Portugal, encouraged Prussia and Austria to begin re-arming in view of yet another coalition against the French. Although Napoleon's armies remained victorious on the battlefield right through 1812, maintaining control of an ever more extensive European empire took its toll: constant war sapped enthusiasm at home as demands for men and money proved unceasing, the levies on the various satellite and client states provoked growing opposition, and some local populations refused to submit and violently pushed back against their colonization by the French.

What brought down the eagle in the end? The outsized effort to definitively crush Russia in 1812 failed not only because too many French troops had been lost and many others still were bogged down by the savage fighting in Spain and Portugal but also because the logistics of marching to Moscow proved insuperable for an early nineteenth-century army. Yet even then, Napoleon was not defeated. That could only be accomplished once the European powers finally united, not once, but twice, first in 1813–1814 and then again in 1815. One of the greatest military commanders seen in the history of the world would not go quietly, and his legacy proved even more enduring. Napoleon had set into motion all kinds of ripples, and the waves that resulted would crash against the traditional order for generations to come.

The police state

One of the most consequential of those ripples was the police state. Napoleon did not have a preconceived plan to develop one, but even after 1807 he could not simply rely on his personal popularity to maintain his power at home. The emergent police state combined repression of dissent with a cult of the leader. Napoleon controlled all expressions of public opinion, such as the press; he ordered the development of a secret network of paid agents to report on any potential disruption; and he did not hesitate to exile or imprison critics without trial. Yet he never used terror or torture to get his way. Instead, he taught all would-be authoritarian rulers after him how best to use the media to make the leader's presence ubiquitous, even when he was not to be seen in person (see Document 6.1).

Fouché, as Minister of Police, ran a network of secret agents to keep tabs on any possible opposition and provided the emperor with daily reports on activities throughout the Empire. Brigandage, riots, strikes, resistance to conscription, and smuggling topped the list but Napoleon wanted to know about everything from public opinion to accounts of religious pilgrimages and local festivals. The government expected café owners to spy on customers but also paid countless moles to mingle in crowds, go to recruitment stations, infiltrate workers' associations, report on plays, and sniff out what socially prominent people were saying at home. In 1807 the government reduced the number of theaters in Paris from 33 to eight and set limits on the kinds of plays or operas each could perform. Big cities in the rest of France could have only two theaters, and they had to be authorized by the prefect. Control over print was even more stringent. The four newspapers allowed in Paris after 1811 and the one for each department were closely watched by authorities. A newly appointed Director of the Book Trade had the power to approve or reject every proposed book publication. French officials frequently banned newspapers in the satellite states as well.[1]

Given the fear of dissent that prompted the development of a police state, it is not surprising that Napoleon did not trust his officials or even his police. He fired Talleyrand as Foreign Minister in 1807 because the former Catholic bishop opposed Napoleon's incessant war-making. Although Talleyrand received an honorific position as compensation and continued to advise the emperor, he also began to league with the Russian tsar, urging him to save Europe from Napoleon's "madness." Napoleon did not trust Fouché, so he hired his own men to inform him separately. He even got his own reports from double agents that Fouché sent out to make contact with counter-revolutionary aristocrats and enemy diplomats. In 1810 the emperor removed the former Jacobin for negotiating on his own authority with the British about possible peace terms. He sent him off to be governor of Rome. Both Fouché and Talleyrand would go on to play important roles in the downfall of the emperor and the transition to a restored monarchy.

Needless to say, Napoleon's use of a secret police aroused criticism, especially once the regime had fallen. Germaine de Staël, one of the emperor's fiercest critics, singled out the secret police: "This very police, for which we have not terms contemptuous enough, terms which put a sufficient distance between an honest man and the creature who could enter into such a den, was entrusted by Bonaparte with the charge of directing the public mind in France." The newspapers, she complained, were "faithful to the spirit of servitude" and "contrived to be insipid."[2] The vast majority of the population accepted such tactics in return for political stability and social order, especially since the government lowered rates on direct taxes on property. It made up for them by increasing taxes on consumption, transferring items of the budget to the local level (thus increasing local taxes and tariffs), and relying more and more on levies in the conquered territories. The official budget nearly doubled between 1801 and 1813, and the proportion spent on the military increased steadily to 60 percent and finally 80 percent. Levies in conquered territories contributed at least one-third of the budget in 1807 and increased afterward, though the exact figures are impossible to establish since many conquered peoples refused to pay what was demanded of them (see Document 6.2).

Napoleon constantly monitored his prefects to make sure that they did everything possible to root out draft dodgers, deserters, tax evaders, smugglers, and armed bands who attacked travelers or mail coaches. Yet he also urged them to pursue projects for improving agriculture and industry that might aid peasants and workers. For most of the common people, as for the ordinary soldier, Napoleon was "their" emperor, not a distant or remote figure. Moreover, even after the government set up eight fortresses as state prisons in 1810, the number of true political prisoners (not would-be assassins, rebels, or common criminals) in them numbered in the hundreds, not thousands. The regime certainly had its share of enemies, but the police relied on constant surveillance, the threat of imprisonment without trial, and forced exile rather than on mass incarceration to keep them at bay.

Napoleon had a remarkable talent for pulling a velvet glove over his iron fist of power. Artists, poets, songwriters, and official accounts alike now referred to him as Napoleon the Great, a label not used since Louis XIV, and in 1807 a law officially changed the name of the Civil Code to Code Napoleon. Images of Napoleon appeared everywhere. The new national museum in the Louvre had been known as the Napoleon Museum since 1804, and the letter N or Napoleon's face could be seen on public buildings and monuments, dinner plates, snuffboxes, coins, and commemorative medals. Although no public statues of him were erected, prints with his image or small busts of him could be found even in peasants' cottages. Napoleon used the newspapers that remained, especially the Paris *Moniteur*, for government propaganda; like his bulletins from the front, the *Moniteur* exaggerated victories and minimized defeats in order to maintain confidence in the army.

Iberian misadventures

The emperor's obsession with knowing everything that was happening in France occupied only a small fraction of his day, for he usually slept only four hours a night, spent as little as 20 minutes on a meal, called his ministers to account at any hour day or night, and dictated staggering numbers of letters to his secretaries. A true workaholic, he confessed, "Work is my element." He needed to be constantly alert in order to keep track of all his commitments, at home and abroad, especially as those commitments seemed to have a way of multiplying on their own. In 1807 Napoleon still had high hopes for his newly instituted Continental System, that is, a continent-wide blockade of Great Britain designed to finally bring down his remaining enemy. After his victories in eastern Europe, few holdouts remained: Portugal, an ally of Great Britain since the fourteenth century, Sweden, and Denmark. Britain made sure of Denmark by bombarding Copenhagen and taking over the Danish fleet. Napoleon expected Russia to take care of Sweden while he dealt with Portugal himself.

Portugal would lead the French emperor ineluctably to Spain, and "the Spanish ulcer" would prove impervious to treatment. Napoleon eventually had to keep more than 300,000 soldiers in Spain during the Peninsular War, as it came to be known, and though the French often had the upper hand, popular uprisings, guerrilla warfare, and British invading forces held them at bay for seven years. As Germaine de Staël later concluded, "The first step that

Bonaparte made toward his ruin was the enterprise on Spain . . . he had not learned to dread the only invincible power—the enthusiasm of a whole nation."

OCCUPATION OF PORTUGAL   When Portugal did not close its ports to the British on his order, Napoleon sent an army through the territory of his ally Spain. France had reason to expect a quick resolution. As First Consul, Bonaparte had induced the Spanish to invade Portugal in 1801 with the help of a French contingent; Spain got a sliver of land and Bonaparte got the closing of Portuguese harbors to British ships. Portugal tried a policy of appeasement thereafter but in 1807 Napoleon decided Portugal was ripe for the picking and agreed with Spain to partition the country. French General Jean-Andoche Junot marched through Spain with 25,000 French troops in November and took over Lisbon without resistance. The regent, Prince John, fled with his family and thousands of supporters to Portugal's richest colony Brazil, leaving the British to try to get Portugal back for him. Napoleon named Junot Duke of Abrantès and Governor of Portugal and as usual demanded Portuguese troops for his army and a contribution of 100 million francs.

As the Spanish King Charles IV and his son Ferdinand began to fight each other for his favor, Napoleon bounced from one more ambitious plan to another. Even as he was proposing to the Russian tsar that they take over the Ottoman Empire and march together toward India, he was funneling more troops into Spain claiming they were reinforcements for those in Portugal. He then proposed to give back the northern third of Spain his troops had occupied in exchange for all of Portugal. Having taken Ferdinand officially under his protection, he named Murat commander of the army of Spain and lieutenant-general of Spain. The king prepared to flee to South America, but the supporters of Ferdinand forced him to abdicate in favor of his son. To complicate matters further, Murat entered Madrid and tried to get Charles to withdraw his abdication; Murat hoped that he would be named king, but by the end of March 1808 Napoleon had decided to name one of his brothers king of Spain. At the same time, he put aside the conquest of the Ottoman Empire because the Russian tsar wanted too much in return. Louis and then Jerome Bonaparte turned down their brother's offer.

MADRID UPRISING   On May 2, 1808, as Napoleon was meeting with Ferdinand and Charles in Bayonne, just across the border in France, Madrid rose up in revolt (Figure 6.1). Hearing the rumor that the last of Charles's sons, a 13-year-old, was being forced to go to Bayonne, too, crowds of ordinary people armed themselves with whatever was to hand and began attacking French soldiers in front of the palace. As soon as Murat got control, he used firing squads to execute supposed rebels. Fourteen French soldiers died in contrast to 400–500 Spaniards. In Bayonne, Charles ceded his rights to the throne to Napoleon, while Ferdinand abdicated and was sent to house arrest at Talleyrand's estate 160 miles southwest of Paris. Napoleon finally got

FIGURE 6.1 *Repression of the Madrid Revolt*
In this painting titled *The Second of May 1808*, the Spanish artist Francisco de Goya chose to focus on the charge of Mameluke cavalry for the French. Napoleon had used Mameluke units since the invasion of Egypt in 1799. They were made up of captured or purchased Greeks, Egyptians, Georgians, and Turks and considered especially ferocious by locals who faced them. One served as Napoleon's bodyguard for 15 years. Oil on canvas, 1814.

his brother Joseph to take the throne. Murat left and was named King of Naples.

Joseph immediately saw the peril of his situation, made grimmer by the news that uprisings were multiplying across the country. He wrote to his brother in July, "My position . . . is one in which a king never was before—I have not a single partisan." He insisted that "to prevent further insurrections and to have less blood to shed and fewer tears to dry, enormous force must be employed." Joseph did have some support among the educated middle classes and intellectuals influenced by the Enlightenment, but in the countryside nobles and priests roused the peasants against the "Antichrist." A Spanish catechism explained, "Where does Napoleon come from? From hell and sin." A Spanish cardinal in Rome wrote to the Archbishop of Grenada, "we cannot recognize as our king someone who is a Freemason, a heretic, and a

Lutheran as are all the Bonapartes and all the French nation." The combination of this kind of religious intensity with resentment of French requisitions and garden-variety patriotism exploded into a fury against the French.[3]

Before Joseph could even install himself in Madrid, the hastily reconstituted Spanish army defeated a French army at Bailén, 180 miles south of Madrid, and forced the French commander to surrender his 18,000 men, most of whom died in Spanish captivity. This first capitulation of a French imperial army lit the fires of resistance around Europe. Prussia and Austria began secret meetings, and many in the Prussian elite joined secret nationalist societies to prepare the struggle against French domination. In early August, the British landed 13,000 soldiers in Portugal under the command of General Arthur Wellesley (later the Viscount, then Duke of Wellington), an Anglo-Irish veteran of the 1799 battle against Tipu Sultan in India. In a clear signal of Britain's worldwide interests, Wellesley had been ordered originally to take his force to South America to help Venezuelan revolutionary Francisco de Miranda liberate his country from the Spanish, but the British government now saw the prospects of supporting Spain as well as Portugal. At the end of the month, with an army now 18,000 strong (2,000 of them Portuguese), Wellesley defeated Junot's French force of 13,000. The British allowed Junot to repatriate his troops to France.

Stunned and furious, Napoleon intended to take charge himself, but first he sped off to visit Tsar Alexander I to make sure of an increasingly fragile alliance. Together they revisited the battlefield of Napoleon's defeat of the Prussians at Jena to remind the Germans of their subjugation. Napoleon agreed to the Russian takeover of Finland, Wallachia, and Moldavia in exchange for a free hand in Spain. He ordered 130,000 soldiers to leave the German states and proceed to Spain, where in November 1808 he joined his army, now 300,000 strong with the addition of a new class of recruits from France. By early December he had regained control, entered Madrid, and ignoring his brother, decreed on his authority the abolition of seigneurial rights, the reduction by two-thirds in the number of monasteries and convents, and the suppression of the Inquisition. Before long his army was marching against the British, who were forced to evacuate from northwestern Spain in January 1809. By early January, the emperor was on his way back to Paris, never to return.

Despite French dominance for the next three years, Spain and Portugal constantly drained imperial resources. In November 1809 Napoleon wrote one of his innumerable letters to Joseph, complaining, "how is it possible that with so large and so good an army, opposed to enemies so little formidable, that so little progress should be made?" French armies repeatedly smashed the Spanish regular army in battle only to confront a more obstinate foe in the shape of guerrilla bands. The guerrillas were terrorist-style fighters without uniforms who used their knowledge of the terrain to harass, ambush, murder, and mutilate French soldiers caught unaware. The word *guerrilla* (Spanish for "little war") comes from this Spanish insurgency. The motives of guerrillas varied; some were smugglers or bandits, but all of them loathed the French occupiers. The modern reader will immediately recognize how the quagmire deepened; when viciously assaulted with no warning by unseen men, the French retaliated against local populations with their own acts of terror, forcing villagers to flee their homes or simply massacring them.

A Polish soldier in the French army, Andrzej Daleki, recounted one of his experiences in chilling detail. While foraging with his mates, he got drunk and woke up to find two Spanish peasants standing over him. Playing dead, he heard one say, ". . . here is a big stone. Smash his head in with it quick!" Daleki denied having sacked any houses but knew in fact that he had two shirts in his pack that he had stolen. He had seen a captive with his ears, nose, and fingers chopped off, buried to the waist, and feared for the worst. A small crowd gathered and a priest decided to interrogate him. Seeing his devotional scapular worn under his shirt, confirming his Catholicism, the priest ordered up sausage and brandy and warned the villagers that the French would have sacked the town again if Daleki had been killed. The soldier returned to his unit but when they came back to reward the priest for his action, "there was nobody in the place. . . . The church had been ransacked and stood with its doors open. . . . My heart stopped at the sight of such devastation in a holy place. But there was a war on, so what could one do?"[4] Human decency barely survived in such circumstances.

The soldiers in the French army rivaled the insurgents in wanton brutality. From a warship off the coast, a British naval officer witnessed the punitive massacre of Spanish townspeople by the French. The locals rushed toward the sea, partially clothed, screaming and trying to dodge the gunfire. There was no escaping, and the French then burnt down the town. If the French suspected that women were helping guerrillas they did not hesitate to shoot them and their children. The French considered the Spanish superstitious, fanatical, backward, and savage, and even the British described the Portuguese, their allies, in similar terms. A British soldier described Portuguese civilians after one battle as "birds of prey" devouring the dead and making off with anything of value. At nightfall, they made a bonfire and sat around it all night, "shouting like as many savages." It was like watching a "feast of cannibals."

Portugal and the British general Wellesley would prove to be the undoing of the Iberian enterprise. Wellesley had been replaced after the initial British victory in August 1808 but returned in April of the following year to rebuild the joint British–Portuguese forces. In August 1809 he was named Viscount Wellington as a reward for pushing the French out of Portugal and defeating Joseph's army inside Spain. One after another French general tried to retake Portugal but each time the British withdrew to their best defended places, waited for reinforcements, and eventually forced the French themselves to retreat. The stalemate might have continued if Napoleon had not needed his troops for fighting in the east, but he did. Still, he had keep 300,000 men in Spain to maintain even the semblance of control, but so many of them were tied down fighting guerrillas here and there that he could not mass a big enough army to defeat the joint British–Portuguese forces. In 1810 and 1811 alone, the French suffered 70,000 casualties in Spain and Portugal. The British pushed the French out of Portugal for the last time in 1811, and the next year Wellington began a relentless push into Spain itself. By the end of 1813 he had reached all the way to the French frontier, and the Peninsular War was winding down.

Austria, from foe to friend?

Napoleon had raced back to Paris in January 1809 to confront two very different challenges: he had discovered that Fouché and Talleyrand were conspiring about who should succeed him as emperor (Murat was their choice) should he die in battle, and Austria was preparing for war again, thinking that Prussia would provide assistance. The emperor kept Fouché on for the moment but denigrated Talleyrand to his face, calling him "a thief," "a coward," and in a final outburst in front of his privy council, "shit in a silk stocking." The Old Regime aristocrat distanced himself from Napoleon after that, but still kept his ear to the ground in preparation for the future.

The Austrians drew their own lessons from events in Spain. Might the uprisings against the French be repeated in German lands? The Austrian government covertly supported a peasant uprising in Tyrol, a mountainous region that was originally part of Austria but ceded to Bavaria in 1806 (Bavaria was a French ally). The rebels won a number of surprising victories in the spring and summer of 1809 and only gave up in 1810. The only other German uprising came to nothing; Westphalia defeated a small band trying to reclaim Brunswick for its dispossessed Duke, who was the nephew of Britain's King George III. In general, however, the Austrians regarded incipient nationalist sentiment with ambivalence since Austria was by definition a multi-national empire. Taking courage from the promise of British financial aid, but without Prussian support, the Austrians attacked Bavaria and northern Italy in April 1809. Napoleon was still reorganizing his army, depleted by the departures for Spain, but he promised his troops, "I am coming with the speed of lightning. . . . Let's march and have the enemy see in your faces its conquerors."

In contrast, the large Austrian army of nearly 300,000 men moved with the speed of a herd of cows, goaded forward by vacillating generals, and once again Napoleon turned the tables. Despite being outnumbered, he pushed the

Austrians all the way back to Vienna, which he bombarded and occupied. His army of Italy, commanded by his stepson Eugene, stopped the Austrians in northern Italy, too. Still outmanned, even though the army of Italy had rejoined him, Napoleon hastened to engage a final, decisive conflict in early July 1809 at Wagram, a few miles from Vienna across the Danube. He won, but losses on both sides were great, in part because of especially intense artillery fire; 70,000 casualties were more or less evenly divided. Four Austrian generals were killed alongside five French ones. Despite facing heavy fire, Napoleon remained unscathed. One of the French brigadier-generals wrote home to his wife, "I do not believe that, in modern times, a more terrible battle has been given."[5]

After escaping an assassination attempt by a 17-year-old German son of a Lutheran pastor while he was reviewing his troops in Vienna, Napoleon finally got the Austrians to agree to peace terms in October 1809. They gave up territories inhabited by 20 percent of their population (3.5 million people), which included access to the Adriatic Sea. The lands were divided among France and her allies, including Russia. Austria agreed to limit its army to 150,000 men and pay an indemnity of 85 million gulden. Because the French had given some Austrian territory to the Grand Duchy of Warsaw, Russia remained suspicious of French intentions in regard to Poland. Only one Pole was on Napoleon's mind at this moment, however, his 22-year-old Polish mistress, Countess Marie Walewska, who had just become pregnant by him.

JOSÉPHINE DIVORCED The pregnancy would change many things, though not for Marie, who was already married. Like all hereditary rulers, Napoleon needed an heir, and he much preferred a son to his brothers, who were officially next in line. Since his marriage with Joséphine had not produced any children, though she had two from a previous marriage, he assumed at first that he was infertile. One of his mistresses had already given birth to a child, but Marie's was clearly his, since she had come to live near him in Vienna, and now he determined to divorce. Already in 1807 Fouché had been spreading rumors of an impending divorce, but Napoleon did not decide on the break until the end of 1809, in part because he genuinely loved Joséphine despite the tension created by their various infidelities. He wrote to her constantly while away on campaign and continued to write to her affectionately after their divorce. An act of the Senate finalized the civil divorce in December 1809 and settled on her an annual income of 2 million francs. A religious annulment was granted by Catholic officials in Paris in early January 1810; in principle, the Pope's approval was required for annulment but had to be bypassed in this case because the Pope had excommunicated Napoleon just months before when French troops took over the papal states.

MARRIAGE WITH MARIE-LOUISE Desperate for the legitimatization that would come with marriage into one of Europe's leading dynasties, Napoleon had been seeking a marriage alliance with either the Russian or

Austrian ruling families. Seeing an occasion for Austria to adapt itself to French dominance, the Austrian foreign minister, Klemens von Metternich, negotiated the marriage of one of the daughters of the Austrian emperor Francis II to Napoleon. Marie-Louise of Habsburg was 18; Napoleon 40. Marie-Antoinette was her great aunt, and the young girl grew up thinking of Napoleon as a cannibal and usurper. She nevertheless obeyed her father and trundled off to France in March 1810, where Napoleon concluded after the marriage, "We suit each other perfectly."

NAPOLEON'S SON   Within the year, she gave birth to the much desired son (Figure 6.2); he was named Napoleon and immediately designated King of Rome in another slap in the face of the Pope. The French had arrested Pope Pius VII in Rome after he excommunicated the emperor in 1809 for taking over the papal states, and they kept him under house arrest first in Liguria and then just outside Paris.

The emperor's new wife distracted him for a while, and he could not bring himself to go back to Spain as planned. Sweden made peace with France, joined the Continental System, and with Napoleon's consent named his Marshal Jean Bernadotte as heir apparent because the Swedish king had no heir. Since the king was also senile, Bernadotte ruled as regent until 1818 when the king died and he became king. In order to shore up the Continental System even further, Napoleon forced his brother Louis to abdicate the throne in Holland and then simply annexed the country to the French empire. The Russians were busy fighting the Turks over control of the Balkan principalities, Wallachia and Moldavia, so the only festering problem for the moment was Spain and Portugal, where despite the return of many units from the army in Austria, victory eluded the French.

Collaboration and resistance in the satellite states

At the absolute height of the French Empire in 1811 (see Map 6.1), Napoleon had in effect colonized much of Europe. The French had annexed Belgium, the Dutch Republic, German territories on the Rhine and those running up to Denmark, as well as a chunk of northwestern Italy and the Dalmatian coast. Family members ruled over nominally independent kingdoms in Italy, Spain, and Westphalia. The Confederation of the Rhine, Switzerland, and the Grand Duchy of Warsaw were subservient while much of the rest of Europe had been forced to ally with the French emperor. Appearances can be deceiving, however. The seemingly uniform shading on the map covers over a much more complicated reality on the ground.

F. Gérard Pinxit.   A. Desnoyers Sculp.ᵗ

S. M. LE ROI   DE ROME,

Dédié à S. M.ᵉ   Imp.ᵗ et Royale

Marie   Louise

Archiduchesse   d'Autriche

Par son très humble et Fidèle Sujet

Auguste Boucher Desnoyers

Membre des Académies de Vienne et de Genève.

FIGURE 6.2 *Napoleon's Infant Son, 1813*
In this celebratory print of 1813, dedicated to Napoleon's new wife Marie-Louise, we
see not only the child but on top the essential Napoleonic symbol, the "N" surrounded
by a laurel wreath. The title, "His Majesty, the King of Rome," speaks for loyalties of
the draughtsman, François Gérard, and the engraver, Auguste Boucher-Desnoyers.

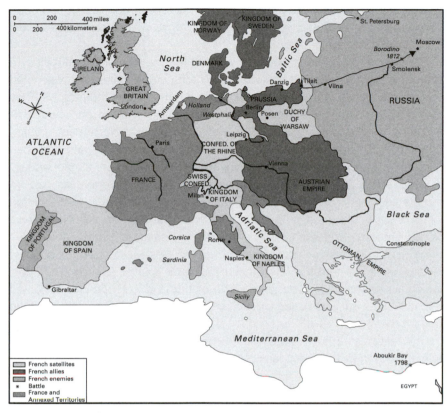

MAP 6.1 *Napoleon's Empire, 1812*

The contradictions in Napoleon's policies ultimately created insurmountable tensions. On the one hand, his officials imposed the same kind of rationalizing policies already pursued by the Convention and Directory governments, but now using the Napoleonic Code as the template: abolition of feudalism, equality under the law, suppression of guilds, confiscation of church properties, and religious toleration. On the other hand, the Napoleonic military machine required even more men and money than had the revolutionary armies, and the emperor saw in conquered territories a reservoir of lands that he could seize to build up his imperial nobility and reward the faithful. The second set of policies often overrode the first; the French desperation for resources undermined reform efforts. The impact was greatest in the lands closest to France that had been the longest under French control: Belgium, the left bank of the Rhine, and the annexed parts of northwest Italy (Piedmont and Liguria). They were fully incorporated into French administrative, financial, and judicial structures; they had their own prefects, paid French taxes, litigated in French courts, and participated fully in the French market. Territories that had been conquered after 1807 and were farther from France were more likely to avoid French rationalization and domination.[6]

Yet even where elites collaborated with the French, they did so on their own terms as much as possible. Leading merchants in the Rhineland welcomed French innovations, especially access to French markets without tariffs. They also saw a chance for the middle classes to make a claim on power that had long been jealously guarded by aristocrats. A local cloth manufacturer, Ludwig Rigal, was thrilled to be appointed to the French Senate and then named Count, but he continued to agitate for local interests as did virtually all local officials. Those who worked for the French nevertheless had no trouble cooperating with the Prussians when they took over in 1815, though local officials did petition successfully for retention of the Napoleonic Code. Similarly, in Piedmont local elites continued to pursue their own reformist and conservative agendas. French reforms accelerated the ongoing decline of feudal forms of land tenure, and the sale of Church properties, which accounted for no less than a fifth of the land in Piedmont, benefited the local elite of landowners, merchants, bankers, and high officials who bought them.

The readiness of local elites in the Rhineland and Piedmont to accept the rulers imposed by the European powers in 1815 shows that collaboration with occupying France was a pragmatic decision, perhaps the only possible decision under the circumstances. Accommodating elites could also be found in places further from Paris, such as the Kingdom of Italy and the Kingdom of Naples, but as the distance from Paris increased so too did the prospect of resistance. While landowning and commercial elites snapped up church and former rulers' properties sold off by the French in the Italian kingdoms, peasants turned increasingly recalcitrant starting in 1809. In the area around Bologna peasants joined with deserters to fight a new tax on milling grain; they killed local officials and burned administrators' papers in villages across the region and even tried to attack Bologna itself, without success.

As it had in 1799, defiance turned more deadly in southern Italy in 1809; refusal of conscription transmuted into a guerrilla war in Calabria that resembled the fighting in Spain with rapes, murders, and castration taking place on both sides. The British and the former Bourbon rulers, now in Sicily, sent aid and encouragement to the rebels. By 1811 General Murat, the French King of Naples, controlled only the towns and depended heavily on the 40,000 French soldiers that had to be garrisoned in the kingdom to keep order. Even so, Napoleon made his financial demands explicit; any attempt to improve roads or education must come after support for French troops, funding of Neapolitan soldiers for the French war effort, and the building of six new ships of the line for the French navy. The emperor did not hesitate, moreover, to double tariffs on Neapolitan cotton exported to France while demanding that no duties be placed on French imports to Naples.

Napoleon may have begun with good intentions, but he ended up squeezing out as many resources as he could. In the Kingdom of Westphalia and the Grand Duchy of Warsaw legal and social reforms almost immediately took a back seat to Napoleon's developing spoils system. Westphalia had been set up to be a test case of the benefits of applying the Napoleonic Code; Napoleon admonished his brother Jerome, the king, "Your people must enjoy a liberty, an equality, a prosperity, unknown to the peoples of Germany." This did not stop Napoleon from giving away a quarter of the confiscated feudal lands to his sister Pauline, the widow of General Leclerc who had married a Roman prince, and to various leading generals and other military officers. Many seigneurial rights were maintained in order to preserve the revenues of the estates, which were administered by French agents. Napoleon arranged for Jerome's papers to be secretly searched by his servants and repeatedly complained about Jerome's laxity in enforcing the Continental System.

In Poland, 27 French marshals and generals received endowments that amounted to a fifth of the revenue anticipated from confiscated lands. The Grand Duchy also had to bear the cost of supporting 80,000 troops, which drained away three-quarters of the new state's budget. The introduction of the Napoleonic Code created its own tensions; the Catholic Poles disliked the Code's establishment of civil marriages and divorce (however limited), and lawyers and judges had a hard time adapting to French notions not to mention French phrases and terms. To cap it off, the Continental blockade cut off trade with Poland's leading customer for grain, Great Britain, and so threatened to ruin the noble landowning class.

The balance sheet had much to recommend it, especially in retrospect. The rationalizing effort of the French paid dividends everywhere, if only in the memory that traditional routines could be smashed. Napoleon broke through the barriers of feudal and aristocratic privilege that had held back reforms. The implementation of the Napoleonic Code and the confiscation of church lands put secularization on an irresistible path. Germans and Italians got first-hand experience of constitutions, and along with the Poles they also witnessed the advantages of more unified forms of state building. Italy had not been so unified for centuries. Most educated Poles seized upon the establishment of a separate Polish government as a way of returning to active civic participation, which included the founding of more than 900 new elementary schools in just seven years. Everywhere the French ruled, plans were made, if not implemented, to extend education. For the Poles, in particular, the Napoleonic state remained throughout the nineteenth century the only bright spot in an otherwise bleak history of subjugation by Austria, Prussia, and especially Russia.[7]

Even among France's sworn enemies, the impact of some French-style reforms proved irresistible. In 1808 Austria introduced a militia, the *Landwehr*, to compete with the French *levée en masse*, and in 1812 undertook a reorganization of the Austrian Civil Code. The government also pursued various bureaucratic and military reforms in the name of greater efficiency in the fight against Napoleon. A much more direct and immediate impact can be seen in Prussia after its defeat in 1806. Like Austria, or like Napoleon for that matter, Prussia intended to reform from above. The Stein–Hardenberg reforms, named after their two initiators, Karl vom Stein, Minister of the Economy, and State Chancellor Karl August von Hardenberg, promoted far-reaching changes that basically took power away from the feudal aristocracy and placed it in the hands of the government bureaucracy. Serfdom was abolished; peasants were freed from seigneurial dues and gained full property rights to two-thirds of their land (the other third was reserved for compensation). Guilds lost their monopolies, taxes were standardized, and Jews gained full citizenship rights. The state took control of education and in 1810 established a new university in Berlin called the Humboldt University after one of the great educational reformers of Prussia, Wilhelm von Humboldt.

The French economy in wartime

Napoleon made onerous demands on the satellite states to compensate for a French economy in trouble. France's losses at sea and the Continental System's blockade disrupted and in some cases nearly destroyed France's overseas commerce. Saint-Domingue's role in international trade had been wrecked even before France lost complete control in 1804, and French ports and their hinterlands suffered great losses with the disruption of most trade to the Caribbean after the resumption of war with Britain in 1803. At first neutral shipping, especially from the United States, provided some commerce, but after 1807, when the United States Congress passed an embargo act restricting all trade with Europe, even that declined. Shipments in and out of Bordeaux and Nantes collapsed and with it went the livelihoods of ropemakers, sailmakers, sugar refinery workers, and even flour mill operators who had provided flour to the colonies.

As the center of gravity of French trade had shifted to the continent, eastern cities such as Strasbourg saw their prosperity increase because they could serve as entrepôts for trade between the Mediterranean and the German and Italian states controlled by France. With British goods excluded, the French manufacturing of cotton expanded dramatically in northern and eastern France. The number of cotton manufacturers in Mulhouse, once a Swiss city but annexed to France in 1798, tripled between 1786 and 1810. Mechanization and therefore industrialization spread in these regions; the number of mechanized cotton mills in France increased from 37 in 1799 to 266 by 1810. Even Paris benefited with 44 cotton mills by 1814. The gigantic Richard-Lenoir textile firm in Paris employed 15,000 workers in 1815. Napoleon went out of his way, moreover, to insist that the French people favor all things French-made, whether silks and cottons, embroidery, or lace.

In 1810–1811, however, a slump threatened these gains. Richard-Lenoir complained in January 1811, "sales have almost ceased, and payments are slow and uncertain. My credit is ruined." Bankruptcies ravaged the textile and banking sectors alike; there were 270 bankruptcies just in the Seine department where Paris was located. The government had to step in with loans, purchases, and public works projects, including a loan to rescue Richard-Lenoir. Two-thirds of the textile workers in Mulhouse lost their jobs. A contraction in exports combined with harvest shortages in 1812 to create serious popular discontent. In response to a food riot in Caen, a town in northern France, a military commission sent by Napoleon condemned four men and two women to be shot; the rioters had done 7,000 francs damage to a local mill. Napoleon proclaimed price maximums on grain, largely for propaganda purposes, as the measures worked even less well than those of 1793–1794. The government also set up soup kitchens and organized workshops for the unemployed. In these difficult times, festivals to celebrate the anniversary of Napoleon's coronation included the distribution of free bread to the poor.

Not everyone was discontent. The price of wheat had risen about one-third since the averages for the early 1790s, which meant that peasant producers got more for their grain. Wages meanwhile had gone up 70 percent, in large measure because conscription took away so many able-bodied men from the labor market. Outside the periods of downturn, then, the ordinary people of France were better off. Yet every time the economy picked up, it remained at the mercy of the increasingly fickle fortunes of war. Moreover, even the solace provided by the Catholic Church seemed in danger. Despite the regime's iron grip on the press, everyone knew that Napoleon had strong-armed the French Catholic hierarchy into accepting his nomination of bishops without papal investiture, and the lower clergy in France was beginning to express its discontent with the blatant manipulation of the Pope. In 1812 the emperor had the Pope moved from Italy to Fontainebleau, just outside Paris, where he hoped to exert pressure in person. The Russian campaign would make that more difficult.[8]

The fateful march to Moscow

Even as the back and forth in Spain and Portugal continued to gobble up resources, Napoleon had begun to prepare for an attack on Russia. His erstwhile partner had withdrawn from the Continental System in 1810 and resumed trade with Britain. The romance had definitely cooled; the French emperor, "the curse of the human race, daily becomes more abominable," complained Alexander in a letter to his sister. Napoleon forced Prussia and Austria to ally with France and promise 50,000 troops for the campaign, and he called up an additional 120,000 Frenchmen. He convinced himself that he could repeat the rapid victories of 1807; Tsar Alexander counted on the similarities with Spain. Russia made peace with the Turks and sought allies of its own but only managed to sign on Sweden, ruled by the former French Marshal Bernadotte, who now busied himself with his new country, hoping to get Norway away from Denmark in the bargain. Bernadotte's defection ended Napoleon's hope of a three-pronged attack with Sweden and the Ottoman Empire as his allies.

Three weeks before declaring war on Russia, Napoleon joined his army in Poland. He had narrowly avoided having to fight the United States, where rapidly growing exports were being threatened by both French and British blockades. The fury of Congress fell ultimately on Britain because the British policy of forced recruitment had led to the impressment of 6,000 American sailors over a decade. The United States declared war on Britain in June 1812, but with an army of only about 7,000 men and no ships of the line, it could only benefit from Britain's attention being drawn elsewhere.

Britain faced its own economic problems at home but was nonetheless expanding its dominance overseas. The British East India Company reached further into India, and the British invaded and took over Java (part of present-day Indonesia) and other islands from the Dutch.

SOUTH AMERICAN INDEPENDENCE British traders developed a booming commerce with the Spanish South American colonies first by supporting the deposed Spanish king and then by maintaining neutrality when colonists who supported the deposed king began to demand independence in 1810. Revolts broke out in Caracas, Buenos-Aires, Bogotá, and Santiago. Napoleon's undertaking in Iberia ricocheted across the Atlantic; by revealing the weakness of the Spanish monarchy, it opened the door to independence.[9]

RUSSIAN CAMPAIGN On June 24, 1812 the 450,000 men of Napoleon's first line crossed the Niemen River, the Russian frontier, at five different points. Eventually, 680,000 men would cross the frontier. Murat, Napoleon's brother Jerome, and his stepson Eugene commanded different units alongside Ney and other generals. Only one-third of the soldiers were French. Massive supplies had been stockpiled in the Baltic ports, and 25,000 carts and wagons and 90,000 horses had been assembled in the supply train. With a deployment stretching across 480 kilometers (300 miles), supplies would not last for long, so Napoleon aimed for a short, decisive campaign. The Russians refused to be lured into battle, however, and retreated steadily eastward. After suffering through stifling heat and drenching rains, Napoleon's main force had gone more than half the way to Moscow by the end of August, but had already been reduced to 130,000 men through casualties, desertion, and sickness. They had fought only one battle of any consequence, at the fortress town of Smolensk, where the two sides lost the same number of men.

TAKING MOSCOW   Napoleon pressed forward even as hunger and thirst crumpled thousands more men and horses. The Russian army swept up all the local food and forage as they fell back toward Moscow. In early September, the 67-year-old Russian commander Mikhail Kutuzov decided to make his stand 75 miles west of Moscow at Borodino. He was so fat his men had to hoist him up to his horse. Still, Kutuzov was no fool, and the Russians had at least as many men and cannon as Napoleon. After furious fighting that killed thousands on each side, both commanders claimed victory. On September 14 the *Grande Armée* marched into Moscow with 95,000 men only to find an empty city. The army and most of the population had moved south. Fires set by Russians soon consumed the city built of wood. Napoleon expected Alexander to sue for peace. Kutuzov's occasional missives seemed to promise some resolution, and in any case what options did the French emperor have? His brother Jerome had already returned to Westphalia because he did not feel his opinions counted for enough. The Prussians and Austrians would bolt at the first sign of weakness. The approach of winter made further fighting impossible for months.

Napoleon decided to set up winter quarters back in Smolensk and proceed there by a southern route in order to find supplies, but Russian forces blocked him and he had to retrace his steps. In the last week in October the French finally began to move westward in earnest. In the first week in November snow began falling and temperatures dropped well below freezing. The Russian army pursued and constantly harassed French forces. A colonel described the situation in the rearguard comprised of Ney's third corps. "Those who had resisted cold and fatigue fell beneath the extremity of hunger. Those who had preserved a little food had not the strength left to march, and fell into the enemy's hands. Some had their limbs frost-bitten, and died stretched on the snow."[10] Only 50,000 men made it to Smolensk and by then the survivors were half-crazed with what they had witnessed along the way, as starving comrades hacked at frozen horses and left the wounded to die because there were not enough horses left to pull the wagons.

After soldiers looted the storage depots in Smolensk, the army had to retreat further westward to Vilna to find supplies. Napoleon returned to Paris, ever worried about what might be happening in his absence and never having admitted to the scale of his losses. He put Murat in charge. After getting the men to Vilna in early December, Murat decided to continue westward for fear that the Russian pursuers would catch him. In early January 1813, having arrived in Posen in the Duchy of Warsaw with 40,000 troops, Murat himself went home to Naples and left Eugene in charge. Some 500,000 men had been lost, including 170,000 who had been taken prisoner by the Russians during the nightmarish return march. The French, not counting those from allied nations, lost 210,000 men, many of them dead from disease, exposure, or starvation. The Russian army pushed on to Warsaw and dissolved the Grand Duchy. Prussia allied with Russia as soon as Russian troops approached, and when Eugene moved the French army out of Berlin, the king of Prussia declared war on France. Austria and the states of the German Confederation refused to provide further troops to the French and waited to see what would happen next.

The eagle falls to earth

Napoleon was far from finished, even though Murat was secretly negotiating with Metternich, and Bernadotte had allied with Britain. By April 1813, France had added to the tattered remnants of the returning army enough new conscripts and National Guardsmen to reconstitute a force of 200,000 men for fighting in the German lands. Napoleon quickly pushed more than 200 miles past the Rhine, winning battle after battle, and compelled the Prussians and Russians to request an armistice. The respite allowed the allies to firm up their alliances; the British promised huge subsidies to Prussia and Russia, and Austria finally decided to join the Sixth Coalition, which would now outnumber the French. Moreover, Napoleon's new men were untested and untrained. The British were about to invade France from Spain where they had finally gained control. So intimidated, still, were the allies, however, that they determined to fight the French wherever Napoleon himself was not present and by defeating his subordinates to eventually gain the upper hand.

BATTLE OF LEIPZIG   Although Napoleon managed to increase his troop strength to 440,000 men in August 1813, he now faced combined armies of 600,000 soldiers. He continued to pull out victories but elsewhere his generals began to lose ground. The soldiers provided by his satellite states started deserting in large numbers. Bernadotte now fought for the allies, and Bavaria concluded an armistice with them. The decisive battle, the greatest seen before World War I, took place just south of Leipzig in mid-October. During the aptly named Battle of the Nations, 500,000 men from ten nations fought for four days supported by 3,000 cannon. Four rulers personally commanded their troops in this conflict that raged in a space of less than 4 square miles. Even though the coalition forces lost more men—80,000 killed and wounded compared to 27,000 for the French—they took thousands more prisoners when 35,000 French and Polish soldiers had to be left behind in Leipzig after the French prematurely blew up a bridge across the river separating the city from the battlefield. The allies had more men to lose, moreover, and fresh supplies at the ready. With his munitions and men exhausted, Napoleon had to move back all the way across the Rhine.

END OF EMPIRE　The end came relatively quickly. Jerome fled Westphalia as the allies took it over. France's remaining German friends switched sides. An uprising in Holland in support of the stadholder prepared the way for his arrival with a British army. As the British invaded Tuscany and moved into France from Spain, Ferdinand VII regained the Spanish throne. Murat defected to the allies, and the Swiss declared neutrality. The allies then invaded France and moved steadily toward Paris. On April 2, 1814 Talleyrand got the French Senate to depose Napoleon, who had foolishly refused an earlier peace offer that would have left him in power. His marshals then convinced him to abdicate. Marie-Louise and his son had fled Paris and eventually rejoined her father, the emperor of Austria. Napoleon never saw them again. Murat prepared to move against Eugene's forces of the kingdom of Italy, but Eugene could see that there was little point and he too abdicated.

CONGRESS OF VIENNA　Faced with the enormity of reversing revolutionary and Napoleonic changes in governments all over Europe, which were reverberating from North and South America to Asia, the allies decided to hold a congress in Vienna to settle their differences and figure out how to reintegrate France into a restored monarchical order. Before it even began meeting, the allies exiled Napoleon to the island of Elba, while the brother of Louis XVI reclaimed the French throne for the Bourbons and named the chameleon Talleyrand his Foreign Minister. Louis XVIII kept most of the Napoleonic Code and promised a constitutional charter. By the peace treaty of May 1814 France was able to retain those territories incorporated up to January 1, 1792. The new monarchical government demobilized the army and put 12,000 officers on half pay, while *émigré* aristocrats returned to take up their military ranks at the level they had attained in the *émigré* armies. A massive rollback was coming.

The Hundred Days and Waterloo

The meetings dragged on at the Congress of Vienna, where Talleyrand did everything possible to ensure France's standing. On Elba, Napoleon heard of growing French resentment at the return of former aristocrats, refractory clergy, and a Bourbon king. Restless and impatient and still only 45 years old, Napoleon plotted his return.

ESCAPE FROM ELBA　At the end of February 1815 he told Murat of his plans and issued proclamations to the French people, the National Guard, and the army. "The eagle," he promised, "will fly from clock tower to clock tower right up to the towers of Notre-Dame." On March 1 the former emperor landed on the French coast near Cannes to begin that strange interregnum called the Hundred Days because that is how long it lasted. He moved north greeting rapturous crowds in Grenoble and Lyon, and when he arrived in Paris on March 20 Louis XVIII had fled. Not a shot had been fired. Writing from Paris in April, the British intellectual Helen Maria Williams exclaimed, "The rapidity of his march appears a prodigy of which history offers no example." Napoleon made Fouché Minister of Police and Carnot Minister of the Interior, abolished censorship of the press, and asked his former enemy Benjamin Constant to prepare a new more liberal constitution. The Vendée rose in revolt again, and the allies regrouped with the intention of punishing France this time.

BATTLE OF WATERLOO   After vainly hoping for peace, Napoleon raised yet another army and went off to fight the allies in Belgium. He had with him Marshal Ney, who first aligned himself with Louis XVIII and then defected, and his brother Jerome, but refused the help of Murat, who had abandoned him in 1814 in order to keep his kingdom only to return to the fold and lose to the Austrians. Following his signature strategy, Napoleon sought a brief decisive battle before the Russians and Austrians could bring up their armies. He hoped to keep the Prussians separate from the main allied force of British, Dutch, and other Germans commanded by Wellington, since once again he was outnumbered, but only if the coalition armies combined. This brilliant strategy was undermined by the tactical weaknesses of his lieutenants, especially Ney, who failed to capture the crucial wedge territory between the British and Prussians even though he enjoyed a temporary numerical advantage. Over three days of battle, known as the Battle of Waterloo after a nearby Belgian village, French fortunes rose and fell, but in the end, in the mud and stench, the Prussians arrived in time to reinforce Wellington's forces which were being repeatedly pummeled by artillery fire and desperate infantry and cavalry charges. Wellington could hold on because he occupied a ridge and he packed his infantry into squares that stubbornly held off cavalry attacks coming up the hill. By 8 p.m. on June 18 the French had given up; they suffered 30,000 casualties in the battle, the allies 24,000.

Napoleon abdicated again, but this time the British deported him as a prisoner of war to the far-away island of Saint-Helena, located in the South Atlantic between Brazil and Africa, an almost inconceivable 4,500 miles from Paris and very far from any continent. Elba, in contrast, was less than 800 miles from Paris and off the Italian coast not far from Napoleon's native Corsica. Louis XVIII returned and granted amnesty to all except those who had actively helped "the Usurper." Ney was executed by firing squad in the Luxembourg Gardens of Paris. Talleyrand took up his post as Foreign Minister and Fouché continued as Minister of Police, but the two lasted only for a few months until Louis consolidated his power. The new peace treaty dictated by the coalition returned France to its borders of 1790 and required the French to pay an indemnity of 700 million francs and maintain an occupying army until it was paid. France now had to return art treasures confiscated during the conquests. The bronze horses went back to Venice, once again under the control of Austria.

The Congress of Vienna, which met from November 1814 until early June 1815, reset the course of European history after more than 25 years of revolution and nearly constant warfare. Meeting under the watchful eye of the Austrian minister Metternich, who still had time to pursue one of his many affairs with aristocratic women, the Congress brought together the major powers of Europe: Great Britain, Russia, Austria, and Prussia. Unlike the peace negotiations after World War I, the victorious allies included in the negotiations the defeated power, France. The coalition partners agreed to include France because each one feared the predominance of others, and the inclusion of France ensured some kind of balance between competing interests. All the other places with a stake in the outcome, no matter how small, sent delegations, more than 200 in all. Salons, *soirées*, and balls occupied so much attention that some joked about the "dancing" congress.

The men in charge would have liked to turn back the clock but they could not. So they restored where they could, such as bringing the Bourbons back to France as hereditary kings and returning the king of Sicily to Naples, and cobbled together other solutions where they could not return to the past. The most significant of the new solutions was the creation of a Kingdom of the Netherlands that included the former Dutch Republic and Belgium, previously part of the Austrian Empire (see Map 6.2). The stadholder became king. Some territorial changes could not be undone, and the Congress had to undertake still others to ensure the peace. Russia kept Finland, taken from Sweden in 1809, and in exchange Sweden got Norway from Denmark which had allied with France. In a sign of how much had in fact changed, the Norwegians gained the right to write their own constitution. Louis XVIII had had to agree to draft a constitutional charter that guaranteed the rule of law and maintained a two-chamber legislature, and the new king of the Netherlands approved a constitution that guaranteed religious toleration and the separation of church and state.

The Duchy of Warsaw disappeared, with most of its territory incorporated into a Kingdom of Poland ruled by Russia. Prussia got back some of its Polish lands, two-fifths of Saxony, and much of the Rhineland. Austria lost Belgium but reclaimed Tyrol, Lombardy and Venetia, and the Dalmatian provinces taken over by Napoleon. The King of Sardinia regained Piedmont, Nice, and Savoy and added Genoa. The Pope recovered his papal states but not the papal territories inside France which remained with France. Britain returned the

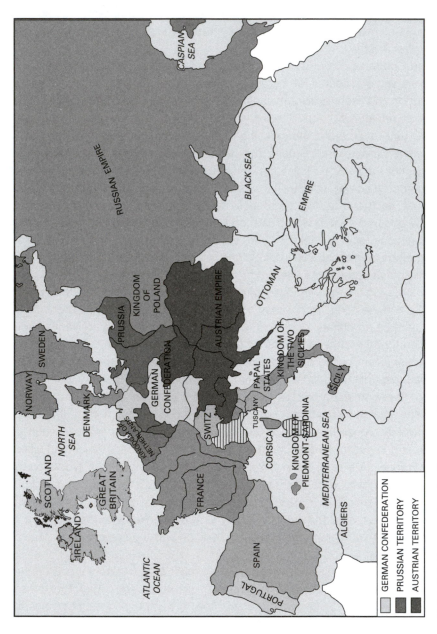

MAP 6.2 *Europe after the Congress of Vienna*

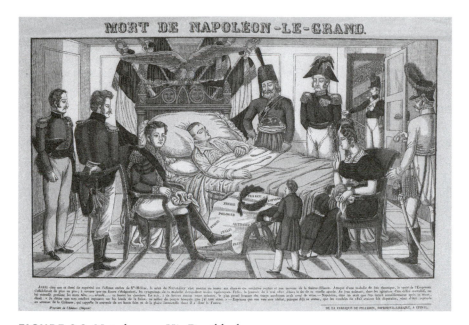

FIGURE 6.3 *Napoleon on His Deathbed*
Popular images of Napoleon proliferated during his lifetime and if anything increased in popularity even after his death. Wood engraving.

Dutch East Indies islands to the Netherlands but kept the Cape Colony in southern Africa and Ceylon (present-day Sri Lanka) in exchange for financial compensation. The British gave back Guadeloupe and Martinique to France as well as the Indian Ocean colony of Reunion Island. Reunion's name changes followed events; originally Bourbon Island, in 1793 it became Reunion Island, then Bonaparte Island, and once again Bourbon Island in 1815. The British kept Mauritius, which they had captured in 1810. Abolitionists convinced the British Parliament to abolish the slave trade in 1807, and Britain got the Vienna Congress to agree to its abolition in principle everywhere, but the French, Spanish, and Portuguese continued the trade. The Congress guaranteed the neutrality of the Swiss Confederation and the freedom of navigation on many rivers including the Rhine, the Danube, and the Scheldt.

DEATH OF NAPOLEON After he arrived at desolate and distant Saint-Helena, Napoleon began burnishing his own legend by dictating a mixture of diary and reflections to his private secretary, Emmanuel, Count de Las Cases. Published in 1823, two years after his death from a stomach ailment whose causes are still in doubt, the four-volume *Memorial of Saint-Helena* became an immediate international bestseller (Figure 6.3). Needless to say, the former emperor exaggerated his triumphs and downplayed his defeats, and sought to excuse himself from the blame for such controversial acts as the execution of the Duke of Enghien in 1804 or the crushing of the Madrid revolt in 1808. He disdained the renewed interest in constitutions and claimed a special kinship with the French people: "The taste for constitutions, debates, harangues, seems to return. . . . [ellipses in original] However, it is only the minority that desires it, do not deceive yourself. The people, or if you like it better, the mob, desire me alone: you have not seen them, this mob, crowding after me, rushing from the tops of the mountains, calling me, seeking me, saluting me."[11] He was defiant to the end.

Documents

DOCUMENT 6.1

Napoleon's defense on the subject of the police state

When Napoleon was exiled to Saint-Helena, he was accompanied by Count Emmanuel-Augustin-Dieudonné-Joseph de Las Cases who served as his private secretary and recorded his thoughts and recollections for posterity. Las Cases was an unlikely follower, as he was an aristocratic naval officer who emigrated at the beginning of the French Revolution and even participated in an attempted royalist invasion in 1795. He returned to France under the Consulate, was made a count by the emperor in 1810, and joined him during the Hundred Days. His career shows that Napoleon did succeed in rallying some of the Old Regime nobles to his cause.

As to the grand machinery of espionage and police, which has been so much talked of, what State on the Continent could boast of having less of such evils than France; and yet what country stood more in need of them? What circumstances more imperiously called for them? Every pamphlet published in Europe, was directed against France, with a view of rendering odious in another country, that which it was thought advisable to conceal at home. Still, however, these measures so necessary in principle, though doubtless hateful in their details, were looked at merely in a general way by the Emperor, and always with a strict observance of his constant maxim, that nothing should be done that is not absolutely indispensable. . . .

With regard to the inspection of letters under the government of Napoleon, whatever may have been publicly said on that subject, the Emperor declared, that certainly very few letters were read at the post-offices. Those which were delivered either open or sealed, to private persons, had, for the most part, not been read: to read all would have been an endless task. The system of examining letters was adopted with the view of preventing, rather than discovering, dangerous correspondence. . . .

The Emperor was far from knowing all the measures taken by the police, in his name, with respect to writings and individuals; he had neither time nor opportunity to enquire into them. Thus he daily learned from his ministers, or from the pamphlets that happened to fall in his way, the arrests of individuals, or the suppression of works of which he had never before heard.

Source: Emmanuel-Auguste-Dieudonné-Joseph Count de Las Cases, *Mémorial de Sainte Hélène: Journal of the Private Life and Conversations of the Emperor Napoleon at Saint Helena* (Boston, 1823), 8 vols in 4, II: 31–33.

Questions on Napoleon's defense on the subject of the police state

1 Why did Napoleon think it vital to defend himself against critics of his police state?

2 What were the excuses that Napoleon cited in his favor?

DOCUMENT 6.2
Germaine de Staël, critic of Napoleon

Anne-Louise-Germaine Necker, Baroness of Staël-Holstein is one of the most fascinating figures of the entire epoch. The daughter of Louis XVI's Swiss finance minister, Jacques Necker, she married the Swedish ambassador in Paris, Baron Erik de Staël-Holstein, but legally separated from him after 11 years. She began writing at a young age and had already made a name for herself by the age of 22. Her literary reputation grew by leaps and bounds in the 1790s as did the notoriety of her love affairs, especially with Benjamin Constant, a Franco-Swiss novelist and political theorist. While Constant briefly rallied to Napoleon during the Hundred Days, Staël remained critical of the emperor throughout, but she found the restored Bourbons equally intolerable. In this passage, she dissects Napoleon's artful political tactics.

Never had a man the art of multiplying the ties of dependence more ably than Bonaparte. He surpassed everybody in his knowledge of the great and the little means of despotism; he concerned himself perseveringly with the dress of the women, that their husbands, ruined by their expense, might be obliged to have recourse to him more frequently. He wished likewise to strike the imaginations of the French by the pomp of his court. The old soldier who smoked at the door of Frederick II [King of Prussia, 1740–1786] was sufficient to make him respected by all Europe. Bonaparte without doubt had enough of military talents to obtain the same result by the same means: but to be master was not all that he desired; he wished also to be a tyrant: to oppress Europe and France, recourse was necessarily had to all the means of degrading the human species; and accordingly the wretch has succeeded but too well . . .

Yet the calculations of ambition and avarice would not have been sufficient to render France submissive to Bonaparte: something great is requisite to excite masses of people, and it was military glory which intoxicated the nation, while the nets of despotism were spread out by some men, whose meanness and corruption cannot be sufficiently branded. They treated constitutional principles as a chimera, like the courtiers of the old governments of Europe, whose places they aspire to occupy. But their master, as we shall soon see, coveted more than the crown of France, and did not limit himself to that plain vulgar despotism with which his civil agents would have wished him to be satisfied at home.

Source: Madame de Staël (Anne-Louise-Germaine), *Considerations on the Principal Events of the French Revolution: Posthumous Work of the Baroness de Stael*, 2 vols. (New York, 1818), II: 66–67.

Questions on Germaine de Staël

1   What are the qualities of Napoleon's rule that Staël emphasizes in this passage?

2   Consider Documents 1 and 2 together. Why did contemporaries have such diverging views of Napoleon?

TIMELINE TO CHAPTER 6

November 1807	French army occupies Portugal.
May 2–3, 1808	French repress an uprising in Madrid.
December 1809	Napoleon divorces Joséphine.
March 1810	Napoleon marries Marie-Louise of Habsburg (Austria).
April–Sep. 1810	South American independence movements begin in former Spanish colonies.
March 1811	Napoleon's son and heir is born.
June 24, 1812	Russian Campaign begins.

Sep. 14, 1812	*Grande Armée* enters Moscow, then retreats with heavy losses.
Oct. 16–19, 1813	Napoleon regroups, then defeated at Leipzig by coalition forces.
April 1814	Senate proclaims end of the Empire; Louis XVIII, the brother of Louis XVI, becomes king.
November 1814– June 1815	Congress of Vienna creates a post-Napoleonic settlement.
March 1815	Escaping exile, Napoleon returns and raises an army.
June 18, 1815	Napoleon defeated at the Battle of Waterloo.
March 5, 1821	Napoleon dies in exile on the island of Saint-Helena.

QUESTIONS ABOUT CHAPTER 6

1   Why were French people willing to support Napoleon even when he took steps to establish a police state?

2   Consider Napoleon's invasions of Portugal and Spain. Why did he take these moves? Why did they fail in the end?

3   What were Napoleon's motives in setting up a system of client and satellite states?

4   Why did Napoleon ultimately fall from power? Consider both international and domestic factors.

5   What do you think is the most important legacy of Napoleon's regime?

Conclusion

Crucible of the modern world

The range and complexity of the decisions made at the Congress of Vienna in 1814–1815 give some indication of the threats that the French Revolution and Napoleonic empire posed to the traditional order. The French not only revolutionized warfare by inaugurating what some have called "total war" but also transformed any possible terms of peace by creating new popular expectations about the nature of government and its relationship to the nation. War touched every state in Europe and the European colonies around the world. So, too, did new political hopes, which included democracy, nationalism, human rights, and aspirations for greater social equality. The great powers hoped to clamp a lid on the expectations by finally winning the war but the lid kept threatening to fly off as demands for greater liberty and participation bubbled up over and over again.

The French revolutionary and Napoleonic wars were not total wars in the modern sense, that is, they did not mobilize the entire citizenry for an ideologically driven war of extermination against the enemy. Some of these elements were present at various times, no doubt, notably in France on both sides of the civil war of the Vendée and in the French armies fighting the coalition between 1792 and 1794. The brutal conflicts in Spain between 1808 and 1813 also engendered a kind of war of extermination, again on both sides. Finally, the Prussian mobilization against Napoleon in 1813 showed how newly energized patriotism and hatred of the enemy could foster a savage fighting spirit. Nevertheless, the structure of the Napoleonic and allied armies militated against a total war based on ideological conviction; each side called upon soldiers from diverse nations, who could not therefore be united by a single strand of patriotism or nationalism. Moreover, rates of draft avoidance and desertion were strikingly high, ranging in France from as low as 5 percent in some departments to more than 40 percent in others. Many chose not to fight.[1]

There is no question, however, that the massive mobilization of troops, pioneered by the French, inevitably encouraged the fighting of ever more gigantic, intense, and therefore deadly battles. The great theorist of war, Carl von Clausewitz, captured the essence of the change in his writings of the 1820s. War assumed a "new nature" as a result of the French Revolution, he wrote, and reached a kind of "absolute perfection" of war:

> The means then called forth had no visible limit, the limit losing itself in the energy and enthusiasm of the Government and its subjects. By the extent of the means and the wide field of possible results, as well as by the powerful excitement of feeling which prevailed, energy in the conduct of War was immensely increased; the object of its action was the downfall of the foe; and not until the enemy lay powerless on the ground was it supposed to be possible to stop.[2]

Clausewitz knew this from first-hand experience since he was a Prussian officer who fought at the epic battles of Jena, Borodino (for the Russians), and Waterloo.

The all-out nature of war produced more than 1 million French military deaths and perhaps as many as 2 million deaths among other combatants, some of whom fought for the French. Civilian deaths must have numbered well more than a million. No one will ever know the exact death count, but it is clear that most men in the military did not die in combat but rather of disease. Between 1793 and 1815 240,000 soldiers in the British army died but only 27,000 of them died in combat or of their wounds. Yellow fever and malaria decimated both the British and French armies in the Caribbean; typhus and dysentery afflicted civilians and soldiers wherever fighting took place; scurvy had not been eradicated from the navies despite new knowledge about the need for lemon or lime juice in sailors' diets; and venereal disease, scabies, depression, and suicide accompanied every march. The damage to houses, huts, farms, and fields was incalculable, and when the fighting required more laborious marches and foraging for food, it fostered looting and rape.

The combination of constant warfare and new expectations of government ignited a series of explosions across the globe. The French invasion of Spain in 1808 produced some of the most striking consequences as Spain's many South American colonies had to choose between Napoleon's brother Joseph, allegiance to the Spanish opposition in favor of Ferdinand, or independence (see Map 7.1). Most of them chose independence; armed movements that began in 1810 had liberated most of South America by 1828. Many leaders of the independence movements, such as Simón Bolívar in Venezuela and Manuel Belgrano in Argentina, had been educated in Europe and exposed to Enlightenment ideals. Many of them, like their counterparts in France, had joined masonic lodges. Belgrano joined the first masonic lodge established in Buenos Aires in 1795.

MAP 7.1 *The World in the 1820s*

These men closely followed French events. Belgrano explained, "the ideas of liberty, equality, security, and property took a firm hold on me, and I saw only tyrants in those who could prevent a man, wherever he might be, from enjoying the rights with which God and Nature had endowed him." French residents in the Spanish colonies became suspect in the 1790s and underground writings threatened Spanish colonial officials with the guillotine if they opposed the progress of *la Libertad*. Like many in Europe, however, the opinions of the future independence leaders changed as regimes changed in France. Bolívar was in France at the moment of Napoleon's self-coronation but did not attend. Later he told an aide, "from that day on, I looked upon him as a hypocritical tyrant."

Once the independence movements began in South America, however, they confronted many of the same problems faced by the French. Although independence leaders from Mexico to Colombia granted at least some rights to the indigenous Indian populations and in much of South America outside of Brazil independence went hand in hand with the abolition of slavery, none of the new regimes managed to found a durable democratic republican tradition. Even Bolívar, despite his criticisms of Napoleon, moved toward authoritarianism. "In view of the lack of racial, social, or geographical homogeneity," he wrote, "it was important to hold tendencies toward disorder in check by creating strong centralized power." Because the struggle for independence involved nearly constant battles with pro-Spanish authorities, military dictatorships popped up in Chile, Argentina, and Peru. In Mexico, the leader of the revolt, Agustín de Iturbide first became President and then constitutional Emperor. At his coronation in 1822 Agustín I even took the crown from the hands of the archbishop and put it on his own head. The Napoleonic paradigm of authoritarianism directed by a revolutionary general proved to be one of the most imitated models of political authority in the modern world. It included the continuing denial of rights to women.

The restored Spanish King Ferdinand VII wanted to crush the colonial rebellions but he could not because he faced his own problems at home. The soldiers in his army, many of them freemasons, were pushing for the proclamation of a constitution written in 1812 by the Spanish opponents of Napoleon; it called not only for the restoration of Ferdinand VII but also for the abolition of privilege, a free press, and a one-house legislature elected by universal manhood suffrage. Ferdinand wanted no part of it, but he was only able to keep his throne when the French invaded in 1823 with the approval of the Vienna powers to crush the opposition to him.

French occupation had produced nationalist reactions nearly everywhere but nowhere were their effects greater than in the German and Italian states, where the emergence of nationalism fed into slow-growing movements for national unification. When the French occupied Berlin in 1807–1808, Johann Gottlieb Fichte delivered his *Lectures to the German Nation* to an eager audience; he urged the Germans, who were divided into many different states, to fight for their freedom as a people with a quasi-religious mission. The poet Ernst Moritz Arndt made his anti-French sentiments clear: "let hatred of the French be your religion, let Freedom and Fatherland be your saints." A secret society in the Italian states called the *Carbonari* (literally charcoal-burners) formed during Napoleonic rule and continued to agitate after 1815 for the unity and independence of the Italians. Some supported monarchy and others a republican form of government but all of them wanted a constitution. Metternich was obsessed with them and pressured the Pope to condemn them in a papal brief in 1821. Throughout his long years in office (until 1848), Metternich made it his priority to crush any sign of resistance to his policy of conserving the status quo.

Although Napoleon had not aimed to create an independent Italy or Germany, he actually unified the Germans and Italians to a previously unimaginable extent. French occupation showed that it could be done, and various elements of French rule remained in the German and Italian states after 1815. The Holy Roman Empire was not restored, and a new, larger German Confederation now included parts of Prussia and Austria. The Austrians in northern Italy and even the restored king of Naples kept many of the civil servants from the Napoleonic period. New law codes enacted for the kingdom of Naples in 1819 preserved many elements of the Napoleonic codes. Although Metternich dismissed the idea of Italy as only "a geographical expression," the middle classes that benefited from the sale of church lands would provide the backbone of unification in the future. Uprisings in Naples in 1820 and Piedmont in 1821 demanded constitutions on the model of the Spanish one of 1812, and though they failed, they showed that memories of the revolutionary and Napoleonic changes remained vivid.

The Spanish South American colonies were not the only ones affected by the long period of war and upheaval. The fighting between French and British naval and land forces created nearly constant upheaval in colonies located in the West Indies (Caribbean), East Indies (South and Southeast Asia), and Africa. The French Caribbean colony of Guadeloupe, for example, changed hands four times between 1794 and 1815; the French first abolished slavery, then re-instituted it under Napoleon, and did not finally abolish it until 1848. The Dutch colony of Java in the East Indies suffered even more dramatic changes because local Javanese rulers had retained considerable power. When the French got control of the Dutch Republic they established a joint French–Dutch regime in Java but it lost out to the British who captured most Dutch possessions in Southeast Asia. The British invaded Java in 1811, plundered the court of one of the local rulers, exiled him, and incorporated many of the princely states into their administration (1811–1816), which meant opening them to trade and taxation. After the Dutch returned and tried to maintain the same kind of control, they ended up facing widespread popular rebellions in the 1820s. The French trading outposts of Saint Louis and Gorée, islands just off West Africa that had been critical to the slave trade, fared somewhat better because as they went from French to British and back to French possession during the Napoleonic wars, mixed Euro-African families began to dominate the trade with the interior.

The worldwide fighting for control of territory produced four major international developments with long-lasting global consequences: Spain and Portugal lost their empires in the Americas (Brazil announced its independence from Portugal in 1822); Britain established its hegemony over the seas; France turned away from the Caribbean and North America toward Africa; and the new United States, which made peace with Britain in 1815, was able to use the distractions of the fighting in Europe and elsewhere to begin its westward expansion. The British had already made a "swing to the east" after the loss of their North American colonies in 1783 and devoted more of their resources to maintaining and developing India. At the very moment that the Industrial Revolution was taking off in Britain, British naval dominance also ensured Britain's international commerce, not only in the east but also in the west, where Britain became the most important trading partner of the new South American governments. Faced with the loss of Saint-Domingue and the Louisiana Territory, French colonial ambitions eventually turned toward Africa. France invaded Algeria in 1830 and began a long and deep colonization with French and other European settlers. The United States sent out the Lewis and Clark expedition to the Pacific the same year that it bought the Louisiana Territory from the French, and by 1820 its population had doubled to 10 million and the union included nine new states.

As might be expected, the legacy of the French Revolution and Napoleon would remain especially strong in France. The fallen eagle aroused strong feelings in the French, as the returning Bourbons discovered. Despite the efforts of the monarchy's police, millions of prints, busts, and medals of Napoleon circulated clandestinely throughout France over the next fifteen years. The French never entirely shook off the Napoleonic virus. Napoleon's nephew, Louis-Napoleon, got himself elected President of the Second French Republic in 1848, largely on the strength of his name, and a plebiscite ratified him as Emperor Napoleon III in 1852. He was known as Napoleon III because Napoleon's son died in Vienna in 1832. Although Napoleon III did not have a military background, generals played important roles in French politics right into the twentieth century, most notably during and after World War II. Marshal Philippe Pétain, a hero of World War I, became head of the government in France that collaborated with the German occupiers after 1940, and General Charles de Gaulle, who had fled to London to carry on the fight against the Germans, became head of the post-war provisional government and then President of the Fifth Republic between 1959 and 1969.

The Napoleon cult was not the only legacy of the period from 1789 to 1815, though it certainly resonated most loudly in the immediate aftermath of Waterloo. It would always have to contend, however, with the revolutionary legacy driven underground after 1799 and especially after 1804. Napoleon did continue the revolution in some areas, most notably by making war against most of Europe; maintaining equality before the law, the abolition of feudalism, and religious toleration; guaranteeing the sales of church property; and extending government control over marriage, education, taxation, law codes, and relations with the churches including Protestant and Jewish congregations. In other respects, however, he shut down the revolution by reducing political participation, restricting freedom of expression, limiting divorce and the rights of women, and reinstituting various forms of hierarchy and subservience from the revival of noble titles to the monitoring of workers' movements. Thomas Jefferson offered a harsh appraisal of "the Attila of the age" in a letter he wrote after Napoleon's exile to Elba. He captured the view of many convinced democrats; Napoleon was "the ruthless destroyer of 10 Millions of the human race, . . . the great oppressor of the rights and liberties of the world."

The revolutionary forms of democratic participation, proliferating news-papers and popular prints, and satirical send-ups of clergy and aristocrats never entirely disappeared, despite the best efforts of police from Napoleon and Metternich onward. Nor for that matter did the memories of Terror, civil war in the Vendée, National Guards, republican mobilization, or Committees of Public Safety. These memories seethed underground in France and much of the rest of Europe throughout the nineteenth century and into the twentieth. In 1797, for example, Greeks began meeting secretly in many Greek cities with the hope that the French would help them gain their independence from the Ottoman Empire. A Greek Jacobin even drew up a constitution for a Greek republic modeled on the French constitution of 1793. Revolutionaries in Vienna in 1848 set up their own committee of public safety and so, too, did revolutionaries in Paris in 1871 and socialist revolutionaries in Russia in 1917. Indeed, revolutions modeled on 1789 or 1793 broke out again in France, in 1830, 1848, and again in 1871 after Napoleon III fell from power. Once it had escaped from the bottle of tradition, the genie of revolution had a way of diffusing in unpredictable fashion.

Despite the tumultuous power of the revolutionary and Napoleonic heritage, everything did not change overnight in France. France remained a nation of peasants, made even more entrenched by the sales of church and aristocratic lands. The nation stayed overwhelmingly Catholic, though it would take years for the Catholic Church to fully recover; between 1802 and 1814 there were 6,000 ordinations of Catholic clergy in France—about the same number as took place in an average year at the end of the Old Regime. The population grew only modestly; though the marriage rate increased the birth rate may have actually declined. Urbanization and industrialization had yet to take off despite some signs of change.

Yet so much in the hearts and minds had changed. Millions of young Europeans had tramped around the continent or served on naval vessels or expeditionary forces. Youngsters who had not left their neighborhood now saw a staggering variety of places and peoples. But most of all, new ideals and new practices had taken root, not everywhere in the same fashion, but in many different places nonetheless. Revolution, human rights, democracy, government economic controls, political propaganda, terror, the military draft, equality under the law, careers open to the talent, wars of liberation, guerrillas: the list of innovations, from the labels "left" and "right" to the establishment of the modern police state, is simply astounding. Just why the French set off this kind of political, cultural, military, and social chain reaction in 1789 continues to excite scholarly debate, with good reason. So many global consequences followed from a debt crisis created by the imperial competition between France and Great Britain. The effects that poured out of the crucible of the modern world seem out of proportion with the causes that went into it. Yet, could there be a more perfect place to end than with an invitation to continue to explore?

Notes

* In the endnotes and bibliography we chose to cite only English language works that are easily consultable. French language studies form the bedrock of any analysis of the French Revolution and Napoleon. Recent works can be followed in the journal *Annales historiques de la Révolution française* or via the blog of the Société des Études Robespierristes at http://ser.hypotheses. org/.

Preface

1   Yarong Jiang and David Ashley, *Mao's Children in the New China: Voices From the Red Guard Generation* (New York: Routledge, 2000), p. 66.

2   Edmund Burke, *Reflections on the Revolution in France: And on the Proceedings in Certain Societies in London Relative to That Event*, 3rd edn. (London: J. Dodsley, 1790), p. 11.

3   Jules Michelet, *History of the French Revolution*, tr. C. Cocks (London: H. G. Bohn, 1847), p. 3.

4   Hippolyte Taine, *The French Revolution*, tr. John Durand, 3 vols. (New York: H. Holt, 1878–85), I: v, 34.

5   The volume on Napoleon can be found at http://www.gutenberg.org/ files/2581/2581-h/2581-h.htm#link2H_4_0015.

Chapter 1

1   Hans-Jürgen Lüsebrink and Rolf Reichardt, *The Bastille: A History of a Symbol of Despotism and Freedom* (Durham, NC: Duke University Press, 1997).

2   Suzanne Desan, Lynn Hunt, and William Max Nelson, eds., *The French Revolution in Global Perspective* (Ithaca, NY: Cornell University Press, 2013).

3   Robert Darnton, *The Forbidden Best-Sellers of Pre-Revolutionary France* (New York: W. W. Norton, 1996).

4   The amount of land owned by nobles and even the *number* of nobles in France is uncertain. We are following Michel Nassiet, "Le problème des

effetifs de la noblesse dans la France du XVIIIe siècle," in *Traditions et innovations dans la société française du XVIIIe siècle: Actes du colloque d'Angers, 1993* (Paris: Presses de l'Université de Paris-Sorbonne, 1995), pp. 97–121. His figures are accepted by William Doyle, who concludes that about 40,000 were ennobled through the purchase of ennobling offices (such as those in parlements) over the course of the eighteenth century. See William Doyle, *Venality: The Sale of Offices in Eighteenth-Century France* (Oxford, UK: Clarendon Press, 1996), p. 165. According to Doyle, there were only 462 families in 1790 that could trace their noble lineage back to 1400. William Doyle, *Aristocracy and Its Enemies in the Age of Revolution* (Oxford, UK: Oxford University Press, 2009), p. 11.

5   Jean Egret, *The French Pre-Revolution, 1787–1788*, tr. Wesley D. Camp (Chicago, IL: University of Chicago Press, 1977); Vivian R. Gruder, *The Notables and the Nation: The Political Schooling of the French, 1787–1788* (Cambridge, MA: Harvard University Press, 2007).

6   P. Boissonnade, ed., *Cahiers de doléances de la sénéchaussée d'Angoulême et du siège royal de Cognac pour les Etats-Généraux de 1789: département de la Charente* (Paris: Imprimerie Nationale, 1907), p. 43.

7   George F. E. Rudé, *The Crowd in the French Revolution* (Oxford, UK: Oxford University Press, 1959).

8   Jeremy D. Popkin, *Revolutionary News: The Press in France, 1789–1799* (Durham, NC: Duke University Press, 1990).

9   Timothy Tackett, *Becoming a Revolutionary: The Deputies of the French National Assembly and the Emergence of a Revolutionary Culture (1789–1790)* (Princeton, NJ: Princeton University Press, 1996).

10   Georges Lefebvre, *The Great Fear of 1789: Rural Panic in Revolutionary France*, tr. Joan White (Princeton, NJ: Princeton University Press, 1973).

11   Rafe Blaufarb, *The Great Demarcation: The French Revolution and the Invention of Modern Property* (New York: Oxford University Press, 2016).

Chapter 2

1   For Benjamin Franklin's use of the term, see his letter of July 7, 1773 to Samuel Mather at http://franklinpapers.org/franklin//framedVolumes.jsp (retrieved April 13, 2015).

2   Janet Polasky, *Revolutions without Borders: The Call to Liberty in the Atlantic World* (New Haven, CT: Yale University Press, 2015).

3   Abigail Adams in a letter of October 1787 to Mary Smith Cranch in Lyman Henry Butterfield, *Adams Family Correspondence: March 1787–December 1789* (Cambridge, MA: Harvard University Press, 2007), p. 193.

4   Lord Sheffield to Lord Auckland, January 8, 1790, in *The Journal and Correspondence of William, Lord Auckland*, 2 vols. (London, 1861), II: 366.

5   During the last half of 1789 the French began to refer to the state of affairs before the revolution as the *ancien régime*, that is, as the former or old

regime. By contrast, then, the revolution looked toward the future rather than the past.

6 Timothy Tackett, *Religion, Revolution, and Regional Culture in Eighteenth-Century France: The Ecclesiastical Oath of 1791* (Princeton, NJ: Princeton University Press, 1986).

7 Michael P. Fitzsimmons, *The Remaking of France: The National Assembly and the Constitution of 1791* (Cambridge, UK: Cambridge University Press, 1994).

8 Mona Ozouf, *Festivals and the French Revolution*, tr. Alan Sheridan (Cambridge, MA: Harvard University Press, 1988).

9 Timothy Tackett, *When the King Took Flight* (Cambridge, MA: Harvard University Press, 2003).

10 Peter McPhee, *Robespierre: A Revolutionary Life* (New Haven, CT: Yale Harvard University Press, 2012).

11 T. C. W. Blanning, *The French Revolutionary Wars, 1787–1802* (London: Arnold, 1996).

12 Siân Reynolds, *Marriage and Revolution: Monsieur and Madame Roland* (Oxford, UK: Oxford University Press, 2012); Gary Kates, *The Cercle Social, the Girondins, and the French Revolution* (Princeton, NJ: Princeton University Press, 1985).

13 M. J. Sydenham, *The Girondins* (London: Athlone, 1961).

14 Albert Soboul, *The Sans-Culottes: The Popular Movement and Revolutionary Government, 1793–1794* (Princeton, NJ: Princeton University Press, 1972).

Chapter 3

1 Lynn Avery Hunt, *Politics, Culture, and Class in the French Revolution* (Berkeley, CA: University of California Press, 1984).

2 David P. Jordan, *The King's Trial: The French Revolution Vs. Louis XVI* (Berkeley, CA: University of California Press, 1979).

3 David Waldstreicher, *In the Midst of Perpetual Fetes: The Making of American Nationalism* (Chapel Hill: University of North Carolina Press, 1997).

4 Charles Tilly, *The Vendée* (Cambridge, MA: Harvard University Press, 1976).

5 David Andress, *The Terror: The Merciless War for Freedom in Revolutionary France* (New York: Farrar, Straus, and Giroux, 2005).

6 Robert Barrie Rose, *The Enragés: Socialists of the French Revolution?* (Carlton, Australia: Melbourne University Press, 1965).

7 Rachel Hammersley, *French Revolutionaries and English Republicans: The Cordeliers Club, 1790–1794* (Rochester, NY: Boydell Press, 2005).

8 Ehrhard Bahr and Thomas P. Saine, eds., *The Internalized Revolution: German Reactions to the French Revolution, 1789–1989* (New York: Garland Publishing, 1992).

9 Paul R. Hanson, *Jacobin Republic Under Fire: The Federalist Revolt in the French Revolution* (University Park, PA: Penn State University Press, 2003).

10 R. R. Palmer, *Twelve Who Ruled: The Year of the Terror in the French Revolution* (Princeton, NJ: Princeton University Press, 2005 [first edition 1941]).

11 Dominique Godineau, *The Women of Paris and Their French Revolution* (Berkeley, CA: University of California Press, 1998).

12 Jeremy D. Popkin, *You Are All Free: The Haitian Revolution and the Abolition of Slavery* (Cambridge, UK: Cambridge University Press, 2010).

13 Ken Alder, *The Measure of All Things: The Seven-Year Odyssey and Hidden Error That Transformed the World* (New York: Free Press, 2002).

14 Michel Vovelle, *The Revolution against the Church: From Reason to the Supreme Being*, tr. Alan José (Columbus, OH: Ohio State University Press, 1991).

15 Timothy Tackett, *The Coming of the Terror in the French Revolution* (Cambridge, MA: Harvard University Press, 2015).

Chapter 4

1 Mary Ashburn Miller, *A Natural History of Revolution: Violence and Nature in the French Revolutionary Imagination, 1789–1794* (Ithaca, NY: Cornell University Press, 2011).

2 Colin Jones, "The Overthrow of Maximilien Robespierre and the 'Indifference' of the People," *The American Historical Review* 119, no. 3 (June 1, 2014): 689–713, doi:10.1093/ahr/119.3.689.

3 Bronislaw Baczko, *Ending the Terror: The French Revolution After Robespierre*, tr. Michel Petheram (Cambridge, UK: Cambridge University Press, 1994).

4 Helen Maria Williams, *A Residence in France, During the Years 1792, 1793, 1794, and 1795: Described in a Series of Letters from an English Lady: With General and Incidental Remarks on the French Character and Manners*, 2 vols. (London: T. N. Longman, 1797), II: 384.

5 D. M. G. Sutherland, *Murder in Aubagne: Lynching, Law, and Justice During the French Revolution* (Cambridge, UK: Cambridge University Press, 2009).

6 Martyn Lyons, *France Under the Directory* (Cambridge, UK: Cambridge Unversity Press, 1975).

7 R. B. Rose, *Gracchus Babeuf: The First Revolutionary Communist* (Palo Alto, CA: Stanford University Press, 1978).

8 David A. Bell, *Napoleon: A Concise Biography* (Oxford, UK: Oxford University Press, 2015).

9 Desmond Gregory, *Napoleon's Italy* (Cranbury, NJ: Fairleigh Dickinson University Press, 2001).

10 Marianne Elliott, *Partners in Revolution: The United Irishmen and France* (New Haven, CT: Yale University Press, 1990).

11 Christopher J. Tozzi, *Nationalizing France's Army: Foreign, Black, and Jewish Troops in the French Military, 1715–1831* (Charlottesville, VA: University of Virginia Press, 2016).

12 John A. Lynn, *The Bayonets of the Republic: Motivation and Tactics in the Army of Revolutionary France, 1791–94* (Urbana, IL: University of Illinois Press, 1984).

13 Alan Forrest, *Conscripts and Deserters: The Army and French Society During the Revolution and Empire* (Oxford, UK: Oxford University Press, 1989).

14 Juan Cole, *Napoleon's Egypt: Invading the Middle East* (New York: Palgrave Macmillan, 2007).

15 Howard G. Brown, *Ending the French Revolution: Violence, Justice, and Repression from the Terror to Napoleon* (Charlottesville, VA: University of Virginia Press, 2007).

Chapter 5

1 Louis Bergeron, *France Under Napoleon*, tr. R. R. Palmer (Princeton, NJ: Princeton University Press, 1981).

2 Michael Broers, *Europe Under Napoleon* (New York: St. Martin's Press, 1996).

3 Nigel Aston, *Religion and Revolution in France, 1780–1804* (Washington, DC: Catholic University of America Press, 2000).

4 Isser Woloch, *Napoleon and His Collaborators: The Making of a Dictatorship* (New York: W. W. Norton, 2002).

5 Martyn Lyons, *Napoleon Bonaparte and the Legacy of the French Revolution* (New York: St. Martin's Press, 1994).

6 Geoffrey J. Ellis, *Napoleon* (New York: Longman, 1997).

7 Robert B. Holtman, *Napoleonic Propaganda* (Baton Rouge, LA: LSU University Press, 1950).

8 Stephen Jones and Charles Molloy Westmacott, eds., *The Spirit of the Public Journals for 1805: Being an Impartial Selection of the Most Exquisite Essays and Jeux D'esprits, Principally Prose, That Appear in the Newspapers and Other Publications*, vol. 9 (London: R. Phillips, 1806), p. 308.

9 Owen Connelly, *Napoleon's Satellite Kingdoms* (New York: Free Press, 1965).

10 David G. Chandler, *The Campaigns of Napoleon* (New York: Macmillan, 1966).

11 Geoffrey James Ellis, *Napoleon's Continental Blockade: The Case of Alsace* (Oxford, UK: Oxford University Press, 1981).

12 Owen Connelly, *Blundering to Glory: Napoleon's Military Campaigns* (Wilmington, DE: Scholarly Resources, 1987).

Chapter 6

1 Philip G. Dwyer, ed., *Napoleon and Europe* (New York: Routledge, 2014). See especially the essay by Michael Sibalis, "The Napoleonic Police State."

2 Madame de Staël (Anne-Louise-Germaine), *Considerations on the Principal Events of the French Revolution: Posthumous Work of the Baroness de Stael*, 2 vols. (New York: James Eastburn and Co., 1818), II: 89 and 91. Germaine de Staël's book, published in French the same year (in London), is one of the most interesting accounts of the French Revolution written by someone who experienced it first-hand.

3 Georges Lefebvre, *Napoleon* (New York: Routledge, 2011).

4 Charles Esdaile, *Peninsular Eyewitnesses: The Experience of War in Spain and Portugal 1808–1813* (Barnsley, UK: Pen & Sword Military, 2008), pp. 122–123.

5 Gunther E. Rothenberg, *The Art of Warfare in the Age of Napoleon* (Bloomington, IN: Indiana University Press, 1978).

6 Ute Planert, ed., *Napoleon's Empire: European Politics in Global Perspective* (New York: Palgrave Macmillan, 2015).

7 Alexander Grab, *Napoleon and the Transformation of Europe* (New York: Palgrave Macmillan, 2003).

8 Philip Dwyer, *Citizen Emperor: Napoleon in Power* (New Haven, CT: Yale University Press, 2013).

9 David Armitage and Sanjay Subrahmanyam, *The Age of Revolutions in Global Context, c. 1760–1840* (New York: Palgrave Macmillan, 2010).

10 Raymond Emery Philippe Joseph de Montesquiou Fezensac (duc de), *A Journal of the Russian Campaign of 1812* (London: Parker, Furnivall & Parker, 1852), p. 89.

11 Emmanuel-Auguste-Dieudonné-Joseph Count de Las Cases, *Memorial de Sainte Hélène: Journal of the Private Life and Conversations of the Emperor Napoleon at Saint Helena* (Boston: H. Colburn and Co, 1823), 8 vol in 4, I: 161.

Conclusion

1 David A. Bell, *The First Total War: Napoleon's Europe and the Birth of Warfare as We Know It* (Boston: Houghton Mifflin, 2007).

2 Carl von Clausewitz, *On War*, tr. J. J. Graham (London: Kegan Paul Trench, Trubner & Co., 1908), 3 vols., III: 102. The book was first published after his death in 1831 but written for the most part in the 1820s.

Bibliography

We have included in the bibliography only works that were not previously cited in the notes to the chapters.

Chapter 1

Before Fiscal Transparency (a website on French finances 1785–1792 with some original documents). http://www.reading.ac.uk/fiscal-history/fhahf-before-fiscal-transparency.aspx.

Forrest, A and Middell, M (Eds.) (2015) *The Routledge Companion to the French Revolution in World History*. New York: Routledge.

Hunt, L (2007) *Inventing Human Rights: A History*. New York: W. W. Norton.

Kaiser, T E and Van Kley, D K (Eds.) (2011) *From Deficit to Deluge: The Origins of the French Revolution*. Stanford, CA: Stanford University Press.

Kates, G (Ed.) (2006) *The French Revolution: Recent Debates and New Controversies*, 2nd edn. New York: Routledge.

Kwass, M (2014) *Contraband: Louis Mandrin and the Making of a Global Underground*. Cambridge, MA: Harvard University Press.

Lefebvre, G (1947) *The Coming of the French Revolution*. Trans. R R Palmer. Princeton, NJ: Princeton University Press.

Sewell, W (1994) *A Rhetoric of Bourgeois Revolution: The Abbè Sieyès and What Is the Third Estate?* Durham, NC: Duke University Press.

Stone, B (2002) *Reinterpreting the French Revolution: A Global-Historical Perspective*. Cambridge, UK: Cambridge University Press.

Tocqueville, A de (2011) *The Ancien Régime and the French Revolution*. Trans. A Goldhammer. Cambridge, UK: Cambridge University Press.

Chapter 2

Andress, D (2013) *Massacre at the Champ de Mars: Popular Dissent and Political Culture in the French Revolution*. London: Boydell Press.

Applewhite, H B and Levy, D G (Eds.) (1990) *Women and Politics in the Age of the Democratic Revolution*. Ann Arbor, MI: University of Michigan Press.

Blanning, T C W (1986) *The Origins of the French Revolutionary Wars*. London: Longman.

Dubois, L (2004) *Avengers of the New World: The Story of the Haitian Revolution*. Cambridge, MA: Harvard University Press.

Ferrer, A (2014) *Freedom's Mirror: Cuba and Haiti in the Age of Revolution*. New York: Cambridge University Press.

Liberty, Equality, Fraternity: Exploring the French Revolution (a website with maps, songs, documents, and brief histories), http://chnm.gmu.edu/revolution/.

Palmer, R R (1959) *The Age of the Democratic Revolution: A Political History of Europe and America, 1760–1800*, 2 vols., I (The Challenge). Princeton, NJ: Princeton University Press.

Plack, N (2009) *Common Land, Wine and the French Revolution: Rural Society and Economy in Southern France, c.1789–1820*. Farnham, UK: Ashgate.

Popkin, J D (2012) *A Concise History of the Haitian Revolution*. Malden, MA: Wiley-Blackwell.

Shapiro, B M (1993) *Revolutionary Justice in Paris, 1789–1790*. Cambridge, UK: Cambridge University Press.

Shusterman, N (2014) *The French Revolution: Faith, Desire and Politics*. New York: Routledge.

Spang, R L (2015) *Stuff and Money in the Time of the French Revolution*. Cambridge, MA: Harvard University Press.

Chapter 3

Baecque, A de (2001) *Glory and Terror: Seven Deaths under the French Revolution*. Trans. C Mandell. New York: Routledge.

Desan, S (2004) *The Family on Trial in Revolutionary France*. Berkeley, CA: University of California Press.

Furet, F (1981) *Interpreting the French Revolution*. Trans. E Forster. Cambridge, UK: Cambridge University Press.

Harris, B (2008) *The Scottish People and the French Revolution*. London: Pickering & Chatto.

Hunt, L (1992) *The Family Romance of the French Revolution*. Berkeley, CA: University of California Press.

Linton, M (2013) *Choosing Terror: Virtue, Friendship, and Authenticity in the French Revolution*. Oxford, UK: Oxford University Press.

Lucas, C (1973) *The Structure of the Terror: The Example of Javogues and the Loire*. London: Oxford University Press.

Perovic, S (2012) *The Calendar in Revolutionary France: Perceptions of Time in Literature, Culture, Politics*. Cambridge, UK: Cambridge University Press.

Roider Jr, K A (1987) *Baron Thugut and Austria's Response to the French Revolution*. Princeton, NJ: Princeton University Press.

Sutherland, D (1982) *The Chouans: The Social Origins of Popular Counter-Revolution in Upper Brittany, 1770–1796*. Oxford, UK: Oxford University Press.

Chapter 4

Bertaud, J -P (1988) *The Army of the French Revolution: From Citizen-Soldiers to Instrument of Power*. Trans. R R Palmer. Princeton, NJ: Princeton University Press.

Blaufarb, R (2002) *The French Army, 1750–1820: Careers, Talent, Merit.* Manchester, UK: Manchester University Press.

Brown, H G (1995) *War, Revolution, and the Bureaucratic State: Politics and Army Administration in France, 1791–1799.* Oxford, UK: Clarendon Press.

Coller, I (2011) *Arab France: Islam and the Making of Modern Europe, 1798–1831.* Berkeley, CA: University of California Press.

Firges, P (2017) *French Revolutionaries in the Ottoman Empire: Diplomacy, Political Culture, and the Limiting of Universal Revolution, 1792–1798.* Oxford, UK: Oxford University Press.

Forrest, A I (1990) *The Soldiers of the French Revolution.* Durham, NC: Duke University Press.

Gueniffey, P (2015) *Bonaparte: 1769–1802.* Trans. S Rendall. Cambridge, MA: Harvard University Press.

Hanley, W (2002) *The Genesis of Napoleonic Propaganda, 1796 to 1799.* New York: Columbia University Press (Gutenberg-e book).

Jainchill, A (2008) *Reimagining Politics after the Terror: The Republican Origins of French Liberalism.* Ithaca, NY: Cornell University Press.

Pichichero, C (2017) *The Military Enlightenment: War and Culture in the French Empire from Louis XIV to Napoleon.* Ithaca, NY: Cornell University Press.

Smyth, J (2016) *Robespierre and the Festival of the Supreme Being: The Search for a Republican Morality.* Manchester, UK: Manchester University Press.

Walshaw, J M (2014) *A Show of Hands for the Republic: Opinion, Information, and Repression in Eighteenth-Century Rural France.* Rochester, NY: University of Rochester Press.

Woronoff, D (1984) *The Thermidorean Regime and the Directory, 1794–1799.* Trans. J Jackson. Cambridge, UK: Cambridge University Press.

Chapter 5

Blaufarb, R (Ed.) (2008) *Napoleon, Symbol for an Age: A Brief History with Documents.* Boston: Bedford/St. Martin's.

Englund, S (2004) *Napoleon: A Political Life.* New York: Scribner.

Geggus, D P (Ed.) (2001) *The Impact of the Haitian Revolution in the Atlantic World.* Columbia, SC: University of South Carolina Press.

Girard, P (2016) *Toussaint Louverture: A Revolutionary Life.* New York: Basic Books.

Hales, E E Y (1962) *Napoleon and the Pope: The Story of Napoleon and Pius VII.* London: Eyre and Spottiswoode.

Hughes, M J (2012) *Forging Napoleon's Grande Armée: Motivation, Military Culture, and Masculinity in the French Army, 1800–1808.* New York: New York University Press.

James, C L R (1938) *The Black Jacobins: Toussaint Louverture and the San Domingo Revolution.* London: Dial Press.

O'Brien, D (2006) *After the Revolution: Antoine-Jean Gros, Painting and Propaganda under Napoleon.* University Park, PA: Penn State University Press.

Serna, P, De Francesco, A, and Miller, J (Eds.) (2013) *Republics at War, 1776–1840: Revolutions, Conflicts, and Geopolitics in Europe and the Atlantic World.* Basingstoke, UK: Palgrave Macmillan.

Chapter 6

Blaufarb, R and Liebeskind, C (2011) *Napoleonic Foot Soldiers and Civilians: A Brief History with Documents*. Boston: Bedford/St. Martin's.

Davidson, D Z (2007) *France after Revolution: Urban Life, Gender, and the New Social Order*. Cambridge, MA: Harvard University Press.

Esdaile, C J (2004) *Fighting Napoleon: Guerrillas, Bandits and Adventurers in Spain, 1808–1814*. New Haven, CT: Yale University Press.

Esdaile, C J (2014) *Women in the Peninsular War*. Norman, OK: University of Oklahoma Press.

Hagemann, K (2015) *Revisiting Prussia's Wars against Napoleon: History, Culture, and Memory*. New York: Cambridge University Press.

Lieven, D (2010) *Russia Against Napoleon: The True Story of the Campaigns of War and Peace*. New York: Viking.

Matteson, K (2015) *Forests in Revolutionary France: Conservation, Community, and Conflict, 1669–1848*. Cambridge, UK: Cambridge University Press.

Zamoyski, A (2007) *Rites of Peace: The Fall of Napoleon and the Congress of Vienna*. New York: Harper Collins.

Conclusion

Belaubre, C, Dym, J, and Savage, J (Eds.) (2010) *Napoleon's Atlantic: The Impact of Napoleonic Empire in the Atlantic World*. Boston: Brill.

Censer, J R (2016) *Debating Modern Revolution: The Evolution of Revolutionary Ideas*. London: Bloomsbury.

Klaits, J and Haltzell, M H (Eds.) (1994) *The Global Ramification of the French Revolution*. Washington, DC: Woodrow Wilson Center Press.

Index

Pages with the suffixes *m, f,* and *t,* refer to maps, figures and tables respectively.